I'm Speaking Now

Black Women Share
Their Truth in
101 Stories of Love,
Courage and Hope

Chicken Soup for the Soul: I'm Speaking Now: Black Women Share Their Truth in
101 Stories of Love, Courage and Hope
Amy Newmark and Breena Clarke

Published by Chicken Soup for the Soul, LLC www.chickensoup.com
Copyright ©2021 by Chicken Soup for the Soul, LLC. All Rights Reserved.

The publisher gratefully acknowledges the many publishers and individuals who granted
Chicken Soup for the Soul permission to reprint the cited material.

Front cover and interior photos of women from top left to right: courtesy of iStockphoto.
com/CarlosDavid.org (©CarlosDavid), courtesy of iStockphoto.com/Avatar_023.org
(©Avatar_023), courtesy of iStockphoto.com/digitalskillet.org (©digitalskillet), courtesy of
iStockphoto.com/uanmonino.org (©uanmonino), courtesy of iStockphoto.com/ajr_images.
org (©ajr_images), courtesy of iStockphoto.com/Ridofranz.org (©Ridofranzimages),
courtesy of iStockphoto.com/digitalskillet.org (©digitalskillet), courtesy of iStockphoto.com/
izkes.org (©izkes).
Photo of Amy Newmark courtesy of Susan Morrow at SwickPix

Cover and Interior by Daniel Zaccari

Distributed to the booktrade by Simon & Schuster. SAN: 200-2442

Publisher's Cataloging-In-Publication Data
(Prepared by The Donohue Group, Inc.)

Names: Newmark, Amy, compiler. | Clarke, Breena, compiler.
Title: Chicken soup for the soul : I'm speaking now : Black women share
    their truth in 101 stories of love, courage and hope / [compiled by]
    Amy Newmark [and] Breena Clarke.
Other Titles: I'm speaking now : Black women share their truth in 101
    stories of love, courage and hope
Description: [Cos Cob, Connecticut] : Chicken Soup for the Soul, LLC,
    [2021]
Identifiers: ISBN 9781611590838 | ISBN 9781611593235 (ebook)
Subjects: LCSH: Women, Black--Literary collections. | Women, Black--
    Anecdotes. | Women, Black--Poetry. | LCGFT: Anecdotes. | Poetry.
Classification: LCC HQ1163 .C45 2021 (print) | LCC HQ1163 (ebook) | DDC
    305.48896/02--dc23
Library of Congress Control Number: 2021931274

PRINTED IN THE UNITED STATES OF AMERICA
on acid∞free paper

30 29 28 27 26 25 24 23 22 21   01 02 03 04 05 06 07 08 09 10

I'm Speaking Now

Black Women Share
Their Truth in
101 Stories of Love,
Courage and Hope

Amy Newmark
Breena Clarke

Chicken Soup for the Soul, LLC
Cos Cob, CT

Changing your world one story at a time®
www.chickensoup.com

Table of Contents

❶

~Stand Up, Speak Out~

❷

~The Shoulders We Stand On~

❸

~Family & Food for the Soul~

❹

~Self-Discovery~

❺

~Where We Come From~

❻

~Everyday Struggles~

❼

~Raising Our Children~

❽

~Taking Care of Me~

⑨

~Sisters, Friends~

⑩

~Loving Black Men~

⓫

~Identity & Roots~

Introduction

*There is material among us for the broadest comedies
and the deepest tragedies, but, besides money and
leisure, it needs patience, perseverance, courage,
and the hand of an artist to weave it into the
literature of the country.*
~Frances Ellen Watkins Harper

"I'm Speaking Now!" You've been there. You've said it or wanted to. You've been seated at the table where everyone but you is being heard and acknowledged because everyone but you is white. When you begin to speak, just like in a bad dream, someone starts talking over you. Maybe they can't hear you? You consider speaking louder. You hesitate because you don't want to be accused of being loud and angry. But you are angry, and you need to raise a fuss. You clear your throat and say, "I'm speaking… now. Now, it is my turn to speak. Can you hear me? Are you ignoring me?"

If you're a Black woman, this has happened to you. Whether you're a business executive or a grocery clerk, you've been ignored, refused courteous treatment, paid less than, policed more than, suspected, unprotected, sexually harassed and exploited and, though a participating witness to the creation of the United States of America since 1619, silenced because you are a Black woman.

Well, we are speaking now. Now. Not for the first time. Now because the moment is now, now in this collection of 101 first-person narratives and twelve poems is an opportunity to hear the often silenced voices of Black women.

The stories in *Chicken Soup for the Soul: I'm Speaking Now — Black Women Share Their Truth in 101 Stories of Love, Courage and Hope* are straightforward accounts of daily lives. Some are bursts of bright recollection of events or incidents from the past that have stamped the authors' lives. Some of the stories are sweet, tender remembrances, evoking pictures of beloved forebears who give us the gritty lessons for survival. Some of the narratives are of dreams and goals the authors set for themselves and their children, juxtaposed with fears and trepidation. Some of these stories are raw, unsettling accounts of trauma. Some are funny, and some are not.

You, whoever you are, will likely find yourself here. Not the least because these are stories about women. Women in this book are writing about you and themselves; they are writing for you and because of you. Many of them tell the truth about themselves plainly and tell it like it is, was, and likely will be. These are stories of universal human experiences but also reflect the specificity of Black women's lives in this country. The scope is broad. This volume includes stories from Canada and the Caribbean as well.

The most compelling stories are those authored by women dealing with the Prison Industrial Complex from inside and outside; narratives of immigration, stories of the Great Migration, stories of international travel, and the adventures of driving around as a Black woman.

I'm speaking now because why should I wait any longer?

It's certainly not the first time we've spoken up. In the early decades of the 20th century, African American women were at the ramparts supporting Woman's Suffrage though they were most often relegated to the side. Later, they witnessed the horrors of white supremacist terror and galvanized their community's resistance to it, though they were given little credit for their work.

We haven't been silent until now. We've had a long history of speaking truth to power. But we've also endured a very long history that devalues our opinions, maligns our point of view, and assaults our dignity daily.

A quote accompanies each story in this volume out of a wellspring of wisdom from historical and contemporary Black women. Settle down with it or read it on the fly. Read. Listen now. I'm speaking now.

— Breena Clarke —
February 7, 2021

The Gift

You're going to walk into many rooms... where you
may be the only one who looks like you... We are
all in that room with you applauding you on...
So you use that voice and be strong.
~Kamala Harris

My gift is my voice
My voice is a gift
It strengthens and encourages
Has the power to uplift

For so long it was stifled
Turned down and smothered
Muted and disregarded
Diminished and covered

All the while inside
Emotions wildly rioted
It was always "Hush li'l Black girl"
Time and time again I was quieted

My voice has many labels
Angry Black woman loud and all-knowing
When really what it is
Is my truth overflowing

I am an amplifier of voices
That were forced into submission
No longer only speaking when spoken to
I don't need permission

From now on I will speak when I desire
And say whatever I please
My voice may move some to action
My voice will bring some to their knees

—Ellen Pinnock—

Stand Up, Speak Out

Breakfast in Northport

When they go low, we go high.
~Michelle Obama

The weathered bell above the white painted-peeling doorway clatters
an unknown tune to the backdrop of morning feet
scuffling in from the excitement of a fenced-in Ferris wheel.
I face the window.
Residents' blushed cheeks turn pink from the autumn breeze the lake
casts off.
Kids with well-funded educations
skip by for ice cream and cotton candy.
Main Street closed off for high school marching bands,
the highest form of entertainment the town allows.
Their children featured in the parade,
Watering plants, watching themselves grow
in this secret white pod of privilege.

Black girl, you don't belong here!
The waitress's body language smolders.
Refusing to water my empty glass,
passing our table serving incoming patrons.
I pass time studying my menu of options, retorts, rebuttals, and complaints

I'm used to it. I just wait.
She finally awaits, impatient
face weathered from a hard life of hate.
No forgiveness,
No eye contact.

What'll you'll have?
A heaping full of respect,
A side of justice and equity...
Decaf coffee with cream. And
the satisfaction of blessing a working-class racist
with a generous tip
From a Black woman.

—Zorina Exie Frey—

Black Girl

You can't be hesitant about who you are.
~Viola Davis

I was in third grade when a classmate decided my name was too hard to pronounce. He said my name wasn't normal anyway, so he wouldn't even bother. "I'll just call you what you are," he'd said.

The next morning, as I hurried down the block, he made good on his promise. "Hey Black girl," he yelled, "better hurry up!"

"Hey white boy," I quipped, "shut up!"

I trudged to the bus stop, not realizing Mama overheard me. When I looked down the street to see if the bus was coming, it was my mama I saw marching down the block in Navy-issued sweatpants and slippers — large pink rollers jostling round her head. When she reached me, she bent at her waist to make sure her face met mine.

"I had better not EVER hear you call someone by the color of their skin again," she whispered harshly. "Do you understand me?"

Her brow furrowed in anger, mine in confusion.

"Yes ma'am," I stammered. I was going to stop there, but when I felt the boy's blue eyes on us — on me, I just needed her to take my side. I explained my word choice: "He called me Black girl and said my name was too hard."

He snickered.

She shot him a look that said, "If I could whip your behind right now, I would." He looked down.

Mama turned back to me; her face softened, but her words didn't. "If you react like this to every ignorant person who crosses your path, you're no better than them." I wanted to tell her I didn't want to be better than them, that I just wanted to do to them what they'd done to me.

My mama wasn't that type of mama, though, so I yes-ma'am'ed the rest of our exchange. I have no idea what else she said before the "I love you" and kiss on my forehead. She stood at the bus stop until the bus came, periodically glancing the boy's way.

He was quiet the entire ride to school. It was like my mama's looks haunted him beyond the neighborhood. I hoped it'd last forever, but the magic ended once we entered our classroom.

"Way to sic your Black mama on me," he spewed, as we hung our coats up.

"Black girl. That's what your mama should've named you," he whispered during attendance.

He even sang, "Black girl" to the tune of the "Star-Spangled Banner." The Pledge of Allegiance provided a brief reprieve from his taunts.

"You'd better be glad your mama taught you some manners. I didn't even know Black mamas could do that."

That one stung more than the others, but I couldn't put my finger on why. Maybe because all the Black mamas I'd ever known had and taught manners. Maybe it was the implication that Black people, Black women — my people and the women who taught them to be — were somehow less than. I bit down hard on my quivering lip and clenched the sides of my desk, willing the weakness of sadness away. I didn't know how I was going to do it, but I resolved to shut him up once and for all — and I wouldn't break Mama's rule, either.

When my teacher called for a bathroom and water break, I decided to stay put. Once the boy saw me sitting, he decided he didn't have to go either. As soon as the class was out of earshot, he began: "Hey, Black girl. Why don't you like being called black girl, when that's what you are?"

"I'm not even black. I'm more like... sienna," I responded in earnest while inspecting my arms.

"If you're not white, you're Black," he shrugged. I continued my inspection.

"Black girl. Did you hear what I said? If you're not white, you're Black." His words were slow and drawn out as if I couldn't understand. I hated my intelligence being questioned.

"You're really dumb. That doesn't even make sense. There are plenty of shades between black and white," I retorted.

"My mama told me that, so it does make sense."

"Guess your mama's dumb too, then," I suggested.

His face grew red as what I'd said churned in his mind. Finally, he was feeling what I felt.

"You don't like that, do you?"

"Black girl, shut your dumb black mouth before I rip your dumb black hair out of your dumb black head just because I'm tired of looking at your dumb. Black. Face."

That did it. That's what finally turned the hurt into anger. I threw paper, pencils, erasers, crayons — they all missed, just as my words had before now. Too small, I thought. I'll have better aim with something bigger. My body took over. I pushed a desk in front of him. Then, I picked up a chair. His eyes widened in surprise, then flattened, daring me to do the unthinkable. I didn't think. The chair hurled through the air. The metal leg of it hit him in his lip and as it tumbled to the floor, our class returned.

"What is going on?" our teacher exclaimed.

"Nothing." The boy hurried back to his seat, sucking the bloodied part of his lip.

I stared in bewilderment at the mess. Instinctively, I went into damage control mode. I hurried around, putting items where they belonged while the boy sat at his desk staring at the blank chalkboard.

Our teacher got the class settled and pulled us both into the hallway.

"Do I need to call your parents?" She looked back and forth between us.

Just the mention of calling Mama scared me. "If you do, tell her I DIDN'T call him white boy!" I blurted. The boy rolled his eyes.

"I'll deal with you in a moment," our teacher ushered the boy back to class. "Not a WORD," she commanded the class.

She returned to the hallway to find me fighting tears.

"Kamala. Tell me what happened," was her stern, but gentle demand.

I laid it out, piece by piece. By the time I got to the part about the flying chair, she almost looked amused. I apologized over and over, full-on sobbing by the time I finished.

To my surprise, she hugged me. It was like one of my aunties had come to my rescue.

"Your mama's right… but I know how you're feeling." She let me cry, her back to the class so no one could see me. She assured me that she would tell my mom that I did not call him "white boy" when she called her to let her know I got detention. My glimmer of hope for not getting in trouble quickly vanished; I looked to the ground.

My teacher cradled my chin and held my head high. "Next time, tell someone before it becomes too much to bear. Can you promise me that?"

"Yes ma'am."

Detention wasn't so bad. As I was leaving, my teacher stopped to tell me that it's not about what they call me, but what I answer to.

"And there is nothing at all in the world wrong with being a Black girl," she added with a smile.

— Kamala Reese —

I Don't See Color

Just remember the world is not a playground
but a schoolroom. Life is not a holiday
but an education. One eternal lesson for us all:
to teach us how better we should love.
~Barbara Jordan

"Hey, did you watch the nigger show last night?" My classmate Tommy, aka Mr. Popular, was most likely referring to the sitcom *A Different World.*

My knee-jerk response was to climb the ladder of the jungle gym because that's what you are conditioned to do when you're the newest kid on the block — and, in fact, are the only Black girl at Stottlemyer Elementary School, located in Westland, Michigan, a suburb twenty miles west of Detroit.

You steel yourself, will away the tears, and keep swallowing until you finally succeed in suppressing the lump in your throat. You see, that playground episode wasn't my first trip to the racial epithet rodeo.

Nearly five years earlier, when I was a kindergartener at a different elementary school less than five miles away, a blond classmate looked me in the eye as we lined up to head to the art room and asked if I was sad. Perplexed, I responded, "No, why?"

"Because," Melissa began, "if I woke up Black I would kill myself."

My five-year-old brain didn't have the capacity to fully absorb the heinousness of her words. Still, I told my parents as soon as I got home from school.

What quickly ensued was a heated argument between my parents behind closed doors. I heard it all: My mother wanted to yank me from that school; my father, however, begged to differ. "She stays," he said firmly. "The thicker her skin, the better."

I would go on to develop a particular brand of resilience that comes from having experienced perverse exclusion at school while simultaneously being enveloped in the strongest love at home. Looking back, my parents nurtured my budding self-confidence by supporting my interest in music and athletics.

To know me was to know that I was both silly and cautious, loyal and independent. But to most of my peers, my color alone was what defined me.

And so, a thirteen-year-old me was flat out dumbfounded when my then best friend Renee said what she said after confiding in me about her parents' imminent divorce. "When I look at you, I don't see a Black girl."

Huh? Of course, she saw color.

Moments earlier, we'd debated the merits of spending my babysitting money on pink high-top sneakers versus blue ones. Renee only fancied boys with blue eyes and knew precisely how much Sun In to apply to achieve the shade of blond she wanted.

Trust me, Renee saw color. As did Tommy, Melissa, and my other classmates who preceded her.

I continued to hear "I don't see color" in high school and college, and it followed me clear into adulthood. The older I got, the more insistent many of my white friends were about not seeing my most obvious physical characteristic aside from my gender.

Most recently, it came from a fellow karate mom while I waited in the lobby during my son Scotty's weekly martial arts class: "I swear, Courtney, I don't see color."

Some background on these moms and me: Our children had been practicing together for three years, and we'd grown to genuinely like and respect each other. We talk about ourselves in such a way that makes it impossible not to acknowledge the obvious.

These moms have inquired about the products I use on my naturally curly hair; what it's like to have a former NFL football player husband; how likely it is that Scotty will surpass me in height by age twelve (hello, his father is 6' 7").

To ignore my color — or to claim not to see it — is a decision, even if it's a subconscious one. And while I don't think there is a hint of malice behind it, it comes across as such, and here's why: Imagine going on a shopping spree and acquiring the most beautiful ensemble you could imagine, one that you are downright proud of… only for a friend to say, "I don't see a thing."

Are they saying my color makes them so uncomfortable, they have to pretend I don't look like me? For many of my former classmates, I was the rarity, the only Black person they had ever really become acquainted with. They retained their generalizations and stereotypes about Black people; I was just the exception.

So, then, what happens when those classmates meet a Black woman who was raised in a two-parent household, who graduated from college, who — like them — volunteers weekly at her children's elementary school, and who listens to Def Leppard and Loverboy as well as Ohio Players and War?

Enter something else I've heard my entire life: "You're Black, but you're not Black."

But I am Black. And it's okay for you to see it.

Black people are not a monolith. I can be all the things you like about me — as well as Black. All can — and do — co-exist.

Seeing a person's color is not racist; but acting on any prejudiced attitudes because of that person's color is — whether one does this deliberately or has been culturally conditioned over time to do so.

The question is not whether we see color — because we all see it. The question is: Why would anyone choose not to?

The key, I believe, is recognizing — and challenging — these thoughts when they occur. Nipping assumptions in the bud is a good thing, too.

Please, see my color. Better yet, embrace it. Just as I'd hope you would come to appreciate my wry sense of humor and penchant for extra-hot café au lait.

But, if you must find something to ignore, go ahead and overlook my gray hairs. Because to know me is also to know that I just don't care enough about dying them.

— Courtney Conover —

Brave on the Inside

Who you are today… that's who you are. Be brave.
Be amazing. Be worthy. Be heard.
~Shonda Rhimes

When I entered the living room that night, she looked up and tilted her head curiously at me. Certainly, she must have wondered why I looked scared. I took the smallest steps toward her as I prepared to face her. She sat on the couch, paging through the old Bible that crackled beneath the weight of her thumb.

I was holding three copies of the Friday edition of the *Atlanta Journal-Constitution* against my chest. A few days ago, I'd received the good news. The editor said it was an "important and timely message" and it would be in the print and online editions. He was especially impressed with the perspective I brought, having professional connections to the police.

I gingerly extended one of the folded papers to her. "Mom, I wrote something. It was published as a guest column in our local paper. Will you please read it and let me know what you think?"

My mother read the headline aloud and her eyebrows furrowed slightly as she did so. "Protests Are an Overdue Wake-up Call."

I searched her face for even the faintest signs of approval or disapproval while she read the 700 words of my article. At times I caught what looked like a grin starting up, but at other times she looked more pensive. She raised her head and met my nervous gaze.

"When you said in this part of your column that 'bias in policing is a problematic symptom, but it's not the root cause,' what did you mean exactly?"

I swallowed weakly. "Well, what I meant was that the racial biases and discrimination that pervade many law enforcement systems are just the more prominent signs of a large-scale moral sickness in our society. It's bigger though than any one institution or any police force. We're talking about a dangerous double standard that has been in play for generations."

Mom nodded her head understandingly and returned to reading. I quietly exhaled. When I first thought of writing an op-ed praising the message of the Black Lives Matter movement and expounding on how the social protests happening in my city were long overdue, I knew I'd have to be brave. I knew there might be a backlash.

I'd worked in public safety as an emergency call taker and police dispatcher for more than five years. I do this job because I believe there are still more good, honest, and virtuous people behind the badge than bad people.

I'd always believed in the righteousness of law enforcement until the news about Breonna Taylor practically broke my heart in two. Something about this young, loving African American female who served her community as an EMT weighed heavily on my emotions. Even more incredibly, on what would have been Breonna Taylor's twenty-seventh birthday, I watched my little sister celebrate her twenty-fourth birthday and blow out the candles on her vanilla-and-buttercream sprinkled cupcakes. Breonna would never get to do that again.

So, what could I do to lend my support to the Black Lives Matter movement? I decided I would write an essay baring my heart and explaining what it means to me specifically; being a racial minority who identifies with public safety but wants to see some much-needed reform.

My mom lay the newspaper down with a mix of concern and, dare I say it, pride on her face.

"You took a chance writing this, you know?"

"I know."

"This was a big risk. Do you realize that?"

"I know."

"What if the people at your job read this?"

"They might. I don't know… I don't care if they do, I suppose." She was sounding more exasperated.

"Did you even think to consider how this might reflect back on you, or on us, your family? What were you trying to accomplish by sending this essay to be published for so many eyes to see?" She shook her finger at me.

I hung my head.

"This is bigger than you wanting to get your opinion out there. You put your job in jeopardy. I really wish you had consulted me first."

"If I had consulted you, you would have talked me out of it. You would have told me that I shouldn't put myself out there in the line of fire. Mom, I knew this was something I had to do. This is my form of protest. I can't swarm the city square with demonstrators, chanting, and hoisting a sign high into the air. But I can write my local newspaper. I can share this message of support and understanding for those who are marching, raising heck, and making noise. I wanted to write this column because staying dead silent wasn't an option any longer for me."

Her lips quivered. This time it was her turn to lower her head. She shook it gently and then she stood up from the couch without another word.

The next morning, my mother woke me in bed; her eyes were watery and red. She wiped away a tear as she spoke to me in a hushed voice.

"Your article … it's beautiful. It's bold. But it's something… something I could have never written. How did you get so brave?"

"From you, Mom. You taught me."

They say that we're all reflections of our parents; well, I'm a mirror image of my mom. Strong-willed. Independent. Unwavering. And a whole lot of loud. I can only be as brave as I am because she is the bravest Black woman I know. I learned from her how to be resilient and courageous in the face of anything or anyone. She taught me to never back down from a fight.

She also taught me it takes courage to leave this world better than how I found it. I chose a career of service to my community because I wanted to be a part of the reason why my citizens feel safe. Today, I choose to use my voice and my words bravely to fight back against any injustice I see. I'm not braver than my mother. I'm just my mother's daughter.

—Samantha Hawkins—

In the Dark of Night

If you are silent about your pain, they'll kill you
and say you enjoyed it.
~Zora Neale Hurston

I was headed home from my third shift job at FedEx one Thursday night in 2004. I was excited that I was able to volunteer to leave early, because I had a final exam at 8 a.m. I was pulled over at approximately 4 a.m. When I looked in the side mirror, there were four other police cruisers. The officers all exited their cars, with weapons drawn, and one got on the bullhorn to tell me to turn off my car and throw the keys out the window. I was confused, scared, and alone.

Of course, I complied. I threw my keys out the window and got out the car.

I was immediately swarmed upon and placed in handcuffs. They said my car had been reported stolen. I said it couldn't be reported stolen as it was mine and I was driving it. I was driving a 1993 white Chevy Blazer with Virginia plates. I had recently been honorably discharged from serving four years in the United States Marine Corps, and this was the car I had purchased while stationed in North Carolina. The white officer proceeded to keep interrogating and demanding I tell him who I got the car from. I repeatedly told him that I didn't remember the name of the dealership, that it was in Virginia.

Luckily, an African American female officer arrived on the scene and pulled me to the side as they searched my vehicle without permission. She asked me the same questions and I told her, if they would check my license and registration, they would see that this vehicle was mine. She looked at me and said, "Wait, no one checked your license?" She retrieved my purse from the front seat and brought it to me so I could watch her get my wallet out. She then called over the main officer and said a few words to him. I was then placed in the back of his cruiser while she stood next to me with the door open.

He kept proceeding to ask about my car and why it was reported stolen. He finally ran my plates. He then apologized and said my car fit the description of another reported vehicle. They were looking for a white Suzuki. I said, "A Blazer is way bigger and shaped different, and you should have run the plates first." The African American officer shook her head at him and watched as he removed my handcuffs and apologized.

I filed a formal complaint at the downtown precinct the following day. The officers working the front desk looked up their badge numbers and the incident and noted that the whole thing only lasted fifteen minutes. For me, it seemed like a lifetime.

In fifteen minutes, my life could have been snuffed away due to an overzealous, negligent, racist, protected-by-the-badge cop. Instead, God protected me and sent the African American woman officer there that night.

I could have been Breonna Taylor or Sandra Bland. But, instead, I am LaTonya Watson.

This is why we protest.

— LaTonya R. Watson —

A Black Woman Not Afraid of the South

Effective leaders must be truth seekers,
and that requires a willingness to understand
truths other than our own.
~Stacy Abrams

"I want to create a space of love for the women who have been ostracized from the church because they are labeled unworthy, loose and filthy, unsaved, and trouble. I want to walk the streets with the prostitutes to tell them that they are loved, and I want to hug the diseased to remind them that love is the contagion, not their disease."

This was the statement from my ministry assignment given in my first undergraduate Biblical Studies class. As I boldly announced in my class presentation that I wanted to be a minister to broken women, the students raised their sleepy heads from their desk to look at me with bewilderment. I stood waiting for applause or even a hallelujah. Instead, my professor said, "Take a seat, ma'am. You're failing this assignment because ministry is teaching and preaching the word of God from a pulpit. Considering that you're a woman, from the South — you won't ever be qualified to do that and it's in the Bible."

Twenty years later, I sit typing this story with the titles of Dr. and Pastor in front of my name. I became the pastor that my professor said I would never be, but one thing he was almost right about was that being a woman in the South, with a mission to bring God's love and grace to broken women would be no easy feat.

Not only am I an educated woman pastor in a region of the South that has an alarmingly high illiteracy rate; I'm also a six-foot-tall Black woman with a New York/Mississippi accent. You would have to hear my voice to truly understand how one sentence of my speech can combine slow simmering Southern dialect with a boisterous New York accent.

Back to the real reason you're here.

Several years ago, I walked into ministry in the South with a desire to bring encouragement about God's grace and mercy to women who have been ostracized and stigmatized by society. They've been judged with harsh labels intended to keep them down based on their gender and their past mistakes. Being that I was raised in the South, I saw the negative ramifications of how religion and culture are used to separate and divide our nation; arguably, even more so than race relations.

The first time I felt the calling to be a spiritual advocate for women came when I was twelve years old. My parents were visiting a small southern Black church for an annual summer revival, and the pastor called all sinners to come to the altar. However, on this particular night he called for a specific little girl to come to the altar. I knew this little girl because she and I were playmates. As she and her family walked to the altar, the pastor never called the little girl by her name — he only referred to her as "Sinner." Once the girl and her family made the long and treacherous walk down the aisle, past all those so-called Christian stares, the pastor turned the little girl around to face the congregation. Then he spoke such demeaning words: "This sinner is carrying a sin baby at only fourteen years old. We are going to pray that God rebukes the sex demon out of her, and that her baby's soul will be saved and won't burn."

Still to this day, I break down when I confront that memory. Even as I write these words, I see the shame on that little girl's face, the look of condemnation on the pastor; I smell the dirty baptism pool water, I hear the snickering of the boys sitting in the front pew, and I feel the pull to help this little girl as her eyes zero in on me.

Today, I serve three small churches not too far from the same church where these heinous memories were created. I carry the unspoken narrative of that little girl in the ministry that I am building in the South.

A few years ago, I sat before a panel of Christian leaders within my denomination, and they asked the same question that my undergraduate professor asked in the Biblical studies class: "What is ministry to you?"

As I sat before the panel, I provided the same answer as I did in that cold and dark undergraduate classroom presentation: "I want to create a space of love for the women who have been ostracized from the church because they are labeled unworthy, loose and filthy, unsaved, and trouble. I want to walk the streets with the prostitutes to tell them that they are loved, and I want to hug the diseased to remind them that love is the contagion, not their disease."

A white woman on the panel told me that those kinds of women, or those problems, did not exist in the South. I was told to go build my ministry in a larger city that has issues, because ministry was for the pulpit in the South.

These words cut just as deep as the words of the professor fifteen years ago, but because of the face of that little girl and the many women I have encountered who have been labeled and judged because of their past mistakes, I cannot move. I cannot give up, and I cannot see my gender or race as something bad or shameful.

I am a six-foot-tall educated, Southern, beautiful Black woman advocating for Women of Color in the South, in areas where they're labeled as unworthy. All Women Matter. The mistakes we make in life do not define us; they create testimonies of power, resilience, and sisterhood. I'm using my voice and ministry to provide them the sisterhood they need and deserve.

— Kitsy Marie Dixon —

That 70s Cop

I don't know who I would be if I weren't this child
from Harlem, this woman from Harlem.
It's in me so deep.
~Ruby Dee

A month had passed before Jeremiah summoned the courage to tell me what happened. My nephew thought I'd somehow blame him; accuse him of some misbehavior that had drawn attention to himself. But I knew better.

"You're lucky you got that uniform on," the cop had sneered. Jeremiah had been spared the humiliation — this time. If this encounter had gone sideways, it would've been tricky for the cop to explain to the brass the harassment of a Catholic school kid simply walking home from school. And he knew it.

Listening to Jeremiah dredged up my own long buried memories of cops back in the 1970s. Back then I was the one in the uniform traveling New York City's subways alone to and from school. They didn't call it Stop & Frisk back then, but the effects, the emotional damage, would prove the same. Now, whenever I hear some enlightened official reflect on the city's lawlessness in the 1970s, I wonder how NYC Transit's finest so often found time to confront me.

The excuse, the justification, was always the same — an in-depth physical inspection of my monthly student train pass. Was it the sight of the uniform that irritated them? Did they resent a little Black girl from a Harlem housing project receiving a better education than their kid?

Perhaps I'm mistaken. Maybe that's not where their heads were at all. Afraid to tackle the real criminals, did stopping harmless me suffice as having done their job? Did ruining my morning improve theirs?

Was this a sick twisted fantasy starring a schoolgirl? I spotted an officer who'd harassed me that same afternoon on the train. He was out of uniform and trying to strike up a conversation with a girl my age, only to have her reject his advances. Was announcing he was a cop supposed to reassure her, put her at ease or compel her to comply? He didn't notice her father observing from across the aisle until it was too late. "I don't care what the %!#@ you are. Don't talk to my daughter!" said the irate dad.

As I grew older, I wonder if they noticed that the fear in my eyes morphed into disdain? I allowed my eyes to declare what my mouth couldn't.

My fellow classmate Tosha hadn't reached that level of understanding. I can only imagine her tirade of indignation was most satisfying at the time. Being escorted to the precinct and needlessly detained long enough to miss two of our final exams a week before graduation wasn't.

I'm proud of Jeremiah. It took him only a month to share his story. I never managed enough courage to speak my truth—that is until now.

— Katheryne McMullen —

Crown of Curls

The strength of a mother is in the ears and on the lips.
~Mali Proverb

We walked into the auditorium for meet-the-teacher night for kindergarten. Both of us were feeling nervous and a little excited. I scanned the auditorium full of parents and their children and saw no one who looked like us. This had become an all too familiar theme living in Utah.

I got in line to sign up for the PTA, thinking that was one way to add some diversity and different perspectives. As I stood in the line, other mothers were greeted by the ladies working the table, asking if they would like to volunteer. When my son and I made it to the table, I was neither greeted nor offered the opportunity to sign up. Frustrated, I got out of line and tried to find a seat before the orientation started.

As Jeremiah and I sat down, we began to get stares. The discomfort began to get to me, so I called my husband and told him how out of place I felt. He validated my feelings, encouraged me to stay a little longer, and said he would be praying.

I hung up the phone and in came this little Latino boy and his father. Jeremiah and the boy were excited to see each other and hugged. I asked Jeremiah if he knew him and he said that the boy went to his daycare. His father came over and introduced himself and they were a breath of fresh air. We learned the boys would have the same teacher, which eased my mama heart.

After some remarks and introductions by the principal we were released to go and see our children's classrooms and meet the teacher. Jeremiah and his friend were inseparable, so the Dad and I continued making small talk while waiting in line to speak with the teacher. When Jeremiah and I got to the front, the teacher looked at Jeremiah and loudly said, "Oh my goodness! Look at your hair. I love your curls."

The first day of school, I was standing in line outside the classroom holding Jeremiah's hand. A father and his little girl came and stood beside us and said hello. The father then put his hands in Jeremiah's curly hair. I looked at him and Jeremiah looked at him uncomfortably; and he removed his hand. The teacher came out to greet all the kids and when she saw Jeremiah that same loud squeal and comment about his hair followed.

This, unfortunately, became commonplace. Every interaction I had with her resulted in a comment about Jeremiah's hair, including on a field trip.

The last straw was when we had parent/teacher/student conferences. The teacher went over Jeremiah's progress and then asked me to check his registration card. I noticed they had his race marked as white, so I showed her the mistake and she replied, "Oh we know he's not white; you can tell by looking at his hair." I stared at her blankly, not wanting to make a scene or show any disrespect to my son's teacher in front of him. So, we left and when I received Jeremiah's report card, in the comment section was yet another remark about his hair.

One night, after I washed his hair, Jeremiah was looking in the mirror as I brushed his hair back. He said, "Mommy, I look so cool." And then told me his hair looked like a friend's. The next morning, when his curls were back, he looked in the mirror and said, "I don't like my hair; it doesn't look straight anymore."

I teared up over that. My young son disliked his beautiful crown of curls. He had loved them when we lived in Texas. There he would get comments, but it was different. They were compliments, not remarks that highlighted his difference. I'd had my own experience with this in Utah, when an older woman commented on my curls and then asked me if they were real. When I told her yes, she put her hands right in my hair to see for herself. I couldn't shake how violated I felt that day.

So I could only imagine how Jeremiah had been feeling.

I scheduled a meeting with Jeremiah's teacher. I explained that Jeremiah had begun to dislike his curls, and I walked her through all the times she'd talked about them, including on the report card. I asked if she'd made any comments about the other children's hair on their report cards and she said no. She apologized and stated that it was not her intention to hurt Jeremiah or make him feel uncomfortable. I accepted and told her I believed her, because I did. But I shared that intention does not eliminate the impact. The comments from his teacher about his hair stopped after that meeting.

I ordered some new books and the one that resonated for him was *What I Like About Me!* by Allia Zobel Nolan. I also made up a silly song just for him: "Jeremiah's got the best curls in the world!" I sang it to him every day as I did his hair. Our neighbors told him about Lenny Kravitz and showed him pictures.

After a few days, success! Jeremiah said, "Mommy, I like my hair and I don't want to change it."

— Shawntae Chase —

Code of Silence

If there's one thing I've learned in life,
it's the power of using your voice.
~Michelle Obama, *Becoming*

"Ms. Wyatt, tell me what's going on," the doctor said.

"Well, when I bit into a piece of toast over the weekend, I heard a loud pop and immediately experienced pain out of this world from the lower left side of my face. It hurt so bad I saw stars and now I can't open my mouth to brush my teeth anymore, can't talk properly, can't chew at all, and can't sleep at night without this aching pain. I've been eating vanilla pudding for three days straight and I miss the taste of real food SO MUCH."

"Do you grind your teeth? I know you have a hectic job and I'm sure nowadays the stress is driving everyone crazy," the oral surgeon asked as he examined my jaw X-rays.

It is indeed true, I work in a highly-stressful environment. For us Congressional staffers, charged with helping lawmakers represent their districts and states, the hours are long, the work intense, and because the nation seems to lurch from one crisis to the next, every breaking news story is an urgent emergency. It hasn't helped that the COVID-19 pandemic took away my usual stress alleviators, all my family members are essential workers and going into work every day, and we are in the middle of one of the most politically-charged times in our nation's history. But every day, I just put my head down, move my emotions to the backburner so I can focus, grit my teeth, and get the job done — because public service is my passion. Politics and policymaking aren't for the faint-hearted.

I half denied and half acknowledged the truth, flatly proclaiming, "I have ground my teeth in the past, yes."

Concern flashed across the surgeon's face and he hurriedly left the room. As I waited for him to return, I stared at the stark white ceiling, shivering in that freezing room and trying not to inhale the acrid smell of too many cleaning supplies in one contained area. I let out the breath I didn't realize I was holding and thought more about the surgeon's question.

He wasn't the first to ask — my orthodontist when fitting me for braces in high school asked me the same. I've been a teeth-grinder since middle school and when I went to see a therapist in college, she said, "Trauma lives on in the body. Your teeth grinding is your emotions trying to make their escape. They can't stay silent forever."

With the rush of a white lab coat, the oral surgeon returned, disrupting my thoughts and pulling me back into the present. He delivered the bad news: I had a jaw fracture caused by my recent wisdom teeth removal and many years of teeth grinding weakening my jaw. I vaguely heard him tell me to maintain a strict liquid diet for the next eight weeks as I silently blinked back tears. Walking back to the car, I resolved to take a long drive (a newly discovered pandemic habit) and clear my head.

The same questions reverberated in my mind as street after street disappeared in my rearview mirror: When did I begin grinding my teeth? When did I silence my emotions? And when did they try to make an escape?

When a boy forced his hand up my skirt on the school bus one day without my permission, I knew that to tell anyone would be the ruin of my already shaky reputation at a new school. Speaking up and saying the wrong thing was a sign of weakness, which made you a sure target for relentless bullies. Trying not to fulfill stereotypes as the only Black student in predominantly white classes at Harvard, I continued the silence. Ditto for working in Congress, one of the world's most elite halls of power. I morphed into a Black wallflower, gritting my teeth to keep from saying the wrong thing, at the wrong time. A silencing of myself over and over, until I thought I had nothing valuable left to say: Silenced.

To be smart, educated, vocal, Black, and a woman was not always the paragon it is today.

"You're an enigma to me. I don't know anything about you because you never share anything about your life." my sister said to me once on a road trip. I sat in the front passenger seat dumbfounded that my blood sister and decades-long best friend, the person I'm closest to in the world, felt she didn't know me. She continued, "For example, I have no idea how you felt when we were kids and Mom was diagnosed with breast cancer for the second time."

I ducked my head and stared at the floor: "I really don't remember feeling anything at all. All I knew was that I had to keep it together so that we could keep functioning. There was no time for emotions." Cue the clenched jaw.

I never made a formal vow of silence. No, I made seemingly small compromises between myself and my emotions along the way that belittled my ability to use my voice. Like a muscle atrophied from lack of use, my voice withered away until I no longer knew how to use it. I sacrificed my truth on the altar of others' truths, desired outcomes, and comfort without realizing the disservice I was doing to myself and everyone around me.

That fractured jaw and my ensuing recovery provided physical proof that my silence, a toxic defense mechanism, was hurting me in tangible ways, not helping me. If I wanted to heal physically, change was no longer optional, and I needed to regain my voice.

I began to speak up in big and little ways: at meetings and in salary negotiations. Acknowledging my emotions, advocating for myself, and speaking my truth released some of the jaw tension. Being honest created a space of vulnerability for others to be open with me too. I voiced things I had never said out loud to my family, friends, and even co-workers. And they repaid me in kind with some of the most honest, intimate, and cherished conversations I've ever experienced in my life. In speaking up, they experienced the real Jasmine, not some robot — after all, our voices and experiences are what make us human.

Weeks after my fracture, domestic terrorists and rioters stormed the United States Capitol Building, my workplace for the last five years. As I watched video after video of the destruction and chaos unfolding on TV, my chest tightened, my heart raced, and I couldn't breathe no matter how hard I gasped for air. I gritted my teeth as every illusion of national progress and false sense of security I held tightly crumbled in an instant.

A colleague e-mailed me about the tragic events asking, "How are you holding up?" I started to type my traditional "All is well" answer before I stopped, fingers poised over the keyboard, teeth still gritted, and pain radiating from my jaw. I hit the backspace button, took a deep breath, and instead wrote "I appreciate you asking, to be honest…"

—Jasmine J. Wyatt—

The Fight to Save the Future

If we merge mercy with might, and might with right,
then love becomes our legacy and change
our children's birthright.
~Amanda Gorman, The Hill We Climb

Originally, I went to AfroComicCon because I thought it would be a good place for a date with my man. He's an Afro Caribbean fantasy-novel reading, *World of Warcraft* playing, *Star Trek* and *Star Wars* watching, *Magic: The Gathering* card-collecting, comic book page-flipping type brother. Although we've been together almost twenty years, when we hang at home, you might find us cuddled up reading very different books. I'm a sister who writes heist and spy fiction, so while we both like our action and drama, we are decidedly living in different genres. The only movie we've seen together in the theater in the last decade was *Black Panther*.

I have much love for the sci-fi fantasy writers of color because these folks are holding a powerful vision of Black people in the future. So I took my man to AfroComicCon in 2017, just after Hurricane Maria had devastated Puerto Rico. I'm a Black Puerto Rican, so that year, I began to see everything through a lens of the climate crisis. So, while I was surrounded by Black people talking about superpowers and heroism and the future, I was also thinking about the climate emergency.

Scientists agree that human beings, especially those of us in the

U.S. and the West, have been burning fossil fuels and the carbon in the air is trapping heat. It's warming the planet and causing sea level rise, and all kinds of disasters, with more to come. Scientists are saying that we have to make drastic changes in cutting fossil fuel emissions if we hope to stand a chance of having a planet whose air, and water, and land can actually support human habitation moving into the future.

Things have heightened to a state of emergency. It's like an episode of *Star Trek*: "Oh no, Captain! This planet is gonna blow!" But unlike *Star Trek*, we only have one earth, and can't tour the galaxy to find a better planet, one that's more stable and fit for human habitation. We need to take the action necessary to save this one.

I have to be honest. When I was coming up, I didn't see a lot of Black people talking about the environment. Some of us did talk about pollution in our neighborhoods, and rates of asthma, but it often seemed that the environment wasn't our issue and the climate movement wasn't our movement. We're tired. We're working on racial and economic and gender justice. Our communities are fighting so many issues of danger and survival today. But all that is changing.

Many movements are coming together to fight for climate justice. Because in order to solve the issues of climate, we need justice-based solutions that are so massive, they will also solve many other types of inequities.

When I stood in AfroComicCon and saw a wide array of Black people cosplaying comic book characters and superheroes, I had that expansive feeling that we can be anything, can do anything. Black writers of science fiction and fantasy are creating visions so Black people can see ourselves in the future. I think we need to take it a step further, we are being called upon to save the future. We need to emulate the people of Wakanda and imagine our power outside of the limits that racism has set for us. Because we all know that inside we are that powerful. I'm telling you, people, WE are the vibranium.

And there's this one particular shred of hope that I've been clinging to lately: *The Hero's Journey*. Joseph Campbell talks about a monomyth, a story that has appeared in every culture on the planet, and it's about a reluctant hero who gets called upon to leave their safe comfortable world and venture into an unknown world. This is the plot of so many of our favorite stories: *Star Wars*, *Moana*, *Black Panther*. And in the so-called darkest hour of the story, the hero has lost hope. The crew is turning on each other. The power of the enemy seems unstoppable. And the hero wants to give up.

Really, the hero has given up. They're just gonna stop fighting and let the evil forces win. But someone comes along and tells them that they can do it. Because it turns out that after all the physical obstacles the hero or band of heroes had fought, the final obstacle was within, their hopelessness or guilt or shame or fear of inadequacy holding them back.

And then some kind of mentor or ancestor or magical force comes and tells them that they can do it. They can fight and they can win. And I choose to believe that human beings in every culture in the world have been telling this story for thousands of years because it is our story. Because we are those heroes, and because we can win if we set aside our hopelessness and fight.

At AfroComicCon I looked around at all those fabulous Black people in their cosplay outfits, and I realized, we're gonna have to come out from behind the books and the gaming consoles and the laptop screens. We're gonna have to join the rebellion, the resistance, the movement IRL — in real life. And we can make noise on the Internet, but we also have to organize and strategize and build a movement that is stronger than the forces that want to destroy the planet.

My man and I went to AfroComicCon that first year, and the second year we brought our kid. Now we go every year. I've even started writing some science-fiction and fantasy of my own. But the biggest takeaway is that Black people can do anything, and that the future is in our hands.

— Aya de Leon —

The Only One

*If everyone likes you, it probably means
you aren't saying much.*
~Donna Brazile

My office phone rang. I picked up the receiver and stated my last name. A soft voice on the other end said, "The assistant superintendent would like to see you."

I tried to think of what I had done to get called to my boss' office. "Okay, coming," I said in a weary voice before disconnecting the call.

I took a slow, steady stroll down the hallway, still wondering what I'd done to merit this unusual invitation. The secretary ushered me into the room where I was surprised to find my boss's boss standing in the corner.

My eyes widened, and my heart sank. "Oh, God! What did I do?" I said. Their laughter reassured me that it was okay to breathe.

My boss directed me to have a seat, and I did. Like a child in the principal's office, I waited for the man who held my fate to speak.

"Doc and I are having a discussion about Black Lives Matter, and we would like you to do a presentation on the subject for a group of stakeholders in the district."

My eyes narrowed. "I need more context."

My boss's boss chimed in. "I fear that the anger and animosity in the community surrounding George Floyd's death, and this war all over social media with 'Black Lives Matter,' 'Blue Lives Matter,' and

'All Lives Matter,' is going to spill over into our institution."

He paused, waiting for me to respond, but when I said nothing, he continued. "I'm afraid of what might happen if we don't deal with this now and provide our employees tools to help navigate these times. As a white man, there is still much for me to learn, but I'm willing."

I still sat there with my eyes darting between him and my boss trying to get a feel of the room, trying to gauge truth and intentions, and trying to determine if my organization was really ready for such a topic. I could think of 100 reasons why this was a bad idea, but I finally agreed to do the presentation. I was anxious, but I realized what just occurred: My institution had just handed me, a melanated girl, the mic.

I hurried to my office, created a new presentation, and titled it "A Conversation about Human Race and Realities." In a subtle whisper, I asked myself, "Alright, girl. How are you going to present this so your white colleagues don't shut down and petition for your pink slip, and how are you going to present this so your brothers and sisters won't feel like you didn't go hard enough for the cause?" Perplexed was an understatement.

The day of the presentation, participants trickled in, and my nerves got the best of me. I kept drinking water, which only turned into sweat that bubbled up on my forehead like dew on a leaf at sunrise. I tried to calm myself, but anxiety was winning.

I stood in the corner of the library inhaling a deep breath and releasing tension in my shoulders like a boxer about to step into the ring. As my boss started the introduction, I turned to face the audience. My eyes scanned the room trying to figure out who was excited, who was uncomfortable, and who was mad as a raging firestorm that this discussion was happening. I hardly heard what he said when he handed me the clicker, and I stepped to the center to begin.

I followed protocol. I established a safe space, provided water for grounding exercises, and sprinkled in techniques for their comfort. We walked through slavery, supremacy, and Jim Crow before getting to present-day systemic racism. I was intentional. Methodical. I wanted them to understand that folk didn't get to this bubbling rage and tension overnight. This thing had been brewing.

Trayvon Martin.

Sandra Bland.

Philando Castille.

Tamir Rice.

Eric Garner.

Walter Scott.

Ahmaud Arbery.

Breonna Taylor.

George Floyd.

Individual members in the room read their stories of tragedy aloud. Emotion welled up in my colleagues' eyes. Their necks flushed red from hurt or anger — it was hard to tell. Their voices cracked.

When it was over, a friendly crowd surrounded me with "Thank yous" and "well dones," but even in the midst of this group vying for my attention, there was one white male who caught my attention. This was the same man who barely said a word during the entire two-hour presentation. He sat in his chair with one leg tucked neatly under his thigh while the other leg swung freely, clad in Birkenstocks. He had a sour face the entire time, like the pout of a three-year-old who couldn't get his way. When it was over, he grabbed his bag and all but ran out of the door as if he had just been released from a hellish prison.

The next day, I combed through attendee evaluations. One comment jumped off the page. My wordless friend the day before had written this in the additional comment section of the survey: "No one argued with the presenter, and if they would have, I'm not sure how she would have responded." That comment didn't sit well with me because I engage in discourse on a regular basis in boardrooms with colleagues who view things differently than I, and I have always kept a level head. Nothing in my professional history indicates that I would have acted any differently on this day.

Until recently, I was the only Black person on this team for almost nine years. I carried the burden of being a representative for all of my people while in this higher office — a weight I'm sure any Black woman who has ever been the "only" knows all too well.

So, I stared at the comment, trying to understand its origin, and as I peeled back the layers of the remark, I realized what it was. He was trying to classify me as an angry Black woman. I chuckled at his audacity, filed it away as evidence that there's more work to be done, and readied myself for Round 2.

— Lexcee Reel —

I'm an Attorney

Your story is what you have, what you will always
have. It is something to own.
~Michelle Obama, *Becoming*

As I walked toward the courthouse for the first time since the horrific events of September 11, 2001, I was reminded of how everything would be different going forward. No longer could I walk past the long line of people waiting to enter, show my Attorney I.D. to the officer, and bypass the line of people waiting to enter the building. Under the new rules that privilege was reserved for only judges and court staff.

It took no time at all for me to realize that this new process would not be a smooth one. I would step up when I got to the front of the line and put my purse and case file on the conveyor belt to be screened. Then I would walk through the metal detector, and quite often, it would beep. The officer would then ask me "Do you have anything in your pockets?" I would say no and would be told to step back and walk through the metal detector again. Another beep. I would then be told to step over near the wall and stretch my arms out to the side. There I would be scanned by an officer using a hand-held metal detector. After this, I would be told that I could proceed into the courthouse.

That was my routine whenever I would set off the metal detector at the courthouse. However, many days, as I stood in line waiting to get in, I noticed that some of my white colleagues would also set off the metal detector. An officer would immediately ask, "Are you an attorney?" They would respond "Yes" and they would be allowed inside with no further questioning or screening. Why wasn't I treated this way? Those attorneys were dressed like me. I was dressed like them. We wore business suits and carried case files. Yet I was never asked the question "Are you an attorney?" I'm all for rules but why weren't they being applied consistently?

There were a few times when I walked from my office to the courthouse with a white female co-worker. We were similarly dressed, carried case files, and talked to each other while we waited in line. When we got to the front of the line, I would have to go through my normal screening process if I beeped. But if she beeped she would be asked "Are you an attorney?" and after responding that she was, she would be allowed to enter.

One day in particular, she was directly ahead of me in line and got through in her usual manner. I went through and I heard the dreaded beep. I was sent back and told to remove my belt. I didn't usually wear a belt but the dress I had on that day had a thin belt with a small silver buckle. I had forgotten that I had it on. As careful as I was to try not to set off the metal detector, how did I manage to show up wearing a belt? I took my belt off and put it in the crate and on the conveyor belt.

I walked through again. Beep. I was sent back and told to remove my shoes. My shoes? It was summer and I was wearing pumps with no stockings. My shoes? This had never happened before. Ugh. I took my shoes off and put them in a crate on the conveyor belt. Beltless and barefoot, I walked through the metal detector again, trying to avoid making eye contact with my colleague who was waiting patiently for me. I was embarrassed and angry. It was obvious I was being treated differently.

Finally, I was waved through. I retrieved my purse, case file and belt from the end of the conveyor belt. I slipped my now dusty feet into my pumps and walked toward my co-worker. I immediately started making small talk so that she wouldn't have an opportunity to bring up the fact that my bare feet had touched the filthy courthouse floor.

After that day, I avoided walking to the courthouse with my white colleague. One day as I was leaving the office before her to head to the courthouse, I explained my early departure by telling her that my client was meeting me at the courthouse for some last-minute trial preparation.

Disappointed, she said, "Oh man! I wanted to walk over with you to see what level of disrobing you have to do today." She chuckled. I had always wondered if she noticed what was happening to me at the courthouse. She had never mentioned it and neither did I. But she did notice! She noticed and she thought it was funny! I didn't respond. I turned around and headed to the courthouse.

When I arrived and walked through the metal detector it beeped. Before the officer could say anything, I blurted out "I'm an attorney." There was no response. I was asked to step aside and spread my arms. I was scanned with the handheld monitor and then waved through. After that day, I never spoke up again. I accepted the situation for what it was. I continued to see my white colleagues waved through without any further screening once they identified themselves as attorneys. If I beeped, I continued to be put through additional screening before being allowed to enter.

I regret not speaking up and bringing to light what was happening. I regret not telling my white co-worker how insensitive her comment was and how it made me feel. As a Black person, you don't want to be accused of "playing the race card," but some things are clearly about race and should be called out accordingly. I am grateful to my ancestors who were brave enough to speak up against inequality and injustice in the midst of much more adversity than I have ever faced in my lifetime. If it weren't for them, I wouldn't even be able to practice law.

In the years that followed I moved on to a new job and worked in a different courthouse. There, I am asked "Are you an attorney?" if I set off the metal detector and then I am waved in. I am happy and hopeful that what I used to go through wasn't a systemic problem but instead a result of the ignorant ideology of the particular officers at that courthouse.

Unfortunately, I failed to speak up at the time, but I implore you to do better than I did. Speak up. Speak out. Whether something unjust is happening to you or to someone else, don't remain silent.

Believe me, you don't want to look back and feel the same regret that I do. Speak up and hopefully it will make a difference.

—Alicia F. Williams—

The Shoulders
We Stand On

I Am Not Safe

Seems like every time life starts straightening itself out,
something's gotta go and happen.
~Jacqueline Woodson, Peace, Locomotion

I. Am. Not. Safe.
This is a reality that I wake up to every day. I can't opt out of situations that might not be safe.
Like safe sex, I can make decisions that keep me safer, but there is no safe place for a Black woman in America.
The face of race is a Black man and gender is a white woman. Me?
Ignored
Overlooked
Rendered invisible
Or believed to have the strength of a superhero.
Therefore, I don't cry. I don't hurt. I don't bleed. And I don't die until I do.
So who cries for me when
the face of race is a Black man and gender is a white woman?
I have been stopped by the police for walking in a white neighborhood, driving in a white neighborhood,
for having temporary plates on a new car and for pulling into a hotel driveway.
My car has been flanked by officers on both sides, my nephew in the passenger seat. My crime: a rolling stop.
I was five when Dr. King was assassinated.

Too young to remember much,
but I do remember the sound of wood breaking as the police kicked in our door
chasing my sister who had been standing
on the corner near our house.
I remember them shining their flashlights.
I remember their voices
My sister hid. She was not taken to jail for violating curfew,
but we had a busted front door.
I am not safe.
Saturday night
awakened from my sleep by the sound of sirens
learning that the non-violent protests had turned violent.
Property destroyed.
Protestors,
Rioters
and Looters
Trapped downtown. CTA service cut off.
Bridges raised.
Late Saturday and early Sunday morning,
neighborhoods under attack.
My failed attempt to go to the store on Sunday
because the stores took precautions and closed early.
On my way home,
I watched
as people stuck their hands through broken windows for merchandise.
I went to sleep to the sound of sirens.
On Monday,
I stepped over broken glass from shattered windows.
I am not safe.
I have asthma and hypertension
and I live in a zip code with a high rate of COVID-19.
For me, contraction of the virus can be death.
And yet many in my neighborhood are unmasked.
I hear the cries of those who want their "freedom"

Those who demand we open the state.
Open the country
the most vulnerable among us be damned.
I am not safe.
Mary Turner was eight months pregnant
when she was lynched for speaking out against the lynching of her
husband.
Her unborn baby cut from her belly
and stomped to death.
Recy Taylor, kidnapped at gunpoint
Raped by six white men.
Sandra Bland died while in police custody.
Atatiana Jefferson and Breonna Taylor
killed in their homes.
Six of the victims in the Charleston church shooting
were Black women.
I am a Black woman in America.
And I am not safe.

— Stephanie J. Gates —

A Serendipitous Encounter

Our race-inflected culture not only exists, it thrives.
The question is whether it thrives as a virus or a
bountiful harvest of possibilities.
~Toni Morrison

You likely know how it is: the bustle of getting to the airport and through security, then finally getting settled in your seat. I had just finished a week at Spirit Rock Meditation Center in California. We celebrated The Gathering of more than seventy Buddhist teachers of African descent for five days, followed by two days of training with over 350 Black folks. Tired and beaming, I headed home to Charlotte, North Carolina.

As I boarded the flight and began settling into my aisle seat, I pulled out my read by the late Toni Morrison, *The Source of Self-Regard*. The white man sitting next to me was also settling in, and pulled out his read, Toni Morrison's *Beloved*. We gave each other a smile and continued to settle in. Before takeoff, he ordered a gin and orange juice and I ordered water without ice. We introduced ourselves.

John shared that he was returning from spending a week in Napa golfing with eight college guys he'd known for more than twenty-five years. This was the tenth year in a row they'd met up, and he expressed pride in having such good friends at the age of fifty-three. I looked at him and realized he was the age of my son, although he seemed older.

John seemed energetic and shared that he was eager to get home to his wife and daughters. I wasn't sure he would want to hear about where I had been, or maybe it was that I didn't want to share it with a stranger. Instead, I shared that I had read just about everything Toni Morrison had written and that this current book, apparently the last one published before her recent death, was the most profound in terms of character and craft. I asked John what motivated him to read *Beloved*. He said that he had purchased the book years ago but had never read it, and as he was leaving home for this trip, the book "fell off his shelf." For some reason, a line in *Beloved* flooded my memory: "...*You just can't mishandle creatures and expect success.*" Next, I thought: *What a ride this read will be for him.* He ordered another gin and orange juice before take-off.

After take-off, we settled into our respective books. I had one chapter remaining in *The Source of Self-Regard*. As with Morrison's other publications, it's not a fast read, more a savoring. I often will read and re-read a paragraph, then ponder it for a while before reading on. I'm mostly in awe at how Morrison is persistent in her message to talk "to" Black people, not talk "for" them, and how her focus is not on slavery per se, but rather on Black culture, interior pain, and character. This last chapter had me feeling satiated, sitting up straighter, clear, centered, and fortified by her words. This was on top of feeling deeply satisfied from the field of wise care I had bathed in with other Black Buddhist teachers and practitioners. I wanted for nothing!

I glanced over at John, who was also into *Beloved*. He seemed tight and edgy. I recall feeling that way when I read *Beloved* years ago. He, too, read, then put the book down, then returned to reading. He seemed to be about one-third of the way into the book. He ordered another gin and orange juice. I wonder if he was reading Chapter 16 (yes, I remember it vividly), where Sethe instinctually decides to kill her children instead of allowing them to be taken and sold into slavery. That moment when, once read, we can't help but ask: Is this criminal? What is the greater crime? Or maybe he was squirming in his seat because he was reading about Sethe being held down and beaten while the white boys stole milk from her breast, leaving nothing for her children.

Dinner was served. We rested the books. Surprisingly, John, now quite red-faced, pulled out a photo of his wife and children. I joined him in this prideful moment. I wondered if reading *Beloved* makes privilege palpable, making one cherish their loved ones even more. This was all that was spoken over our meal. I wondered if it felt dangerous or too risky for him to ask me about my life. Or worse, as least for me, that it never occurred to him.

I finished the last few pages of *The Source of Self-Regard* and closed the book, bringing it close to my heart. As an author, I'm deeply inspired by Morrison's example. I marvel at her clarity and brilliance; how close she stays to her inside voice, and how brave she is to trust and share it unapologetically. I am grateful that she lived and that she taught us, and I can taste this goodness. I ordered a glass of red wine to toast the moment.

I glanced over at John, who was napping with *Beloved* on his chest and surrender on his face. Was he napping because this is what one must do from time to time when reading the dense forest of Morrison's work, or was he napping because his gin and orange juice had finally caught up with him? It didn't matter, really. Morrison's work is meant to be meditative. My guess is that we were both somehow in the "scorched earth" of Morrison's wise love. Therein lay the bountiful harvest of possibilities.

— Ruth King —

I Shall Dance

*My body is very different from most of the dancers
I dance with. My hair is different than most I dance
with. But I didn't let that stop me. Black girls rock
and can be ballerinas.*

~Misty Copeland

I always loved to dance. As a child growing up in a Brooklyn housing development I danced as free as a bird — brown arms swinging, feet shuffling, hips swaying. I danced with my eyes closed imagining myself on stage, feeling the music: the R&B music and jazz my father blasted on the weekend, or the music my aunts played at my grandmother's house whenever my family and I came to visit.

Then, even though I had decided I wanted to be a writer when I grew up, I longed to take ballet lessons. But my parents couldn't afford them. Instead, I was given the choice to take piano lessons taught by a woman who lived in an adjacent housing development from ours. Her lessons were practically free and my older sister and I and a few neighborhood children went to her apartment twice a week to learn how to play the piano.

Still, I never lost sight of my dream of being a ballerina. I yearned for the day my parents could afford lessons for me. I couldn't wait to put on my black Danskin leotard and tights, and leap and twirl across the floor in a real dance studio instead of our living room. Unfortunately, that never happened. Money was tight, and other things took priority.

So I focused on writing, filling the blank pages in my black and white notebooks with my stories.

One day though, while in my last year of elementary school — a school we were bused to when white schools were being desegregated — a ballet company came to perform. They were recruiting interested students for their company. They even offered a scholarship to those who couldn't afford lessons. That day every part of my being was filled with hope. I couldn't wait to get the information to take back to my parents.

I watched their performance in awe. Afterwards I gathered with my white classmates around the dancers and shared my dream of studying ballet. After a silence, one of the lead dancers finally said, "Oh, I'm sorry but you're not the right type for ballet."

I wilted like a flower that had once been in full bloom. My long-held dream was put on an even higher, inaccessible shelf because of someone's judgment of who I was and could be as a Black girl. For me, she was in fact saying, *You're not the right color. You don't have the right body type. And you'd have to work hard, practice each day, and be dedicated, and as a person of color you can't do that.*

My hopes were shattered and so was my confidence. Even though the women in my family were anchors, their sage words and inspiration and love couldn't make me feel otherwise. I thought I wasn't enough. Gradually, I let go of my dream of being a ballerina and let my pen pirouette across paper instead, creating a rhythmic dance with my words.

Many years later, I happened upon a documentary on PBS about the Alvin Ailey American Dance Theater. As I watched these brown and black bodies, I was led to dance with them. I pushed the sofa in my living room back and danced, with a newfound determination not to let negative words from my past define me.

I bounded across the floor, not at all gracefully. I danced for all the aspiring Black boys and girls who may have been rejected from learning ballet. I paid homage to the dancers who had made it, and to Misty Copeland, the first African American female principal dancer with the prestigious American Ballet Theatre. She blazed the trail so other Black girls can become ballerinas.

I celebrated because dance has always held specific meaning in the history of Black people. It was often an instrument of communication or an act of resistance to whatever was going on in our lives. It is so much more than just the movement of our bodies.

During these times, when we're feeling the substantial weight from all that has occurred and is still occurring, and are weary emotionally, spiritually, and physically, I dance even more. I play my favorite soulful playlist and dance my heart out, alone or sometimes with my husband, children, and grandchildren. When I dance, I feel free as a bird, brown arms swinging, feet shuffling, hips swaying… just as when I was a little girl. The song in my spirit remains even when my feet stop moving.

Dancing, physically, is breath, laughter, and self-care. It is self-love. It is prayer.

But dancing figuratively in life is important also. It's knowing that we are strong oak trees. It is realizing we have an ancestral rhythm of being overcomers, that because of the seeds planted in us — seeds of greatness, resilience, and unwavering faith — we may sway but will never break.

So… I shall dance. As much as possible, whenever I can. And as I dance, I chant this mantra to myself and send it out into the atmosphere to other Black girls and women; "Dance suga'. You're so beautiful when you dance. Push back that sofa. Kick off them shoes. And dance free as a bird, brown arms swinging, feet shuffling, hips swaying. Dance suga', with all your heart and soul."

— Jeanine L. DeHoney —

14

These Women Mattered

We can and must bend the arc of the moral
universe — toward both justice and unity.
~Susan Rice

O h, how I wish my mother had been alive to see this movement, the cardboard signs saying that Black Lives Matter hoisted high above smiling faces. I can't imagine what that would've meant to her, after eighty-two years of struggling to exist, to uplift herself and her children in a world that seemed intent to degrade, beat and kill them.

I bet she would've cried tears of joy, knowing that social change was coming, and that there would be a reckoning, an accountability that hence forward Black people in America would not be mistreated. Because Black lives do matter and soon justice would be just for us too. Oh, how happy she would've been!

Last summer, as I drove past many small groups of protesters on street corners in Boston, I teared up. They wore masks following COVID-19 protocol and held up handmade signs of racial awareness. All of them heroes without capes, recognizing the injustices that my ancestors had endured. That recent deaths of Black people, by police hands, were not okay.

I honked my car horn and waved jubilantly, because I knew that they were demanding social change that was beneficial to me and people who look like me. I got chills at the energy between us, their conviction to correct a wrong. They pumped their signs up and down even more enthusiastically and chanted: "No justice. No Peace." And in that moment, I believed them. I was reminded of other historical social movements, Ghandi in India and Martin Luther King, Jr. in Selma, and the successes of those movements. I drove slowly away from the feel-good moment until I reached a place where the street corners were empty.

And that's when it hit me; in the quiet of my car I became overwhelmed with emotion. You see, I've never had so many strangers, white people, care about me before. I parked and wept like a baby. You have to understand the joy that was in my heart, after a lifetime of being Black, existing in a world where justice was never just for me and those who looked like me. When I got home, I began to write. I hadn't written in years; it was one of those deferred dreams that Langston Hughes had written about. But on this day, everything seemed possible and so I wanted to write about how the movement and the moment had made me feel. I sighed and taking a deep breath, I suddenly remembered where I had been, where I had come, and everything it had taken to get here.

I was raised by Black queens in a poor housing project in Boston. These single mothers who had been mentally and physically abused, who had escaped their tormentors or had been abandoned and left with multiple children to clothe and feed, were superwomen in every sense of the word. They protected me and all the kids in the projects the best way they knew how.

These women who wrapped their hair in colorful scarves, told stories and sang beautiful songs, were a portrait of civility. I remember sitting on the front steps watching them snap green beans, laughing and telling stories, smiling despite the burden of eviction notices that stuck up from their housecoat pockets. On Sundays, they'd make everything smell good, coaxing old stinky collard greens into deliciousness, heavily seasoned and frequently stirred. They made something out of nothing so often that I believed I could do the same. I could be a writer.

Everywhere I went I carried pencil and paper, trying to put into words their rich stories. The queens talked fast except when they grew weary. Moods change quick when you're growing up poor. I'd get into trouble if I wasn't physically busy, that is cleaning or playing. It was important to the superwomen that their children weren't idle. So, for a long time, I missed out on the mental aspects of becoming a writer, that is the reading and research that's required.

But the best part of growing up was the card parties, when they got to playing whist. After the day was done and everyone had finished their chores, the queens would set up the card table. Two decks of cards would be placed on the table, to be shuffled and used in rotation. They'd light cigarettes and sip beer from their cans and play all night. I learned how to play bid whist by watching and listening, trying to catch the essence of their stories. And when someone had to go to the bathroom, sometimes they'd let me sit in.

"Storm's coming," Miss Dee would announce, as if someone had asked. She was the neighborhood "weather lady," without the gadgetry. Miss Dee studied the sky at dusk and could tell you the weather for the next three days, based on the color, shape and position of the clouds.

"She don't know," Miss Alice would say. "She don't know nothing about the weather, any more than the man on the moon. But what I will say, is since they started sending rockets into space, they messed the weather patterns up."

"Sure seems like it," my mother agreed.

"Anyway, even the meteorologist on TV can't tell what the weather's gonna be, and he's paid to tell it."

"Ain't that the truth." They were in agreement now. "That's the only job I know of, that you can be consistently wrong and not get fired!"

"Every time I turn on channel seven news, there he is grinning and lying."

"But he is good looking," my mother would say. "Easy on the eyes. Who cares about the weather?" She chuckled, and then as if on cue, she started singing Lena Horne's "Stormy Weather." And all the women joined in, lifting their voices as if they were in church or something.

Their conversations would run the gamut from kids to buying clothes and shoes not fitting, then back to love, back to kids, then on to the everyday struggles of life. There was no pity, no time for self-reflection; it was just life, being Black, being born a female, and being poor. Sobering discussions of who had passed, who was in jail, and police beatings met by gutturals, because there just wasn't any words. And then in the spirit of endurance, these queens would stand up and call it a night. They'd go home, crawl into bed, and get up to start again in the morning.

I always believed it; their lives mattered, too.

— DaNice D. Marshall —

15

Sayings for Staying Safe

*I was surrounded by extraordinary women in my life
who taught me about quiet strength and dignity.*
~Michelle Obama

Every mother wants to keep her child safe, especially now, but a Black mother's fear for her children is passed down through generations. A Black mother knows she can't control the world her children grow up in, so she needs to teach them how to navigate a world she knows will be especially unkind.

Sometimes the help comes in the form of love and sometimes it comes in the form of fear. In my house, it was often a mix of both with the scale tipping toward my mother's fears. Yes, we got the talk about not answering back to police and be careful about what we said and did in front of white people. But for my mother, the worst days for Blacks were behind us. Racism and police brutality were not at the top of her list of concerns.

My mother taught me to be on the lookout for anything or anyone who could hurt me. I believe in her mind, if you were careful, you could avoid being hurt or caught off guard. In order to do this, you had to be prepared for a worst-case scenario. When I learned to drive, she told me: "You have to learn to drive for yourself and the fool. Not everyone behind the wheel is paying attention."

Because my mom was born in the South and was a sharecropper's daughter, most of the sayings my siblings and I heard in our home in New England came from her upbringing in Mississippi.

During my adolescent years, my mom's sayings were like parables designed to protect me from social pitfalls. For her, protecting your reputation was just as important as practicing good hygiene. You didn't want anyone saying you smelled bad, and you didn't want to be embarrassed by saying something you could have "kept to yourself," especially if "Mad Day" came along.

What is Mad Day? That's the day when someone gets so upset they try to hurt you by throwing your weaknesses or secrets back in your face. According to my mother, Mad Day will come after you "fall out" with a friend or a family member. Then you'll likely see a totally different side of that person who you'd thought incapable of hurting you.

My mother was a big proponent of "see and don't see." This means you don't have to acknowledge everything you see, especially if it's none of your business. She wanted to make sure we knew how to keep our mouths shut and keep it moving. She didn't want us getting embroiled in other people's problems.

"Beware of a person who brings a bone and carries a bone." This means if someone brings you a piece of gossip, they will most likely take what you say to go gossip someplace else. I was told this when I reached middle school. I passed this one onto my daughter when she reached the same age — to keep her out of the gossip loop.

She taught us to stay quiet when other people were gossiping. If you remembered to "keep your name out of other people's mouths," when they carried away that juicy bone of gossip, your name would not be on it.

"You never give someone a stick to crack your head with." This means don't give anyone any information that could be weaponized against you later. You would also avoid giving someone else said stick to be used against a family member or friend. Once I complained to my mother that a friend shared something I said in private with someone else and hurt their feelings. She looked at me, shook her head, and said, "You gave her the stick." She thought she taught me better.

Keeping yourself and others safe from judgment meant that you kept quiet about "certain things," and you somehow always knew what those "certain things" were. She explained, "Some things are between you and God." You didn't confess your indiscretions to anyone besides God. "No one needs to know everything about you or your past," she added, and I wondered how many secrets my mother had buried.

There were often similar warnings given against trusting anyone completely with all your secrets or personal details. "Don't put anyone totally in your bosom," she said. We were to take precautions with even the closest friendships to avoid being betrayed.

"Take it to your grave" was often said to protect sensitive information that was passed on but should never be repeated. You are never to tell a secret that could jeopardize someone's livelihood, marriage, or reputation in the family.

My mom lived in a different time and a different world, and the wisdom and urgency in her words made me pay attention. I internalized them and used them as a code to live by. She did what she could to keep me safe. Yet, I hadn't realized until recently why it was so difficult for me to trust people, and why it was always easy to stay quiet while others shared. I could keep a secret, and I was always on the lookout for signs of betrayal, bracing myself for what I might discover on "Mad Day."

Even though I had passed down most of these sayings on to my daughter, she doesn't carry the weight of them. She is now in her twenties and not as careful in her relationships as I once was. She doesn't care much about what people think of her and rarely takes things personally. She lives more fearlessly than I did because she lives in a different world, and I'm glad.

I don't want her to be a fool on the roads of life or in her relationships, but I don't want her to be on guard so much that it takes away her ability to love with her whole heart. I want to keep her safe, but I also want her to make her own decisions on the chances she takes. I want her to know that it is okay to trust those that earn it, and that since the beginning, safety has always been an illusion. "Mad Days" will come, but I want her to fully enjoy all her good days ahead.

— Yolande Clark-Jackson —

16

A Servant's Heart

I have found that among its other benefits,
giving liberates the soul of the giver.
~Maya Angelou

"Here baby, take these plates of food over to Miss Lillian and your 'Aunt' Carrie. Let me know if they need anything else. Get going now while it's hot!"

We were the kids with the mother who sent plates all over the neighborhood. It always felt weird to me, but I would no more have questioned my mother than stopped breathing. What I didn't realize was that my mother was showing me what it meant to have a "Servant's Heart." She never talked about it, because there was nothing to say. She saw a need and filled it. She was also the woman who, when faced with a visitor who was getting ready to finalize their visit, would say, "You leavin' so soon," and not as a question. She always had space in her life for visitors, and she understood the need for connection in their lives and hers.

As an adult, I've taken those lessons deeply to heart even as I forge my own way in the world. I've done some things that others would have called crazy, such as taking strangers into my home, feeding them, and sending them on their way. I have given rides to men and women who needed them. I have given money to strangers. And all I asked them was to pay it forward if they could, one day. Never has any one of them not agreed. Generosity begets generosity, and it feels really good to be able to be "generous" to another.

I am a Black woman. I am a vocalist. Some would call me a "sanger." I have probably been one all my life, but only in the mid-'80s did I realize I could do this and fulfill one of my life's dreams. I am also an "emoter" in my singing style. I came to realize that my style of singing was important, because it gave folks, most especially women, the permission to be emotional as well. I've come to realize that some women would never display emotion so freely, but my attitude gave them courage and permission too, especially in public. What a joy!

I have learned that enabling people to safely express themselves is an amazing gift, and one that I have used innumerable times as I progress in my career. It's part of my journey in trying to have a "Servant's Heart." And being able to be available as an entertainer, especially after a show, is one of my highest joys. It never gets old to embrace a woman whose emotions were bottled up inside her until I sang about "Hard Times Coming Again No More."

In 2020, I discovered there was an "accidental activist" inside me. My outrage at the injustices that occurred found an outlet on social media. I realized that I have a huge need to serve and enlighten, but it's been difficult expressing my opinions in a way that does not offend. I don't hit the mark every time and have lost folks I considered friends.

However, I continue to speak up. I've found another voice inside me that doesn't involve singing! I have been trying to find the kernel of commonality in folks while trying to educate them about the realities of our world. Thelma Bryant-Davis talked about this in her National Public Radio piece, "Missed Milestones to Faded Friendships: the unacknowledged grief of 2020." She said, "There is a gift for us in truth-telling. It's urgent that we stop pretending we're not hurting."

We all are.

It's so important that we express those hurts but respect the humanity of the people we're "emoting at." Black folk today are engaging in the very same struggle that our forebears did. The courage I have seen displayed is humbling yet reenergizing. I think what's been hardest, even in my righteous anger and upset, is remembering that we're all human.

It's incredibly humbling to realize that I, but for the Grace of God, could be one of those struggling. Yet here I sit with food, a safe and warm home, and the love of friends and family. I remember the lady who stopped me to thank me after I sang at a Volunteers of America hunger event on Martin Luther King, Jr. Day one year. She said "I wasn't always like this. I had a husband and a good life. But he died, and now here I am."

When I'm tempted to stop my activism, I think of her and the many like her. My words may be the catalyst for someone to step up and volunteer at a shelter. Or lobby our government leaders for more care for the homeless and hungry. Or persuade a foundation to donate funds, or create programs, or grants, to care for our less fortunate. And it's all thanks to my mom's example.

— Erica Brown —

Grandma's Surprise

*Something about memory. It takes you back to where
you were and lets you just be there for a time.*

~Jacqueline Woodson, Red at the Bone

I spent lots of time with my grandparents growing up, as my mother sometimes worked two jobs. My grandfather was cool, calm, collected and fun, but my grandmother was intense. She was very conservative, followed the rules, demanded excellence, and was pretty serious. She brought her strong Arkansas drawl with her to California and combined that with a fierceness that commanded respect everywhere she went.

Imagine my surprise one Sunday afternoon when I was ten and my grandmother announced that she was taking me somewhere for a little fun. I remember looking her up and down thinking she looked comfortable in her jogging suit, tennis shoes, and multi-colored necklace, a far cry from her normal nurses' scrubs or housecoat.

I grabbed my shoes and sweater and dashed for the car behind her. Once in the car we headed toward downtown Long Beach. I must have asked her 100 times what the surprise was. As we entered Shoreline Village there were large crowds everywhere, everyone was dressed in bright colors, and in the distance I could see what looked like a carnival. Giddy with excitement I asked if that's where we were headed and I nearly exploded with joy when she confirmed it.

In my excitement, I don't remember much about the walk to the carnival after we parked, or the line at the ticket booth. What I do remember was walking hand in hand with my grandma, fist full of ride tickets, through what she thought was Long Beach Carnivale.

As we moved further and further into the carnival, I started to notice there weren't any other children present. I mentioned it to my grandma, who was having her own epiphany at the very same moment. She ordered me to keep my eyes on the ground and dragged me back out of the carnival to the ticket booth to demand a refund. The amused worker informed my grandmother that Carnivale was the day before, and today was the Gay Pride Celebration.

Apparently, they intentionally booked the same weekend to share expenses and permits. Ever the Southern belle, my grandmother graciously thanked him for the information and did her best to navigate me back to the car through a sea of fishnet, leather, bare chests, and rainbows, none of which we had noticed earlier in our excitement.

When we got back to the car my grandmother began to apologize profusely while I attempted to hold in my laughter. When I didn't respond, our eyes met and we both exploded into laughter, with her saying, "Please don't tell your grandfather; he'll never let this go."

We headed out and settled for a trip to the ice cream shop instead. Although I had been sworn to secrecy, I blurted it out to my grandfather as soon as we walked in the door. The three of us laughed until we cried, and until the day my grandmother died it was a sure-fire way to make her laugh.

That day my grandmother wasn't intense or serious; she was adventurous and funny. She showed me that it's okay to laugh at yourself every now and then. It's good for your soul.

— Autrilla Gillis —

Role Models Banned

The whole point of being alive is to evolve into the
complete person you were intended to be.
~Oprah Winfrey

y mom, known as "Momma Weekes" by my friends, was the fiercest protector of my dreams. When she and my dad immigrated to the United States from Barbados in the 1970s, they saw themselves raising a child who had endless possibilities within her reach.

Growing up, Momma Weekes had rules for the home that seemed unconventional and just plain crazy. I certainly was not the envy of my high school friends when it came to household rules. My curfew was too early. I was only allowed to watch television two or three hours a week. In the summers, I had to write book reports for my mom in addition to having a job or participating in a leadership camp.

One rule I blindly obeyed was Momma Weekes's ban on having role models. Like most of Mom's rules, I attributed this to her being West Indian. She would always say, "You are allowed to respect certain qualities and characteristics about a person, but you can never place that person on a pedestal." Mom would then lecture me and explain that when you idolize people, their greatest accomplishments can unintentionally become the ceiling of your dreams.

So, while I loved Oprah as a 1980s child, Mom refused to have me strive to be like Oprah. She forbade me from having posters of Oprah or anyone else taped to my walls. The only concession was that watching *The Oprah Winfrey Show* was excluded from my weekly television time quota.

Instead, Mom would ask me, "What are the qualities you like about Oprah that you think make her successful? Why are these qualities important to you? What else do you think you need to be successful that Oprah may not be showing or telling you?" And after her interrogation, she would always say, "There is only one Oprah and only one Dana. So, what are you going to do with your life?"

Even at a young age, I could feel the gravity of my mom's words as her eyes bore into my soul. I would feel unsettled, until eventually her rants began to comfort me and take hold over the years. "Envision your own success, Dana. Don't let Oprah do it for you."

In my late twenties, after graduating from college, working in politics, and graduating from law school, I lost touch with Momma Weekes's lesson. I succumbed to the hustle and bustle of the legal and policy world, and I prioritized striving over thriving. I wanted to be the best, and I exhausted myself trying to make real the visions others had for me. It had become second nature and I was collecting notches in my proverbial belt.

Many times, I was rewarded for mirroring others' lives or meeting their benchmarks of success. That led to bonuses, promotions, accolades, likes on social media, and other affirmations intended to make me feel accomplished. Of course, after my sugar high of accomplishment wore off, I came back to my secret reality of feeling empty, uncertain, and a bit bitter at myself. But I would still put on a smile or post something witty on social media. Little did I know I was distancing myself from the person who knew me best — me.

I had freely given permission to friends, colleagues, mentors, and even strangers to impose their ideas of success on me. I let the people I knew and loved dictate the course of my life when they spoke about my career, my desire to be married, my health, my happiness, and pretty much anything else about me. When it came to the people I didn't know, I used the image they projected of their lives to serve as my GPS.

In my mid-thirties, I began to comply with Momma Weekes's

longstanding ban against living out other people's intentions. I now understand that Mom didn't want any person — no matter how successful — to have dominion over my thoughts, dreams, and aspirations. It was her prayer for me to trust and protect my inner callings, rather than make them vulnerable to the successes and failures of others.

Now more than ever, there is a need to recreate ourselves from within — to become our authentic selves. It is still important that we learn from those who have come before us. Yet, their stories should help to inform our visions, not become them.

As my mom said, "All the tools you need to live your calling are already within you, Dana. No one else can live your life's purpose better than you."

— Dana Tenille Weekes —

Remembering Georgia

Success isn't about how much money you make.
It's about the difference you make in people's lives.
~Michelle Obama

I hadn't seen her picture, yet she was the most fascinating person in the world. I'd heard tales of her greatness. Thousands of babies... she had delivered thousands of babies. What would she look like? After 700 miles of backseat anticipation, I'd get to see her.

Today, I was going to meet my great-grandmother.

I leaped out of our old Chevrolet into the warm water that swirled around my little brown legs. I soldiered on, a brave five-year-old clinging to my mother's hand. My father carried my little brother on his shoulders.

My mom looked down and reassured me. "Doin' good, honey. Water's not too high."

Our short walk in the southern downpour only took minutes but it felt like an eternity until we passed through the rusty chain-link fence and entered the weathered house. I saw faded pictures haphazardly placed on the walls in the poorly lit living room. In the far left corner, my great-grandmother sat in an armchair like a self-appointed Queen Mother. The faded neutrals of her dress covered her entire body, with only her head and hands showing. She summoned me over to her throne with a nod.

I obeyed.

I stood in front of her with my hands behind my back, rocking back and forth nervously. Sensing my unease, she reached behind me and pulled my small hands into hers. My awe reflected in her wire-framed glasses.

"Been waitin' quite a while to meet you," she said in her native drawl. I squeezed her hands and she knew I wanted to know more.

She obliged.

"I doctored up until a few years ago. I brought so many babies into this world, both Black and white. And I never lost no one. Never lost a mother. Never lost a child. Look here."

She flipped her left wrist over and guided my fingers along the side. It felt like half a marble was wedged under her skin.

"I broke this wrist deliverin' babies."

She continued talking but my mind was stuck on her wrist. I couldn't comprehend the intricacies of childbirth. The weight of her accomplishments. As a licensed midwife in rural Arkansas, she was the sole reason generations made it safely into the light. I knew that her work was important.

She held her hand steady and let me trace the marble knot in small circles.

"Nikki!" My mother shouted above the white noise of adult conversation, shaking me out of my reverie. "Water's gone down. We gotta get back before dark."

My great-grandmother patted my hand goodbye. I didn't know that would be our only encounter.

Decades later, sitting in my home office, I tracked my mouse across the highlighted row named "Georgia." The 1910 census confirmed she was twenty-four years old then. Negro. Married. Under occupation it read none. None?

Was my only memory of her a dream?

I frantically opened the census reports for 1920, 1930 and 1940 with the same result. Occupation: none. That stung my soul. I continued to search the columns for answers and saw the words Farm Laborer dozens of times.

My brain clicked.

I remembered my mother talking about how she and all her siblings picked cotton on farms growing up. My mother, her mother, and her grandmother were part of the engine that drove the cotton-is-king economy that permeated the Jim Crow South for years. My great-grandmother had worked on farms picking cotton. Before, after and sometimes during working the fields, she attended to women in labor.

In modern terms this revelation meant midwifing was her side hustle for sixty-seven years. Her side hustle, often unpaid, produced generations. She went to work her side hustle when called, armed with an archaic medicine bag, a lantern and her bible.

Georgia was part goddess, part saint. Her heroics run through my blood. They are the inner voices that whisper wisdom and breathe superpowers into my quest to conquer everyday mountains.

She brought thousands of babies into this world and never lost a mother, never lost a child.

I will always remember to draw strength from this side hustle epiphany.

And never forget tracing the half-marble in her left wrist.

Her sacrifice lives on.

— Nicolette Branch —

Family & Food for the Soul

Garden of Delight

Doing the best at this moment puts you
in the best place for the next moment.
~Oprah Winfrey

In my small plot of backyard garden, I am lady of the land.

The surprising flash of yellow flowers, under wide green leaves, marks
where cucumbers will eventually grow.

Lush arugula, tempting to tiny caterpillars, is already fit for first harvest.

Three varieties of tomatoes, two heirlooms and one Roma, tower over
my microfarm.

Dazzling sunny flowers open and hint at the fruit to come.

I haven't gardened since I was a six-year-old, happily toiling alongside
my mother in the little square under the kitchen window of my
childhood Detroit home.

Born in Louisiana and raised in Tulsa, Oklahoma, Artie Mae never
thought not to grow her own food and flowers.

Leafy collard greens, bountiful enough to share with neighbors, we
ate garden to table long before organic was a thing.

Now grass covers the little square, but crimson Canna lilies she planted
in her last spring have returned faithfully each year since she left,
even though they weren't meant to be perennials.

The grandchildren who adored her are all grown now. The grands and
greats and great-greats are living evidence of her obedience to the
edict to be fruitful and multiply.

The fear of shortages and need for mental clarity drove me to plant
my victory garden in the spring of the quarantine.
The harvest belongs to my southern mother, Artie Mae.

— Sonya Carol Vann DeLoach —

Things My Aunt Nanny Taught Me

Be thankful for what you have; you'll end up having
more. If you concentrate on what you don't have,
you will never, ever have enough.
~Oprah Winfrey

My Aunt Nanny scolds me, because when I open the fridge all I can see are bits and pieces, and not all the things that she claims can be made from them.

It's just an egg, it's just a slice of cheese, it's just a potato.

But no, no, no she says, these bits and pieces were made for making bigger bits and pieces. Made for feeding families.

She scrambles the egg, crisps the potatoes in bubbling oil, lays a layer of cheese on top that wrinkles in the way well-lived skin does. When I pop the potatoes in my mouth, they burst from out of their casings like the hot pulp from a summer-sun roasted plum, all soft-steamy-smooth.

My Aunt Nanny teaches me that whole chickens aren't needed, neither are slices of turkey, or the frozen bags of things that can be quickly slammed inside of an oven. Easily 425-degreed, timed, and done.

"When your family is hungry," she says, "you make a way out of anything, out of everything. Even this can be saved," she says as she holds a bell pepper with spotted skin. And she shaves away the rotting pieces, leaving only the healthy bits behind. "These bits and pieces are not made for throwing away; they're made for making the meals that cannot be so easily seen."

"Can you see it?" she says. "How it all adds up? Can you see the meals that can be made?"

I feel like a bit and piece myself. Not fully anything, but remnants of so many other things that just can't puzzle their way to a solid picture.

The ingredients in the *Chopped* basket that have no place being together — Sauerkraut, Bloody-Mary Mix, and Carrot Ketchup.

Sometimes I feel like I'm not a whole chicken. Like I'm just an egg, maybe.

But eggs can be fertilized, can't they? I want to ask her.

Eggs can go on to grow into full chickens. I want to say to her.

And oh, to become the pretty, brown-skinned poultry-bouquet centered at the dining table.

Not just a meal, but an entire feast.

— Exodus Oktavia Brownlow —

21

Pecans & Power

We have to raise our daughters to be the women they
want to be, not the women they think we should be.
~Jada Pinkett Smith

When I think of Black motherhood, I think of pecans. They evoke many of my favorite memories as one of the South's daughters.

The picture is fuzzy, but I recall sitting with a stainless-steel bowl between my legs on my grandmother's front porch using pliers — which felt like a very grownup tool — to shell pecans. My mother's mother, Grandma Vernell, mother to eleven children in rural, upstate South Carolina, knew what an eight-year-old could handle. We'd sit side by side, watching cars whiz by as she spoke to me like we were old friends, our conversation punctuated by the surgical crack of a pecan's husk.

Growing up, Black mothers were omnipotent, omniscient beings who supported me in a broad diversity of ways using their hard-earned resources.

There was my mom, who made monthly payments on a set of encyclopedias so we could do reports from home.

There was Tammy, my mother's neighborhood friend, who on 9/11 scooped me and my siblings up in case a terrorist had a plot planned for my high school.

Then there was Aunt Kathy, the woman who noticed children nodding off during Sunday School and began serving buttermilk biscuits slathered in jelly to keep us awake.

Carolyn Frye was the academic advisor who made sure I could visit every college I was considering.

"Aunt Karol" wasn't actually my aunt, but she took me in when I moved to D.C. with dreams and plans bigger than my bank account could handle. And on and on.

Black mothers with leisurely Southern accents that kept pace with their sharp minds are the ones who pushed me forward.

But in 2017, I was newly married and in Los Angeles, far from the community that snapped beans to prep them and snapped at teachers to correct them. I was about to join their sorority; I was pregnant. I vacillated between excitement about meeting my baby and fear over the delivery.

And then I learned that Black mothers in America were dying in labor at alarming rates, regardless of income or education. Statistically speaking, a white woman who hadn't earned her high school diploma had a better chance of surviving a delivery than I did, a Black woman with a master's degree and a comfortable income.

Until then, I had considered myself different than the women who'd raised me. I'd "made it" and phone calls and infrequent holiday visits were enough to sustain me.

Now I wasn't so sure. I told myself I wanted to give my mother the news of my pregnancy in person for her benefit.

The truth is I needed her to tell me, it would be okay. I flew in, surprising her by crashing a family holiday party. The footage of my big reveal (a postcard with a sonogram) shows her pulling me in for a crushing hug. It looks like I'm making her day. In reality, it was her excitement that gave me permission to be excited too. Too often, milestones in the lives of Black children ,which might otherwise be marked with joy, are marked with fear for us. A son with peach fuzz coming in makes us worry he'll seem intimidating to others. A daughter assertively negotiating her salary makes us worry if she'll be seen as angry or aggressive.

But my mother who could barely handle having her eyebrows waxed knew what it was like to birth three children. Her pure joy on my behalf gave me the freedom I needed.

I flew back to California, literally and figuratively, feeling lighter even as I grew heavier. I began to proactively focus on what I could do to have a healthy, safe pregnancy.

After extensive research, I decided to give birth with a midwife at a birthing center. My mother-in-law, an immigrant from Ethiopia, was alarmed. "I didn't leave my poor country for my grandchild to be born like a poor person." My mother was also concerned. "Will those hippies be able to handle an emergency?"

My research taught me a surprising fact. Until the 1970s, when most Americans had shifted to hospital births, it was the midwives, or "granny-midwives" as Black midwives were called, that continued to serve poor and rural women in the South. In fact, it hadn't occurred to me to ask until I myself was with child, but my grandmother had birthed her first seven children with the support of a Black midwife.

I'd thought my plans to deliver with a midwife was the Californian in me. It turns out there are few things more Southern and historically Black than my birth plan. This knowledge made my decision feel less like risk aversion and more like a homecoming.

Prior to giving birth, I typed up affirmation statements to help me get through labor. The statements ranged from Biblical "The Lord will never put more on you than you can bear" to quippy — "We're strong enough to bear the children, then get back to business." (from Saint Beyoncé).

At the peak of my labor, my husband reached for those strips of paper, hoping they would encourage me. They did not.

But I did remember that my grandmother, a woman with fewer resources but boundless resolve, had done this eleven times, most in a remarkably similar fashion. And then, my son was here.

Oh, what joy!

There are many important conversations about the difficulties of being a Black mother, particularly in a year of reckoning where mothers from around the world heard George Floyd call out for his. That conversation is one we should never stop having.

But we must also embrace and keep talking about the joy. I'm told that when my son arrived, I cried and repeated over and over again, "I love you I love you I love you." I have no recollection of that, but I remember the bliss.

My son is a toddler now, and we have relocated to North Carolina near my family. When my son waves at every car that drives by, I like to believe that is the Southerner in him. He prefers the R&B remix of "Baby Shark" to the original and I like to believe that's the Black in him.

Even in life's most difficult moments, he is a reminder to us that there is always room for more joy. He doesn't know that the world is raging with a pandemic; he just knows that he gets to hang out at home with Mom and Dad. He doesn't have to wonder if the reason no one joins him in the kiddie pool might be because we're the only Black family present; he thinks the pool was created just for him.

Recently, my mother indulged him, as grandparents do, with some bites of her favorite ice cream—butter pecan. A refreshingly, cool treat with warm flavors and a nutty crunch. He grinned and asked for more, likely beginning to understand what I've known all along.

Black motherhood is more than grief and tribulations; it is also pecans.

— Crystal Marie —

22

It's Not Just Black and White

It is not our differences that divide us. It is our inability
to recognize, accept, and celebrate those differences.
~Audre Lorde

"Single Black female seeks single Black male, preferably 5'9" or taller, height proportionate to weight, who is responsible, confident, mature, caring, has a sense of humor, is a non-smoker, enjoys traveling and sports, and is prudent with money." This is how my advertisement would have read if I had submitted an ad for a husband.

Darrell met every requirement in this ad except one. He's not Black.

I had never dated outside of my race until I met him. At first, I thought we would just be friends. I grew up in a multi-racial area and had white male friends as well as being friends with white males I worked with, but there was something different with Darrell. We never had a "just friends" vibe. I developed strong feelings for him rather quickly. I couldn't wait to talk to him and hang out together.

As our relationship progressed, I began to worry. What would I say to my family and friends? One of my sisters was kind of militant. She would never date outside her race and the only white male she found attractive was John F. Kennedy. Jr. My other sister was married to a Puerto Rican man. I remember my mother making a comment that she wished my sister had married a Black man. I thought if I showed up with a white man, my mother would have a United Nations situation happening with Black, Puerto Rican and white boyfriends or husbands.

Eventually I introduced him to my family. They got along like they were old friends. I don't know if it was genuine on my parents' part, but at that point I didn't care. I just wanted them to like this man who I had come to care for so much.

My militant sister met my husband and she too seemed to accept him. However, I made the mistake once of sending him into the airport to pick her up when she was coming home from a vacation with friends. She got upset with me because I sent him to get her. She feared her friends would think she was dating a white man and didn't speak to me for weeks because of that.

And then there was his family. He told me when his father learned he was dating a Black woman, one he dated before he met me, his father was so upset he was unable to go to work the next day. I never met his father and I never pushed the issue.

I eventually met Darrell's mother, but unfortunately, she had dementia and was living in a nursing home. When he introduced me to her, she looked at me and said to him, "Leave her alone." Since she had dementia, who knows what she meant? I interpreted it literally and assumed she didn't want me with her son.

Other than family, I wondered what the outside world would think of my interracial relationship. Would we get harassed? Would we be able to travel together? If we took a road trip, would we be pulled over? Would we be given the worst hotel room? When we traveled, I sent my husband in alone or I went in alone so that our interracial relationship would not influence the type of room we got.

My husband never thought that way. He says we don't have to worry about those things today. I disagree. He doesn't know what it's like to be followed in a department store for no reason. He doesn't know what it's like to feel like you don't belong because of the color of your skin.

This was another thing I was concerned about when we first met. Would we be able to overcome our different upbringings and our different childhoods? I was raised by a Black woman who didn't allow

me or my sisters to talk back to her. We didn't want to get "the look."
He had no such concerns with his parents growing up.

I also didn't know if we could overcome our different tastes in music.
I grew up listening to rhythm and blues while he grew up listening to
rock. I don't like rock music and he is not fond of mainstream R&B.

We have been together for more than twenty years. My husband
and my parents get along well. My elderly father even sometimes calls
to speak specifically to him. They bond over sports and politics.

While I never got to know his parents, I've gotten to know some
of his cousins pretty well. They seem to accept me.

In general, I don't notice whether or not people stare at us when
we are in public. We lived in Chicago our entire lives before we moved
to a warmer climate in Charlotte, North Carolina recently. Chicago
is a liberal city with plenty of interracial couples, so we didn't stick
out like sore thumbs. I haven't noticed as many interracial couples in
Charlotte, but I believe Charlotte to be one of the more progressive
cities in North Carolina, so I haven't felt judgmental eyes staring at
us there either.

Before 2020, we took at least two week-long vacations a year. We
have traveled all over with minimal issues, but I still send him into
the hotel to check in without me.

I have educated him on what it's like to grow up with a Black
mother, what it's like to look around your college lecture class and
realize you are the only Black person, and what it's like to experience
discrimination because of the color of your skin.

I, in turn, have learned a different way of thinking from him. I
tend to be a pessimist and used to give up easily on things. Now I am
more optimistic and don't throw in the towel right away because of
obstacles in front of me. It took some time, but I started grasping the
art of compromise.

It works. Now when we take a long drive, we'll listen to oldies
like Sixties music or Motown, something we both can enjoy together.

I know we grew up in different environments. We share so much,
but our differences make us who we are. At times, I wish we could
talk about music from back in the day, as well as the Black mother

experience and Black traditions. When I want to reminisce about those things, I go to my sister or a friend.

What I realize now is that whether you're in an interracial relationship or not, you've probably had different experiences. Most of us want a loving relationship where we can grow and be free to be ourselves. And that's the marriage I have.

— Cherise Haggerty —

23

Hum

Love makes your soul crawl out from its hiding place.
~Zora Neale Hurston

Soul food (n) traditional southern African American cuisine. Ever since I was a child, I've hummed when I'm eating. Let me rephrase that: I hum when I eat GOOD food. I'm talking that fresh out the oven, skin still cracklin', pot bubblin', beans so green you can taste the soil that gave them life, good food. I come from a family of good cooks. Soul-food cooks.

Grandmama cooks with love and taught all nine of her children how to do so, who in turn taught their children, my generation, how to do so. And we will teach the next generation.

It had been a while since I had had soul food. I'm horrible about attending family gatherings and don't really know many other Black people in my town. I keep to myself most days. So my access to that good food is limited. Maybe once every other Mother's Day when I made it over to Grandmama's for the after-church meal. I always pile up my plate and dig in, humming the whole time. Aunt Algie has always teased me about it. I just tell her that's how you know it's good food.

So here we are, Thanksgiving 2020. Although it's the time of the year most people usually want to gather and visit with family and loved ones, gatherings have been advised against. And furthermore, I've recently had surgery and am under explicit doctor's orders to stay home. It's already been a long, lonely year, and this definitely isn't helping. So when Aunt Algie called and offered to bring me a plate of food from the dinner at Grandmama's house, I was beyond elated. All that good food delivered to my door with a face-masked hug from Uncle Paul to top it off? Grubhub, eat your heart out.

They swung by late in the evening on Thanksgiving Day. I met Uncle Paul at the door, we took a moment to catch up, and then he left. I had already eaten so I put the bag in the fridge, giddy at how heavy the container inside felt. I could have opened it and peered at my bounty, but the fat kid that I am, I was already imagining what goodies awaited me. It felt like it was Christmas Eve and I was a curious child, shaking presents, imagining what was inside. I didn't want to ruin that magic.

Dinnertime the next day finally rolled around. I had eaten a little earlier while catching up with a friend, but it was more of a snack than a meal. Did the job at the time, but by now I was starving. I hobbled to the kitchen on one crutch, opened the fridge, and pulled out the Walmart bag of deliciousness. One smaller Ziploc bag with four rolls and a stuffed Cracker Barrel to-go container were my prize. Have you ever noticed how it feels like time slows when you're waiting on something? It felt like I could have written this story in the time I stood there, watching that black container spin round and round. Almost in a trance, the gentle humming of the microwave guiding me in song, taking my mind far, far away....

After what felt like a century, it was time. I hobbled my way to the table and immediately started shoveling it in. Juicy, tender brisket cut thick. Mac & cheese so rich and cheesy. My god, the cheesiness. Gravy with the giblets over the stuffing. Creamy green bean casserole with those little fried onions on top that get a little soggy but somehow still stay crispy on the edges. But then the carrots stopped me in my tracks. All my aunties always made them the same way: cut into rounds and baked to tender, melt in your mouth perfection with butter and cinnamon. One bite, and I was a child again, sitting at the kids' table in the corner of Grandmama's kitchen, humming more and more intensely with every bite. And there's something about corn bread with that dense, cake like texture and actual corn in it that sets my soul ablaze. As I polished off that cornbread, I remained that child in the corner, my humming now something more of a victory song than a happy little tune.

By the end of the meal, I didn't feel quite as alone as I had when I began eating. I could feel the love of my family growing in me with every bite, soothing and warming my recently aching soul. I sat there, staring at the now almost empty to-go dish, with so much appreciation for that piece of plastic. Almost moved to tears with how full both my belly and my heart were in that moment. Still humming my victory song.

— Emmy Faith —

Soul Food Is Overrated

The more you praise and celebrate your life,
the more there is in life to celebrate.
~Oprah Winfrey

Thanks to quarantine, expensive holiday flights, and me being 2,400 miles from home, my two housemates and I decided to make the best of Turkey Day/National Day of Mourning together. As we began writing our menu into an iPhone shared note, they asked me what my family usually ate for this day. At this point, I had only been living with them for about three months, so we were still getting to know one another. I closed my eyes, dropped my head back, and pictured the tables crowded with mac and cheese, collard greens, candied yams, baked turkey wings, corn on the cob, fried chicken, baked beans, corn bread, homemade rolls, peach cobbler, sweet potato pie, pound cake, banana pudding, and so much more. With every detail I could think of, I gifted them the smells, textures, and especially the tastes right into their imaginations.

When I lifted my head and opened my eyes, they had theirs closed and saliva creeping out the corners of their mouths. "KAM, YOU HAVE TO MAKE ALL OF THAT!" Uh oh… I'd talked myself right into a trap. My housemates, half-sisters who share Mexican heritage and never had a holiday fixated on soul food, were asking ME to take on a feat fit for a big mama.

Now, some of you may read this and not see a problem. Of course you wouldn't make all of that, but you definitely could whip up the staple items and confidently bless these young ladies with incredibly satisfying home-cooked soul food.

But I, a twenty-five-year-old Black woman from the heart of Detroit who had soul food at every holiday she could think of, had a bad case of stage fright. I'm not sure if it's from my mom never having me help in the kitchen, the boarding school in the suburbs, the introduction to Whole Foods and chia seeds in college, or my short lived, plant-based phase during graduate school, but nothing within me was confident about completing this task.

I had previously had my Black card revoked by a friend for not knowing how to braid hair and for never having watched one episode of *Living Single*. I had to accept this challenge. And I made sure that I was the only one in the house that knew it was going to be a challenge.

After a few phone calls to the aunties and mamas in my life, and some time on the Internet looking up the "Southern" version of every familiar dish, I had some pretty solid recipes. I was ready to try making the staple soul food items: candied yams, collard greens, and the showstopper... mac and cheese. Thankfully, we agreed to have a meatless meal and my housemates wanted to make a couple other side dishes of their own, so I didn't have to rattle my brain with more than this.

I created my e-note grocery list, scurried through three different grocery stores to get the exact ingredients required, paid an absurd amount of money for cheese (did I mention I'm a grad student?), and then made it home to start prepping before the big day. I won't bore you with the hours spent in the kitchen but do know that I understand why Big Mama always needs a foot rub after cooking dinner.

Fast forward to the big day. The meal looked lovely! Nowhere near as much food, and definitely some healthier and more unique options — like fried oyster mushrooms instead of fried chicken — but nonetheless, the meal was looking good! I took pictures and sent them off to my kitchen superiors for validation, and then sent up a prayer that everything would taste as good as it looked.

We made our plates and came to the table, eager to dig in. I closed my eyes as my housemates' forks made their way in slow motion to their mouths. "Dear God, please don't let me get another Black card revoked today!"

"Kam, this is SO good!" My eyes shot open! Did I just level up?! Both of them kept carrying on about how good my dishes were and how amazing the mac and cheese and candied yam combo I taught them was. I was in shock. Finally, I decided to dig in to join the experience. I had a bite of each dish and was surprisingly… underwhelmed. Was soul food overrated? Don't get me wrong, it was good, and it would have fit in just fine in any Black family holiday spread. But it wasn't how I remembered it.

But… there was no spades games playing nearby, no little cousin sitting on my lap trying to use my phone, no thunderous laughter and clinking of drinks from my uncles, no warm hugs followed by cold jokes from my siblings, no hand holding for Grandma's prayer, no aunties asking about my dating life, and no fighting over who would have the last slice of sweet potato pie. The more I ate, the more the feeling of emptiness grew inside me. And then I knew why it was called soul food. It's all the love that happens around you while eating it that makes your imagination remember the food for more than what it really was.

— Kamaria Washington —

25

Heart of Harlem

My mother would look at me and she'd say,
"Kamala, you may be the first to do many things,
but make sure you are not the last."
~Kamala Harris

My husband Reggie and I decided to go to New York City, to use up airline tickets previously booked for an event that had been rescheduled. It would be my first time visiting the city, and we both wanted to check some things off our bucket lists since there's so much to do and see there. Plus, we wanted to visit a good friend in Harlem, Eric B. Turner, a Black Broadway actor, who wears many hats in New York and in other cities around the world.

We arrived at Eric's apartment after spending the morning driving around Manhattan and taking in some of the sights. We were tired and hungry from the long red-eye flight, so the three of us decided to head out on foot to fill our bellies with soul food! We were going to one of the popular Black-owned restaurants Eric recommended in the historical neighborhood.

We hadn't thought about what was going on in the election at the time, so we were surprised when we found ourselves surrounded by people yelling and clapping, blowing their car horns, and generally celebrating. "We did it! We did it!" one white woman on the street corner said. "Joe Biden just won the presidential election!"

Walking around Harlem wasn't what we expected during a pandemic.

I thought everyone would be shut inside, but we passed by tons of street vendors selling everything from clothing to scented oils and homemade CDs. I wanted to stop and shop, but our conversation turned to the history in the making, and quickly I forgot about the vendors. We all began to talk about Kamala Harris becoming the first Black and first female Vice President.

As we continued to walk through Harlem, Eric gave us a tour and showed us where many movies were shot. When we were a block away from the restaurant, we were yet again surprised by the huge community gathering ahead. Kool & The Gang's "Celebration" was playing on a speaker, people were dancing and waving American flags, and bike riders, city workers, police officers, and people of all colors and ages were standing and cheering in unity. Some were crying tears of happiness. Truck drivers passing by participated by honking their horns. Everyone was wearing their face masks, but there were some people who forgot their social distancing in the middle of their joy. They were hugging strangers and giving high fives all around.

We were now at the restaurant, standing on the street corner near the front and waiting to be seated outside for curbside dining. A man from the restaurant opened a bottle of champagne and ran into the crowd spraying bubbly about and shouting, "Yeah!"

Before we knew it, the music changed to "The Cupid Shuffle." Everybody knew what was gonna happen next! *To the right, to the right, to the right, to the right. To the left, to the left, to the left, to the left…* As soon as we heard the song it was like we were all in a trance. *Now kick, now kick, now kick, now kick. Now walk it by yourself, now walk it by yourself….* Those who weren't line dancing were watching others dance!

By this time, we were heading to our seats. Eric ordered appetizers for the table: fried catfish bites and spring rolls filled with collard greens, black-eyed peas, and macaroni and cheese. Sounds tasty? It was! For himself he got fried chicken wings, red beans and rice with oxtail gravy on the side. Mmm. Reggie played it safe and got honey lemon fried chicken strips with waffle fries, since he's not a big soul food eater. Me, I got more of the fried catfish. Sitting at the table, we were in good spirits and continued to people-watch as we discussed our country's future history. Yes, I said "future history." I didn't say much at the table, but if I did choose to stop filling my mouth with that perfectly seasoned, yet soft and flaky, crunchy catfish filet, I would've said this...

"Kamala Harris represents the future we've only hoped for until now, and she will go down in history as the first African American, South Asian female Vice President. This will open doors, and the windows that we've only watched through, since the past wasn't our time. This will destroy the shackled mentality that wouldn't give a place or right to a woman in a leadership role, yet alone running a whole country. This moment now has a significant place in my life and in our unique culture's soul, flowing into the hearts of us all. This is for me, my daughter, and every woman with a mind and voice to say, "Now it's my future, it's my time! As a Black woman, I'm proud to say I'm a citizen of this nation." That's what I should've shared at the table with Reggie and Eric, instead of piling all that food into my mouth!

We finished lunch with a super thick piece of homemade red velvet cake and some sweet potato pie. It couldn't have been a more perfect ending to a beautifully spontaneous morning, filled with good friends, good news, meaningful conversations and tasty soul food. How amazing that we got to celebrate such a significant moment in history in the heart of Harlem. That was the best food for the soul.

— Lavinia Nanetta Holmes —

26

Her Famous
Pound Cake

Each time you love, love as deeply as if it were forever.
~Audre Lorde

I never had the privilege of meeting my grandmother on my mother's side. So how is it possible that a memory of her lingers in my mind? Maybe it's the constant mention of her name or the pictures I've seen. Or maybe it's a sweet, delectable dessert, Annie Belle's Famous Pound Cake, that created a bridge connecting me to my grandmother.

I remember waking up to my mother baking her mother's famous pound cake. The buttery aroma of the batter would fill the house. I would pop up as if my alarm had gone off and make my way down the stairs and into the kitchen where all the magic was happening. My mother would pop the beaters out of the mixer and hand one to me coated with the perfect amount of batter. Immediately my heart was full as I licked the beater clean with no trace of batter remaining.

This pound cake had an extraordinary reputation and orders began rushing in. My mother would make hundreds of cakes and I was always there, waiting for my favorite and most important job. Each time I felt a closeness, like the arms of a grandmother bringing you in close and holding you until you lost track of time.

My mother didn't keep this recipe a secret and although others tried to imitate this work of art, they always found that something was missing. Nobody could make it exactly how my mother and grand-mother could. Every step and each ingredient was listed in a church cookbook, but the outcome was only flawless when my mother was in the kitchen. I wondered if this had anything to do with the special pan my grandmother used and passed down to my mother — or was it deeper than that?

I knew one day I would have to attempt baking this famous pound cake. But what if I failed? What if, like all the others who tried, I didn't have what it takes to successfully make this family recipe?

I told myself, *If you fail, who cares? Just keep trying. If it doesn't come out perfect, it's still a cake! Eat it anyway and enjoy every single bite.*

I purchased all the ingredients and made sure I prepped every-thing the night before. I felt ready. The morning came and I woke up extremely excited and ready to put my skills to the test. I ran into the kitchen and reached into the cabinet to take out that cake pan, the third generation to use it.

My mother knew I was nervous so she guided me through each step via video chat (thank God for technology). Whether it was as simple as gradually adding the sugar or sifting the flour, my mother held my hand virtually throughout the entire experience. As she smiled and watched me do what she did for so many years, I couldn't help but picture that bridge again. The bridge I felt as a child that connected me to the grandmother whom I never met.

At the age of twenty-five, in the midst of the pandemic, I baked my first pound cake! A pound cake that tasted identical to the one that ran through my veins for generations.

Instead of the once so little girl running down the stairs to taste test the cake batter, I was now the one in the kitchen. The one who will one day wake her children with the tantalizing smell of a pound cake being prepared. As I hear the sound of my children's footsteps, I will meet them with a batter coated beater. As they enjoy their treat, I will know that their ancestors are wrapping them in their comfort-ing arms. My children will feel warmth that they won't know how to explain and a love that they haven't been able to touch.

Using the same cake pan that my grandmother used to bake her cakes, I unveiled my flawless replica of our family recipe. I swear for the first time I heard my grandmother's voice. She whispered, "Now you are the carrier of this family tradition."

—Naomi E. Johnson—

27

Uncle Bubby

*If people aren't accepting then they can easily tear
you down if you're not prepared and
comfortable with who you are.*
~Wanda Sykes

Uncle Bubby blessed and brightened my life so deeply,
yet we never had long conversations about anything. He
silently let me know I was precious, sane and safe. I tucked
those feelings in my bag and took them back to Jersey to
carry me through until the next summer.

My first memories of Uncle Bubby began at age four in 1957,
sitting on the porch with him and Brownie, his tan and white Collie,
in Hart County, Kentucky. We watched the fields gently roll into the
pasture across the road, green and yellow, endless and kissing the sky.
I was filled with freedom to just be precious, his precious little niece.
Uncle Bubby was the ONLY man in my childhood of whom I had NO
fear. I was afraid of dogs until Uncle Bubby introduced me to Brownie
and showed me how to dance with him. Brownie put his paws on my
shoulders, and we would dance all afternoon!

Uncle Bubby introduced me to cows, inviting me to walk the
pasture with him and Brownie while they worked. The cows were big
and gentle, just like Uncle Bubby. He stood at least 6'5" and I imag-
ined that the cows would be as tall if they could stand up. I still love
cows, their sagging stomachs always looking pregnant and standing in
meditation all day. I love their huge eyes and how their eyelashes fall

like sheer curtains. Uncle Bubby was like a cow, few worries, doing what needed to be done, a day at a time.

He laughed with me, never at me. I remember him taking me to the barn and letting me think I was milking when I was ten. I anxiously grabbed an udder and drew back in repulsion. That thing was warm and gushy! Silly city girl, expecting it to be cold, like refrigerated milk. Did we laugh!

I really thought I was somebody when he let me drive his tractor! Who else would let me drive anything? He sat me up on his tractor and walked beside me as I smiled and turned that big wheel. I probably only drove a few yards, but in my mind, I drove a country mile!

When Uncle Bubby spoke, he made no-nonsense good sense. Once, I commented that Sport, his Border Collie, was in the pig pen hitting the silo lever with his paw, dispensing corn. He held a cob over one paw and under the other. He even figured out how to turn the corn as he crunched. "Uncle Bubby," I said with alarm, "Sport is eating corn!"

"That's all's in that dog food y'all buy." He said it as dry and bland as animal feed. He looked straight ahead as he spoke the obvious, not moving a facial muscle. I laughed and then his face broke into a broad smile.

When Daddy died, Uncle Bubby came north for the first time, intending to bring his widowed sister and her children to Kentucky to support them.

I wanted to go. Mom explained that she was just fine. The day after the funeral, Mom cooked breakfast for everyone and introduced the Philadelphia Pork Roll, proud of her acculturation to the urban north. "I don't want none," said Uncle Bubby.

"Just try it Bubby, it's good."

"What's rolled up in it?"

"Pork, I guess, well, pork and something."

"Don't nobody know what's rolled up in that thing and I don't want none!"

I stopped eating pork roll after that.

In 1971, I was a freshman at Kentucky State College. About an hour and a half from the farm, I felt a million miles away from love. Miserable, depressed, and anxious, I knew I needed to go home. Uncle Bubby always accepted me at every stage or phase I went through. My mother said that Uncle Bubby called her after my visit and said, "Regina doesn't seem to be happy."

She matter-of-factly told him that I had never been happy. His report to her told me that it DID matter, that I should be happy all the time, not just over the summer. It was fine for me to pursue happiness. I kept that idea in the hope chest of my soul.

A few years later I started to find the happiness that comes from accepting and loving oneself. I made a blundering effort to share it with my family over Thanksgiving break, at Uncle Bubby's house. I talked incessantly, yet vaguely, about how important women were in my life. A few days later I called his daughter, my cousin Mary. She told me that afterwards, Uncle Bubby said, "You think Regina is gay?"

"Yes," she replied.

"I think so too," he said. That was all.

The next time I saw Uncle Bubby, I had my two children in tow. After greetings, we climbed the creaky stairs to heaven in the upper rooms. I loved the smell of heat and the sweating wood in August! I sat in a rocking chair and watched my children sleep in the bed of generations. I inhaled longer and deeper than I had in seven years. I breathed in uninterrupted sky that bowed down to meet the hills. Stars accented the blue-black velvet like champagne bubbles. My grandparents twinkled in those stars. I rocked all night, breathing in the smells of pine, cedar, clothes and the distant smells of cows, manure, corn, chickens and endless greenery. This blessing swaddled me as I fell asleep.

That was the last time I saw my Aunt Virginia. She'd lived with ALS disease for thirteen years. She could no longer move or speak. One does not need words when your husband is Uncle Bubby. When I got up, she was beautifully dressed, sitting in her wheelchair with her hair done, courtesy of her husband. Uncle Bubby rolled her in front of the vanity mirror, decked with several bottles of cologne. He picked them up one at a time, asking her which one she wanted. When she

finally groaned, he sprayed her neck and wrists.
This is the meaning of happiness.

—Regina S. Dyton—

Chapter
4

Self-Discovery

Retail

*Some people say I have attitude — maybe I do...
but I think you have to. You have to believe in
yourself when no one else does —
that makes you a winner right there.*
~Venus Williams

After I'm done working for the man
When I'm done pretending
For white America

I put back on my black face
And leave my mammy tendencies
And forced compliments
At the door

Till tomorrow
When I have to punch back in

They got me working for quarters
Penny pinching so hard
I make Abe scream

I'm a slave to my bills
I guess that's why
I'm working retail

That forty acres and a mule
Would come in good now

My feet get sore
And I thirst for something more
Preferably in the field
I went to school for

In between racks
I hide from white America
With my black face on
I can never wash off
But I can't stay forever
Because I have some transfers
And put backs

So much for a college grad
The new chains is loans
Sallie Mae is my master
Whipping up my phone

They said education
Was "freedom"
But equality means nothing
I'm still Black with a degree

Got me contemplating that debate
Who was right?
My boy W. E. B. Du Bois
Or Booker T

— Sydney Ann Johnson —

28

Bold Beautiful Sakora

The kind of beauty I want most is the hard-to-get kind
that comes from within — strength, courage, dignity.
~Ruby Dee

I lay on the table wincing as my aesthetician, Ranni, moved the white thread over my eyebrows. As she repositioned my fingers I said, "I've been thinking about shaving all my hair off! Will you do it for me?"

Ranni's eyes grew wide, eyebrows reaching for her hairline as if the act I had asked her to commit would ruin our friendship forever.

Next to my Seminary friends and therapist, this woman was the only other person who had known me the entire time I had been at Berkeley. Ranni had been there for celebrations and successful conference presentations, final papers and exams. Deaths and emergency trips back to the continent. Ranni had also been there when threading those eyebrows seemed to be what I needed to get through yet another bipolar episode.

Ranni stopped threading and shook her head at me. "No! I can't. I never received training on how to style Black hair!"

"Well, I can be your guinea pig today!" I said with a smile. She smiled back nervously but agreed that there was no time like the present to try her hand at something new.

Eyebrows done and looking perfect as usual, I lifted my body off the reclining table and followed Ranni out to the main part of the salon. Once seated in a chair I was seized by a momentary panic: What if I hated it? What if the shape of my head was hideous? How long would it take to grow it back?

Ranni wrapped the black cape around me tightly as if hugging me. She patted me on the shoulder and asked one last time, "You sure? You wanna cut it all off?"

I nodded.

I watched as the cutest pair of clippers disentangled itself from the river of cords belonging to all the other clippers. It was pink.

With the first buzz, I prayed I'd have a symmetrical head, and not one with dents and craters. Dimples would be okay. The air rushed in as Ranni moved the clippers around my head. With the air came the questions. What if it didn't grow back the same? How did one handle the spiky stage of growth? How would I take care of my hair? My scalp? Did I really want to have a shaved head for a while or was this a passing fancy encouraged by my new lover?

Ranni touched my shoulders gently to make sure I was okay. I smiled back in the mirror, reassuringly. Ranni continued to buzz away until she raised a pancake of hair from my head and held it out. Ranni felt so proud of herself. I marveled at the effort it took for her to keep all the hair on my head connected until the last bit was shaved. She asked one of the stylists to bring me a bag to store the pancake of curls.

"It looks like a wig, well… more like a judge's wig," I said, smiling at the curious stylists who had gathered around my head.

"You look stunning!" Ranni declared. All the other heads nodded.

I rose slowly from the chair to look at myself in the 360 mirror. Ranni was right. I looked stunning!

My first step after I spun around in front of the mirror was lighter. The breeze that embraced me was energizing. A sudden burst of confidence rode in on the breeze as it gently kissed my scalp. I grabbed my bag of curls, paid Ranni, and skipped out into the El Cerrito sunshine. I was ready to show off my new do.

My first gawkers, two young boys, stared for more than the "approved" polite moment. Next to the corner Starbucks, three women stepped off the sidewalk and averted their eyes as they took in my shaved head. A few minutes later, an older woman smiled and asked how my day was, redeeming my faith in humanity. The few Black men who saw me instantly looked above my head refusing to acknowledge me as though my shaved head was a challenge to them.

Outside a grocery store, a young boy, probably no more than twelve, was selling candy bars. Here we go again I thought, expecting another stare-down.

"Not today," I said as he asked if I could support his school campaign.

"Okay. Have a good day, beautiful!" the young boy replied.

I did a double take. When I recovered from my shock I said, "You do the same, honey," making sure to stress the last word. He grinned at me.

He grinned broader still when twenty minutes later I emerged from the grocery store with my purchase.

I smiled at him as I walked by, still aware of his attention.

"Do you have a boyfriend?" he boldly called after me.

I laughed heartily. What was the world coming to? Well, at least this one wasn't just staring.

"Aren't you just a little too young to be asking this question?"

I chuckled as he responded, "Age ain't nothing but a number!"

"Have a great weekend, honey!" I turned and smiled at him not wanting to deflate his self-confidence.

"You do the same, beautiful!" he responded, blowing me a kiss.

I shook my head as I walked away marveling at his boldness.

As I crossed the parking lot, a woman held her son's hand closer as he stared at my head, doe-eyed. The woman averted her eyes and tried to chastise her son.

I wondered what sort of statement my shaved head was making as I strutted around enjoying the kisses of the breeze on my way to the BART stop. People were certainly reading my Black body differently. Perhaps people were worried about my health or confused about my sexuality.

I wondered if the place I occupied in the world had changed. Perhaps I was performing gender from a far more non-conforming space and that shifted my place in society. It troubled me that even though I saw bald men everywhere, no one paused to stare at them. People's reactions so far had centered around avoidance, blatant staring, or a confused smile. The two people who stopped me to say I was stunning were non-Black women. What did that say about who valued what in this society?

Later that evening, I took selfies, and after posting them on Facebook got an even wider array of negative comments from the Black friends who were from the African continent.

One wrote, "Ah! What happened? Are you okay?"

Another commented, "Yikes! What did you do to your hair?"

Another advised, "Grow your hair back pretty girl."

Yet another said, "You crazy Kuuk, but I love your ummm…"

These comments said a lot about the standards of beauty, what my own people valued, and how this value was diminished by shaving my head. Regardless of what they thought, I was loving it. Of course, it helped that I had my new lover as my cheerleader.

— Kuukua Dzigbordi Yomekpe —

Finish the Race

When anyone tells me I can't do anything,
I'm just not listening anymore.
~Florence Griffith Joyner

In 2010, I experienced multiple life-changing setbacks within a short period of time. My marriage ended after seventeen years, I got laid off, a dear friend and mentor died, and I had an adolescent child who was facing circumstances that were beyond my ability to fix. My physical and emotional health suffered as I attempted to keep my mind straight in the midst of overwhelming pain and uncertainty.

From the outside, my smile, energy and personal accomplishments made others believe that life for me was great, but at night, I took the mask off. That's when I prayed, journaled, and cried myself to sleep.

I made a decision in 2013 that every year I'd do something I'd never done before. Life is a race and "Just Keep Going" became my mantra. I made a decision to LIVE! I started walking in 2013, completed my first 5K in 2014, finished my first half marathon in 2015, and blew my own mind when I conquered a full 26.2-mile marathon in 2016. This was in addition to writing a second children's book that was featured on FOX 5 news. Life was great for a while.

Then I took my dad for a visit to the ER after a cough that had lasted nearly two weeks. Right there in the exam room after only a chest X-ray and CT scan, the attending informed us that the cough was likely related to my dad having what appeared to be stage 4 lung cancer. "Wait… what?"

We had absolutely no idea. The ER physician had delivered the news assuming we already knew my father had lung cancer.

I remember the tears streaming down my face as we drove home from the hospital. My dad asked me to play "Baby Face" on Pandora and we both sang. I cried the entire ride home while singing to him. That was our thing, singing together in the car.

Daddy lost his battle with cancer in 2017. This loss shook me in a way that was far more painful than my combined experiences in 2010. It would've been so easy to fall right back into a state of depression, but my spirit was stronger than it had been back then. I went through my grief but I wasn't paralyzed by it. *Just Keep Going.*

In August 2017, keeping with my decision to be adventurous and ambitious, I decided to sign up for a triathlon. I was curious about what it would require, so some friends joined me on a road trip to see a triathlon that was taking place in the boonies of Maryland. I saw women going into the water and thought, *Are you sure you want to do this thing… there are ducks in the water! And, you don't know how to swim, fool!*

I started pre-training in February 2018, which was the anniversary of my father's transition. I learned from the past that I have the power to make anniversary memories what I want them to be! Feel what you need to feel but don't fall back into a depressed mindset!

I had a minor setback in April after breaking my leg during a run. This meant an interruption of my training. I took the recommended time off to heal and then got right back into my routine. From June through August, I had no pain and no complications. Two weeks before race day, my leg started aching. I was already tapering my training, so I just decided to slow it all the way down and take a break. I'd come too far to drop out.

My nerves weren't as bad as I thought they'd be on race day morning. I had focused on preparing for the swim portion of the event more than biking and running. The goal was to touch land. *You can do this, Temeka… you know how to swim!*

My anxiety eased up when I saw my coach Lloyd Henry and

teammates Kandis Gibson and Maxwell P. Blakeney. *All you have is a half mile... just swim one buoy at a time.* I stepped into the water with my wave and two minutes later, we were off. I was talking in my head the entire time, reminding myself to sight the buoy so I'd know what direction to swim. When I raised my head to sight, I couldn't see because of the fog. *Just Keep Going.*

I finally make it to the first turn but not without having to flip onto my back for a brief recovery position. I did this several times during the swim. The lifeguard in the canoe asked if I was okay. "Yes, I just need a minute."

When I finally made it out of the water, I discovered I was the last person to exit the lake. "How in the world did that happen? There were at least four other waves that came after me. Oh well, I finished without quitting, freaking out and getting pulled.

It was time to move onto the bike portion no matter how tired I was from swimming. *Just Keep Going.*

Kandis helped settle my nerves once my feet touched land. She walked me up the stairs near transition so I could switch into my cycling gear. Thank God for friends. Christy Fenner had introduced me to the world of triathlons; her words of inspiration and encouragement the evening before resonated in my heart now. When I arrived at the transition area, I saw that my bike was the only one there... out of 500. I silenced my thoughts and repeated, *Just Keep Going.*

I took off and heard the volunteer say on the radio, "The last bike is now out of transition." I was too determined to be embarrassed! I started singing Mary Mary's "Can't Give Up Now" in my head.

For a long distance, I was by myself on the road but then I saw other participants. I started passing folks. That last hill was a monster. I had to clip out and walk with my bike, but I didn't stop. *Just Keep Going.*

At the top of the hill, I saw my village which consisted of my fiancé, coach and teammates. Coach was ringing that cowbell. Their presence gave me life and a burst of energy. I hopped back on the bike and made the turn toward the second transition. I saw my children standing on the sideline yelling "That's my mommy... Go, Mommy!"

I survived the swim and the hilly bike ride. Running would be a breeze for me. I could do a 5K in my sleep, that is unless I got a cramp in my quad. I never had this happen before during a race. I was rubbing my leg and running at the same time. I turned the corner and saw the finish line. The cramp was gone and so was I! I flew as fast as I could.

I thought I could do it and I did! I swam, I biked, I ran.

"Look at me, Daddy. I'm a triathlete!"

— Temeka S. Parker —

30

Finding Purpose with Puppies Behind Bars

Service is the rent that you pay for room on this earth.
~Shirley Chisholm

At seventeen I was sentenced to fifty years in prison. I constantly thought how foolish and careless I was for being involved in a crime that took the lives of two innocent people. I made the worst mistake of my life and in doing so altered the trajectory of my life and of all those connected to the victims. The pain that I created through my involvement in the crime forever haunts me.

I sat in a prison cell paying the consequences for the error of my youth. Many nights I lay awake going over the choices that I could have made and beating myself up because I didn't. My life needed to get back to a place where I could create some good, but how was this going to happen in a maximum-security prison for women? Prison was a place where they locked you away and forgot about you. The cells were damp and dark, cold in the winter and hot and humid in the summer, and you spent the majority of your day locked in a cell.

A pilot program called Puppies behind Bars was introduced into the Bedford Hills Correctional Facility in 1997. It was created by Gloria Gilbert Stoga, and it originally trained dogs as guiding eyes for the blind. The program expanded to train and raise service dogs for wounded war veterans and first responders, as well as explosive detection canines for law enforcement.

The puppies entered the prison at eight weeks old and lived with their raisers for about twenty-four months. As the puppies matured into well-loved, well-behaved dogs, their raisers learned what it meant to contribute to society rather than take from it.

In 1999, I had already been in prison for twenty-one years. A memo went out to the prison population for anyone who wanted to join the program. We had to write a letter and explain why we thought we would be a good candidate.

I applied and was accepted. The puppy program changed my life from one of self-pity to self-discovery and service.

The program was very intense, yet very fulfilling. I learned all about dog behavior and how to properly take care of a dog, including crate training, grooming and medical care. I spent twenty-four hours a day with my new puppy. It was an amazing experience teaching him and caring for his needs. The responsibility was enormous and sometimes overwhelming, but the sole objective was to raise a dog for a vet who'd put his or her life on the line for the freedoms we are afforded in the United States. I was honored to have a small part in this process.

On the day of graduation the veterans come to the prison to meet with the puppy raisers. Emotions run high for all involved. The veterans are getting a service dog to help them live a life of independence and security. We puppy raisers learned that contributing to society is far more rewarding than taking from it.

In serving others I actually learned to heal from my own trauma, and I have dedicated my life to continue to serve with a grateful heart.

I was paroled in October 2018.

Now I work for V-Day, a global organization that vows to end violence against women and girls and the planet. I advocate to end mass incarceration and I'm proud to serve my community in these ways.

— Roslyn D. Smith —

31

One In a Million

Decide what you want. Declare it to the world.
See yourself winning. And remember that
if you are persistent as well as patient,
you can get whatever you seek.
~Misty Copeland

"**B**aby Girl, Pettis," these words stared back at me from an old yellow piece of paper. I asked my mom what this was and she told me if I ever wanted to find my biological family, this would help me. It was my birth name. Now I felt like I had the golden ticket to start my search. My mom had given me the green light.

There was so much about myself that I was curious about. I grew up an only child so I wondered if I had biological siblings. If I did, would they even care to connect with me?

To begin, I applied to get my birth certificate. I mailed the forms, and then months went by. Finally, it arrived. I felt chills as I stared at this document. I saw my birth mother's name for the first time in my life.

I immediately got to work. I did a Google search to begin locating my bloodline! I found so many names, numbers, and addresses that I filled an entire sheet of paper! I was shocked to discover that I came from such a huge family on the maternal side! I narrowed it down to one particular person to contact and hoped for the best.

When he answered the phone, I quickly told him this would probably be the strangest call he ever received and then explained my purpose. I found out I was talking to a cousin! He contacted my grandmother to confirm my story and she confirmed that I was who I said.

Before I knew it, my phone was blowing up with phone calls from all kinds of family members! I learned that I was the youngest of four sisters! I had siblings! After speaking with my birth mother, I asked her about my birth father. She told me several different stories, all which were hard to verify and led to a dead end.

At this point, I was unemployed and couldn't afford a DNA test. But that was the only way I was going to solve this mystery… unless I found another way.

An old friend told me that the *Judge Mathis* show was looking for people who were looking for their birth families. I went on the show and tested my sister's father and learned that he was not my biological father. I was disappointed but not that surprised. After walking out the courtroom, the producer told me if I ever needed help with my search, let him know. I confirmed that I would.

I received an overwhelming response on social media from people across the country. I was shocked my story resonated with so many people! The audience was very encouraging. One person suggested that I use AncestryDNA. I could afford it by then, so I went ahead and did that test.

When I received the results, I was connected with more than 600 people! I knew for a fact that my birth father's side of the family was huge as well! I organized the results from the strongest DNA match. My strongest connection was a seventy-six-year-old man. I called my biological grandmother to see if she recognized his name. I knew if she didn't recognize him, he had to be connected to my birth father. She didn't know him.

I called him and learned that he had more than forty siblings, and that we could have had the same father. I called the TV producer again and gave him an update. I asked if there was a way to do a DNA test to verify that that gentleman and I were siblings.

It was time to go back on the show, and I felt more confident than ever. I had done a lot of research and had a better understanding of the genetic data. Then I saw the man with his wife and we looked so much alike! Judge Mathis confirmed that the defendant was indeed my brother! I'm the youngest of more than forty siblings!

I went from "Baby Girl, Pettis" to putting the final piece of the puzzle together. To complete the search, all I needed was what was already inside me — my DNA! Wow! I just needed that one connection out of hundreds to connect me with my birth father's side! Life has a way of showing us just how powerful we are once we tap into what's already inside of us.

— Halona Jackson —

32

Steel Walls

Remember this in the darkest moments, when the work
doesn't seem worth it, and change seems just out
of reach: Out of our willingness to push through
comes a tremendous power... use it.
~Stacey Abrams

At first, I just wanted to be accepted. I graduated from San Francisco State at the top of my class. I walked away with recommendations in hand and a dream of becoming a reporter. It took seven internships, 327 applications and years of rerouting before I accepted my first reporting role.

I blindly left my life in Los Angeles to accept an East Coast position paying $27,000 (before taxes) a year, with no perks or real moving reimbursement. Nevertheless, I was the happiest I had ever been.

Many Black women in this industry and plenty others have gone on record to say they are paid significantly less than their white counterparts — specifically men. In one market, my white male co-worker was paid nearly $15,000 more a year. In that same market, he was promoted, and I got an e-mail saying how much the station appreciated all my hard work. I received more exclusive interviews than any anchor or reporter at the station that year.

Shortly after I started in television news, I went natural. I connected with the meaning behind "the big chop" and I went for it. This was not acceptable for many members of management within my industry.

In one instance, a news director in Virginia approached me about a weekend anchor role. After three long discussions, he called to ask if I would be open to wearing a wig with long straight hair. He added that it would give me a softer look.

My no and the no's that would follow cost me advancement, friends, and, at times, my peace.

In another market, I served as an anchor. Well, at least that's what my contract said; I accepted an anchor/investigative reporter position. After I moved to the state and got settled in, I learned in addition to my roles I would also produce my own show, manage the weekend team and serve as my own photographer. Shortly after I left a very nice white woman took over my role and was given a producer.

It took years before I felt comfortable enough to ask for what I deserved. I had always been stuck behind the steel wall that I had created in my image of what a "strong Black woman" had to be. Behind that wall, I could not warp, split or crack. I had to have the same hairstyle and demeanor every day. I had to be impenetrable, imperturbable.

The pandemic slowed everything down and I took my first real break from the industry. This time of reflection changed my life. My newfound clarity served as the fire needed to melt the steel wall I had strategically placed myself behind.

Once I stopped tiptoeing around what I wanted out of life, I found myself at the very top of my game! I now hold the power. There is no ceiling for me and this truth has set me free.

Now I create steel walls that don't hold me in; instead, they protect me from anything that tries to disrupt my Big Queen Energy.

I wake up now and water flowers that I thought I could never grow. I take my dog on a walk in a neighborhood that I never thought I'd live in.

I get to do the work I love on a platform ten times bigger than before.

My name is Ashonti and I build steel walls, my way.

— Ashonti Ford —

33

I'm Not a Minority

When there are many worlds
you can choose the one
you walk into each day.
~Jacqueline Woodson, Brown Girl Dreaming

We pulled up to the university, our car packed with all the items I thought would make me feel at home. I began wondering if I would fit in. For the first time, I felt somewhat inadequate.

I had been accepted at many other colleges and universities, some of which were HBCUs. I even caught some flak for choosing a PWI instead of an HBCU from a few of my friends. As I scanned the campus, hoping to find someone who looked like me, I wondered if I made the right choice.

I graduated from a predominantly Black high school and chose to go to a predominantly white institution for college. I soon realized that it was a totally different world. I'd never felt like a "minority" before. I had a friend from high school who was going to the same school; however, she was assigned to a dorm across campus.

I hoped my roommate and I would hit it off. My mother had already told me to be prepared to have a roommate that wasn't of my ethnicity. I was okay with that. I had friends who weren't Black. We respected our differences and enjoyed our friendships.

I knew having a roommate would be a challenge in itself. The ethnicity part didn't concern me. I was ready to make it work.

I only wish I could say the same for my roommate, who had disappointment written all over her face when she saw me. She had an air about her and was quick to let me know that she was from upstate New York and that her parents had money. We had nothing in common, except that two weeks was going to be too long to wait to put in for a room switch request.

She told me she didn't have any Black friends and I imagined she probably hadn't had much contact with Black people in general. I remember so clearly, she never unpacked her boxes or bags, as if she thought I would steal something. She stayed up late listening to music and had friends over with no thought that it might bother me.

One day she asked me what my parents did for a living, and asked if I was on financial aid or a scholarship. The nerve of her.

I was in total shock. I can't believe I didn't lose my temper. I sternly told her, "My parents make too much money for me to get financial aid." As if it was any of her business if I was. I asked, "Are you on financial aid?" I think after that conversation, she learned to tread lightly.

I was miserable. Some of my classes had at least 200 students in a lecture hall. You could count the Black students on one hand. I called home one night and my brother answered the phone. I told him how my roommate was acting and how I was tired of being nice. I even shared how I rarely saw a Black person on campus, at least it seemed that way.

That night I did the wrong thing. I started crying on the phone with my brother. He was hard on me. "You chose that school. You better get yourself together and remember why you are in college. Don't you let anyone make you feel like you don't belong. Life is about adjustments; make your adjustments and keep moving."

He said some other things too—unfavorable things about my roommate, so no need to mention them. I never really listened to my brother before; after all, he was only a year older than me. But this time, it was what I needed to hear. That next day, I started talking to my floormates and inquiring about roommate swaps.

The few freshmen that I met on my floor were already satisfied with their roommates. There were a few upper classmen on my floor, but I didn't know them and was slightly intimidated to start a conversation with them.

I guess timing is everything, or my prayers were burning God's ears and he sent an angel my way. I was approached by a Black upperclassman who shared that her white roommate wanted to move out of their room. We arranged for our roommates to meet and they hit it off.

My new roommate personified how I foresaw myself as a student. She was beautiful and smart, and confident. She made me feel at home. School didn't seem so big anymore. As I moved my last piece of clothing from my old room, I said, "See you around" to my old roommate.

Surprisingly, she said, "It was nice meeting you." Maybe we made some progress, I thought.

I never felt like I was a minority again on that campus.

— Andrea Taylor —

34

Telling My Jamaican Mom I'm Not Going to Be a Nurse

*The thing you fear most has no power. Your fear of it is
what has the power. Facing the truth
really will set you free.*
~Oprah Winfrey

I paced my dorm room floor. Back and forth, back and forth. Today, I was declaring my independence. "I am going to the counseling office and changing my major. I don't care what Mommy says."

It was the spring of 2012, and I was in the middle of my second semester at Georgia State University, studying pre-nursing and extremely unhappy. Why? Because my Jamaican mother wanted me to become a nurse — which was not my passion.

You see, since I was thirteen years old, becoming a journalist was my dream. In my downtime, I would watch Soledad O'Brien on CNN for leisure. I wanted to be informed, tell the stories that needed to be told, and be a trailblazer for Black women in media. But, I had a traditional Jamaican mother.

For those who have immigrant parents, you understand my issue. Doctor, lawyer, nurse, and anything else that screams dollar signs were the only encouraged professions in my household. Journalism was not seen as a viable career that provides a stable income to support myself. Also, no one else in my family (except maybe a distant cousin) pursued journalism, so my mother did not have any knowledge about my dream job. She was a nurse, and in her mind, this was the best option for me.

When I was applying to college, my dreams of becoming a future Soledad were shut down by my mom, and I didn't dare protest. I was lucky enough to have parents that were funding my schooling, and in my household, the child had no say. My parents and grandparents came to this country as immigrants and worked hard to provide a comfortable life for their families. If not for them, I wouldn't have the opportunities I have today. I respected my parents and reluctantly took the submissive role.

But now, enough was enough. I was failing human anatomy and physiology (for the second time), feeling defeated, and I even had a mental breakdown a few days before at the nail salon with my aunty. Yeah, I reached my breaking point.

So, there I was in my dorm room, pacing back and forth, hands shaking and palms sweating. I rehearsed the words that I was going to tell my Jamaican mother.

I closed my eyes, pressed my mom's name on my contact list and the phone rang. It was the longest five seconds of my life. I felt the tears start in my eyes. My heart was racing. My mom was strict. I just knew I was dead meat.

"Hi dumpling," my mom answered in a cheerful voice.

I was prepared to crush her good mood and stand my ground.

I proceeded to tell her that I was going to change my major, my breakdown in the nail salon, and how nothing was going to stop me in my pursuit to be a journalist.

I was ready. Nothing could stop me now… until my mother said, "Okay."

Shocked does not even begin to describe how I felt. My mom proceeded to tell me that my aunty called and told her what happened in the nail salon. She apologized for pushing me to pursue nursing and told me that she only wanted the best for me. I don't think my mother truly understood how unhappy I was. But it took a conversation from her older sister to finally understand. For that, I was grateful.

My mom dreamed of me becoming an independent woman and supporting myself without the need for anyone. She believed that nursing was my ticket to financial independence; however, she understood that journalism was my passion and if I'm going to do it, she knows I'll do it well. Nursing is not the only ticket to living independently.

Just like that, the tears started to flow. My mom was letting go of control and passing the baton to me. She was giving me my freedom to choose, and for a first-generation kid, that was a big deal.

Later on that year, Mommy passed away from cancer. At her bedside, I made a promise that I would become the best journalist that I can be. I went on to get two degrees (one from one of the top journalism schools in the country), and work at one of the top television networks in America. My journey has just begun.

—Sarai Ashari Thompson—

35

Church Folk
Postscripts

*If I didn't define myself for myself, I would be crunched
into other people's fantasies for me and eaten alive.*
~Audre Lorde

C o-worker knows I'm new to Fort Lauderdale. Beneath her Asian weave and immovable forehead, I am eyed like a fresh soul; cordially invited into her fold. She smiles, says: "Take Federal Highway into Hollywood. Come as you are. We love everybody. I'd love to see you there."

Ten Sundays pass. I come as I am: showered, vintage, Bohemian, dreadlocks. No pressed powder. No red lipstick. No Sunday hat. No Sunday shoes. No wig. No weave.

Searching the rear of the sanctuary for solitude, I find a hip-room seat near a young mother with two under two in tow. Her face: charcoal blotted eye sockets confess sleepless nights, hard times; chewed up and swallowed by emotional trauma. I sit, note indentations of ragged tree branches on her wrists: evidence of life gone bad.

She shifts, smiles, nods in my direction. Newborn reeking of baby oil and spit-up squirms in her lap. Tired young mother uncages the nipple of left water-balloon breast with I'm-not-new-to-this precision. No evidence of third-finger-left-hand commitment. My heart saddens.

Heavy oak double doors in back groan as humid air ushers in musk of a man from who-knows-whose party just hours before. He creeps in, spies the front pews through hard-blinking eyes of avoidance. Lifts his arm. Eyes the time on expensive watch: Breitling? Drops his head. Sits quietly on the other side of tired Mom. I lean forward. He turns, nods in acknowledgement of my presence, and shrugs shoulders beneath a jacket that confesses a deficiency in order or neatness. Tired Mom's baby continues suckling. His left eye massages the water balloons.

Preacher man revs up, says "We're all sinners!" His suit: expensive. Tired Mom weeps at hearing the words, burps suckling baby, shoves Disney-decorated bottle into mouth of the toddler. Musty party man again shrugs. I nod in silent confession.

Older kid slings juice-filled bottle to the floor; grabs at water balloon and cries "Milk, Mommy, milk!" Heads turn. Eyes roll. Hisses of "Shhh" and "Why can't she keep them quiet?" reach us from throughout the sanctuary. Tired Mom's face becomes mask of embarrassment. I extend my arms and take suckling baby. Tired Mom exhales hard, comforts toddler by rocking. She continues to weep.

Preacher man's lips unleash fire and brimstone. He points out sinners. Calls out liars. Unmasks adulterers and fornicators. Quotes Leviticus to shame homosexuals. How does he know who's done what to whom?

Uneasiness makes a beeline for our pew and thrusts musty party man into good posture. I shift in my seat, rock sucking baby; shake my head, ease out a "Lawd have mercy on this man" …the preacher man, that is. Party man's eyes go wide.

Tired Mom raises her testifying hand and falls to her knees. Preacher man in expensive suit's words of unjustified and unqualified opinion force my neighbors to cringe in shame. "Humph. Ain't this a regular Sunday," my heart bleeds.

Preacher man's hips earthquake; his body zigzags across the pulpit on Tinker Bell toes. I whisper "show time" through lips squeezed tight. My eyebrows struggle to touch. He grunts, sweats like a woman over fifty, resuscitates a James Brown move, and then falls to his knees.

The choir stands. Preacher man's Maceo Parker posse escorts him to his feet. The choir moans lyrics from a collage of soul-twisting-and-pulling gospel hymns. They rock side-to-side, wave their hands for special effect. Preacher man lets out a sixty-second "Whoooah!" then takes a breath. White-dress woman in a loose wig runs to the pulpit, wipes preacher man's brow in slow, slow motion. She winks, smiles, exits.

My mouth forms a gaping "O". Tired Mom gets up, takes now-fussy baby. A cell phone rings. Nearby heads turn; faces twist in disgust as if the babies' disturbance was enough distraction for one service. Ringtone is old school: Wilson Pickett's "Funky Broadway." It's a shout-out from party man's disheveled yet expensive jacket. Relaxing my "O" gaping lips, I comment: "Bredren, that's too cool. Where'd you dig up Pickett?"

Eyes from turned heads roll. Wigs shift. Strong exhales are released. Party man's body stiffens, yet his eyes roam. The ringtone continues. He plays deaf. Tired Mom sighs at the judging eyes; lowers her chin in an attempt to avoid them. Rocks cranky suckling baby. Toddler, on the cusp of waking, stretches.

Tired Mom's face shifts in my direction. It reads: "I just came for the Word." Her eyes are moist. I mouth: "Me too." We smile. No teeth. I cross and uncross my legs. Half shrug my shoulders. Our eyes refocus on the religious circus. Mine are twin shallow pools of dampness. Party man's eyes squeeze shut.

Co-worker's hat catches the dust from my breeze outside of the church. "Where you going so fast? Stay for the fellowship luncheon — meet some people. Where did you sit?" She takes a breath between border-line accusing questions, hugs me, leans back, does the up-and-down you're-a-fat-girl scan as the grip tightens on her insignificant-in-the-world-of-real-things Sunday pearls. I don't hug her back.

"Why didn't you tell me you didn't have anything to wear? And I could have had my girl, you know, do a little something with, how can I say it without being misunderstood, your hair."

Inside I respond: "Diarrhea lips of judgment."

Outside I say in one breath: "This was fine. Thanks for inviting me. We aren't the same size. I'm mad cool with dreads; they are a part of, how do I say it without being misunderstood: who I am."

Co-worker flinches, blinks hard. Behind my back, my middle finger struggles to extend. I snatch it back and instead squeeze my fist tight. This judgment stuff ain't for me. My head turns. My eyes trail sounds of Wilson Pickett calling from musty, expensive jacket. On his heels: church-hat woman from the front pew — in a state of obvious agitation.

I just wanted to hear the Word.

—Cynthia A. Roby—

36

Who Am I to Be a Yoga Teacher?

*I'm working out just as much for my girls as I
am for me, because I want them to see a mother
who loves them dearly, who invests in them,
but who also invests in herself.*
~Michelle Obama

So, after nine months of training, learning the poses, understanding the Sanskrit terms, sweating, digging into my emotions, crying, complaining, crying some more, committing to the fact that I'm not here to teach but to learn… yup, I'm standing in the front of the class as the instructor. This was the grand finale of my 200-hour yoga teacher training. Needless to say, showing up to class was the biggest hurdle for me. I wasn't sure how I would relate, being overweight, not very flexible, full of insecurities, feeling broken most days and yes, I am a Black woman. I would probably be the only one.

Now yoga wasn't a part of my childhood; not many spoke of it when I was growing up. Always interested in sports and health, I stumbled across an article about the benefits of yoga and started reading about the philosophy. Honestly, the pictures were of young or middle-aged white women that I didn't relate to, or old Indian men that did ridiculous contortions with their bodies. Modern-day yoga journals showed what looked like dancers or gymnasts, nothing like the overweight, brown frame I was working with.

Yoga was something that "they" did. Eventually, I came across an Instagram of a yoga teacher who did some amazing poses, and she was bigger than me. I followed her stories and classes, practiced her flow, and digested the words of encouragement she offered. She was authentic.

My journey to health was a long and brutal one. Diet and exercise my entire adult life were never enough. Kinda confirmed how I felt about myself — never enough. True to form I kept trying, failure after failure. Moments of change, but overall I was still failing.

Getting married and having kids pushed me to figure this out. I had people depending on me. How could my kids think I had value if I couldn't even get this body under control? How could I preach health and better choices if clearly I couldn't stick to anything that worked for me? My weight was proof of my lack of discipline and control; everyone could see it. So, more diets, running, lifting, small wins. Changing food choices. A few more wins. Then the aches and pains of pounding workouts began to catch up, and in came yoga. It was time to revisit the benefits, mentally and physically. Still after many years, there weren't many like me on the scene. I needed some healing, so it was time to break barriers.

It was months of stalking the class before I took my first step inside. The mental hurdles my mind went through to get me into that class were monumental. That first step led me to an awareness that has changed my life forever. The instructor warmly greeted us and invited us to get into child's pose. She said there was "nothing to prove here" and "you are enough so just breathe."

Now I am the teacher. As people file in, I am in my head. A polite smile to greet each participant, all the while wondering *Who am I to teach this class?* I've had a lifelong battle with self-image, and after all, still being overweight was a manifestation of my failure to be in control, right?

I talk about healthy choices all the time but still struggle to run faster, control my cravings, secure strong relationships in my life. I'm overworked, struggling with debt, and the kids are, honestly, being teenage kids — a pain in the ass. I am still learning to manage stress, still having moments of despair. I am continuously working to be better. *They do know that, right?* I say to myself. I keep smiling, hoping I won't be discovered as a fraud. *Don't forget the order of the poses. Look like you know what you're doing. Fake it, fake it.*

The preparation for this class was equal only to the final exam in the anatomy and physiology course for the last class of the last semester of my bachelor's degree. I studied, found references, practiced, studied more; it was going to be perfect. That's what I thought. I have every move and term in my head and as backup I wrote it down. My journal falls to the floor and opens to a page with this quote from Ernest Hemingway: "The world breaks everyone and afterward many are strong at the broken places."

My nerves are getting the best of me and panic is setting in when I notice everyone is on their mat, in their heads, some about being in a yoga class for the first time, some with the stress from their broken relationships, others overwhelmed with work. I can see it so clearly: the tense shoulders, closed hearts, anxiety and just plain denial that self-care was what we needed. I throw my lesson aside, take a deep breath, and with a warm greeting I invite them to get into child's pose. Child's pose serves two purposes, one, it takes everyone's eyes off me, and secondly, it helps them breathe into their own space.

I tell them the story of Janine Shepherd, an Olympic athlete who was paralyzed and eventually rebranded herself and became the first female aviation aerobatics instructor. I tell them how we walk into a room defined by our titles as mother, father, woman or man, student, business owner, athlete, with expectations from ourselves and the world. I tell them of my failures and my insecurity about leading in this moment, but how I choose to breathe into this space. I invite them to lay down their titles, strip away their limiting beliefs of who they're supposed to be — and just be. Just breathe.

A collective exhale wafts over the class like a wave coming to the shore. You can see them letting go, a long-awaited moment for some, a welcome reminder for others. It's a confirmation for me that I am exactly where I need to be. This is not a place of competition. I am no longer concerned with what qualifies me to lead. It doesn't matter how much I weigh, the color of my skin, my level of experience. I was able to see what this class needed, and I spoke to them from a place of love and authenticity. I wasn't here to be perfect; this was not about me. I am here as a guide and this is authentically me.

We exhale together and class begins.

—Rozelle Clark—

37

Finding My Roots

The biggest adventure you can ever take is to live
the life of your dreams.
~Oprah Winfrey

The goal was to concentrate so intently on drawing big breaths that I wouldn't notice the needle pricking my skin. Yellow fever. Check. Typhoid. Check.   ·

I had to leave by month's end when my work visa ran out. All I needed was a flight reservation.

I hadn't told a soul about my plan. Mostly because it was half-baked — more aspirational than real.

I'd been living in Washington, D.C. for three years. I was so entrenched on Capitol Hill that I started using words like "aspirational" and "circling back." I told people I came to D.C. for graduate school. The truth is, I wanted out of the excruciating boredom of working in a government bureaucracy in Canada. I wanted out of my city, out of my country, out of my life.

I used to spend hours devising ways to avoid the office. People think bureaucrats have an easy, cushy job. *Au contraire!* Try smiling while you pretend not to hear slurs, being passed over for promotion after promotion for less qualified, overgrown frat boys, or slaving away on projects you know are utterly useless.

Iconic South African leader Nelson Mandela once described the mind-numbing labour he was forced to undertake at Robben Island. His overlords placed a mountain of heavy rocks in one corner of the quarry. Mandela and his cohorts would spend six months dragging, rolling, or carrying the rocks to the opposite corner of the large quarry yard. Upon completion of the task, the prisoners were forced to move the rocks back to their original location.

It's a form of torture.

That's how it felt to work in public service: breaking your back to move heavy rocks around for no reason.

I was biding my time, moving rocks around, during the eleven months per year that I wasn't on vacation. There came a point where no number of Lenny Kravitz concerts could fill the emptiness of a wasted life.

Maybe it was a mid-life crisis.

I sold everything I owned, including my home and car, and skipped town under the guise of "furthering my education." This explanation conveniently nipped in the bud any follow-up questions.

In Washington, I bloomed like the cherry blossoms around the Tidal Basin. The city was bursting with opportunity, culture, and good weather. Not to mention the Obamas: The First Lady went to the gym down the street from my overpriced shoebox apartment.

Washingtonians complain about gentrification and the loss of the district's Black footprint. Yet it was the Blackest city I'd ever lived in. The mayor was Black. The Police Chief was Black. The Attorney General was Black. I had a Black professor for the first time in my life.

All good things must end and so would my work permit. My employer exhausted all options to keep me in America legally.

"I'm going home," I told my boss. "Thanks for all your efforts."

"I've given it some thought," he responded. "We need you to finish the cycle. Can you go back to Canada and work remotely for the next six months?"

"Sure. I can make it work."

I played it cool though I had no idea how I would manage a team of five to eight people remotely. Our interns required various levels of handholding. I couldn't do that via Skype. If I returned to Canada, where would I live? I'd sold my house prior to moving to D.C.

I had two weeks to figure out a Plan B.

With no particular place to go, I'd have to leave all my stuff in D.C. I listed my closet-sized apartment on AirBnB.

Three years prior, I had signed the lease sight-unseen. I had hired interior decorators to turn a drab English basement into an elegant refuge where I could make believe I wasn't a poor grad student. They managed to combine the pair of designer lamps and mirrored night-tables I brought from home with an eclectic array of crême-coloured pieces that gave the space a sophisticated French flair. Yes, that's "crême," not "cream."

My Dupont Circle neighbourhood was considered posh, so I quickly found a subletter. I'd leave my home furnishings and clear out one of the two closets for the tenant.

I could work remotely from anywhere in the world. Why the hell would I go back home? Ottawa, Canada: The Coldest Capital City in the World. The White Man's haven. I'd escaped three dreadful Ottawa winters. It was time to make it four.

Where would I go? Rome. Paris. London. Buenos Aires. Rio. Amsterdam. Milan. Panama City. San Juan. Aruba. Barcelona. Istanbul. Havana. Corfu. Venice. Frankfurt. Santiago. Lima. Montevideo. Athens. San Salvador.

Been there, done that.

I drew my inspiration from my ancestry DNA test. I had genetic "cousins" in a large swath of land that stretched from present-day Mali to Angola. Going to the Motherland had been a dream ever since I got my test results. Going there was also scary. We've all been told a lot of negative things about Africa and Africans: violence, sexism, political instability. I had to decolonize my mind and decide to go and visit all the good stuff about Africa. After all, that's where we're from.

I booked a flight to Dakar.

I thought I would get emotional when the plane touched down. I was reconnecting with the land my ancestors were forced to leave in the bowels of ships, never to return again. Shouldn't I have felt something? I didn't.

I managed to get through customs and out the door in what seemed like minutes. Then I recorded my first steps on African soil, 250 years after my last ancestor set foot here. The tarmac was windswept with reddish sand. The sun was about to rise.

I started feeling it.

After posting my desire for a "room and board" in Dakar on social media, a friend of a friend of a friend of a friend had found me a place to stay. A Ghanaian-American lady living in a well-to-do neighborhood of Dakar had an extra bedroom. She allowed me to rent it for a month. She even arranged a taxi to fetch me at the Dakar airport.

My driver spoke a version of French that was vaguely familiar. He welcomed me politely and took my bags to his car.

"How long is the drive to the house?"

"Dakar est à 50 kilomètres d'ici."

We were on the road for less than twenty minutes when the car got a flat tire in what seemed like the middle of nowhere. This, I said to myself, was the kind of unexpected, time-consuming mishap I'd have to get accustomed to in Africa.

The driver didn't seem surprised or alarmed. This must happen often. As he replaced the flat tire with the spare, I wandered on the edge of the highway. In the distance, there were joggers taking advantage of the cooler dawn air. I swear on my grandma's grave, I saw the same birds that fly at the beginning of *Lion King*.

"Naaaaaaaah! Tsi Venyaaaaaaah! Bagadi thibaba!" I quickly shooed the *Lion King* opening song out of my mind, like a cobweb you want to disappear. I was mad at myself for starting my journey to the Motherland with a Disney soundtrack. An Elton John song… Ugh. How colonized was my mind that this was the first tune that came to my spirit?

Did I know any authentic African songs?

Does "The Lion Sleeps Tonight" count if the original African singer never saw a royalty cheque?

"Mama say, mama sah, mama koo sah?" I didn't even know if that meant anything.

As I took a deep dive into my mental catalogue of non-*Lion King* music, the taxi driver called me back. The tire was fixed.

"Allons-y." Let's go.

The countryside gave way to the suburbs, then the congested

cityscape. Through the taxi's window, I got my first glimpse of African people in their natural setting. They walked at a slow pace. They didn't seem stressed. They didn't look famished. There were no flies milling about their faces like the TV commercials for Foster Parents Plan.

In fact, it was nothing like what I imagined.

As I observed women going about their morning routines, I noticed they were impeccably coiffed. Every woman's headdress matched her garment. Her earrings matched, too. I noted the unmistakable sway of their hips, their stoic, fearless glares, their age-defying, sun-soaked skin. The familiar way they pursed their lips while queuing up at a bus stop.

They all looked like me. Dressed like me. Walked like me.

It was like looking in an infinity mirror. I was dizzy from the shock of it all.

It suddenly dawned on me: Had I finally found my tribe?

— Rachel Decoste —

38

God Is a Black Woman

*Learn to be quiet enough to hear the genuine within
yourself so that you can hear it in others.*
~Marian Wright Edelman

My introduction to God happened when a woman passed out in front of the altar at church. Only moments before, she had been whirling down the carpeted aisle, screaming out the name "Jesus!" as if she expected him to physically manifest in the sanctuary. Then, as quickly as she had jumped up out of her pew, she dropped to the floor, a fall so graceful that she managed to cover her legs so that no one could see up her skirt. Women dressed in white circled her with a bottle of water in hand, a lace cloth to cover her legs, and a napkin to wipe her sweaty brow.

My Sunday school teacher called it "catching the spirit," and explained that it was something that happened when you were so full of God and the Holy Ghost that you had to run and shout about it. I would experience the same one day if I was truly a child of God, if I were lucky. But this process seemed too violent for me. I wanted no part of an entity taking over my whole body to the point that I lost control, but the physical expression was presented as a mandatory requirement.

If I didn't feel God to the point of spiritual ecstasy, could I call myself a true believer? The God of my youth had too many commandments: women couldn't wear pants; women couldn't preach; no one could be gay; children couldn't question (Why is God a "he?"). The list was endless. Hell always remained in close proximity for individuals who stepped out of line, so I quickly learned to pray with a hopeful repentance in order to secure my seat in heaven. But despite decades of following all of the "rules," I felt a deep emptiness that no amount of church could fill.

"I think I'm depressed," I revealed to a family member.

"Depression is a sin," she stated matter-of-factly, "And if you kill yourself, you're going to hell." She then proceeded to recite a biblical scripture about finding joy in the Lord and I never mentioned it again.

For most of my young adult life I went through the motions of communion, revivals, and re-dedications trying to feel something—something that would make me feel God like the women who caught the Holy Ghost. God seemed so easy to access during church service. I could hear him through the cries and wails of the congregation and even in the fire and brimstone teaching from the pulpit. But it was when I was alone that the space between me and heaven seemed insurmountable.

In November 2020, I carried this void to Snellville, Georgia when I signed up for a spiritual retreat with ten other Black women I'd never met before. For seven days we eliminated meat and processed foods, drank a gallon of water each day, meditated, participated in traditional African religious rituals, and unpacked generational trauma in front of an ancestral altar.

For the first time, I saw how spirit existed outside a pulpit. The restrictive paradigms that encompassed my Baptist upbringing began to shatter completely. Everything I was taught about religion and spirituality proved to be skewed by interpretation and colonization. The oppressive nature of the religion I grew to know stemmed from generations of my own people being oppressed under the guise of God's will. It was by turning toward ancestral practices that I was able to experience true liberation.

On the last day of the retreat we dressed in white and gathered at Yellow River. Earlier that day we'd written down all the things we wanted to release — on dissolvable paper. But before we could throw our worries into the water, we performed a ritual for Oshun. We poured honey into the cold water, gave a fruit offering, and sang without a script. The freedom of it all made me hesitate. There had to be more that I needed to do to surrender to the experience; but as I turned to the other women around me I understood it all clearly.

God is everywhere.

I felt spirit in the wind that tugged at my skirt. I heard the same in the voices of the women surrounding me. Despite the frigid temperature, I had taken my shoes off and stepped into the river; I felt God there, too.

At the age of thirty-two, I found a new truth. I could run around a sanctuary and lie prostrate at the altar begging for blessings and forgiveness, and I could also take a walk along a shaded trail and talk to God as a friend. I could fear God and do good things out of reverence, and I could love God and do things for others so that they could experience the same love.

No matter what way I chose, the foundation of it all was understanding that my spirit, my ancestors, my dreams and failures all encompassed the Being of me. God didn't have to be a "he" or a specific structure. There were no rules or machinations to be one with God. God was not separate from me. She could be something that understood my personal journey. Something that required me to find myself in order to conceptualize all that she is. God could be 5'3" with a wide nose, a gap tooth smile, and skin kissed by the sun. She was right inside me all along.

— Morgan Cruise —

Where We Come From

An Introduction

There will be people who say to you,
"You are out of your lane." They are burdened
by only having the capacity to see what
has always been instead of what can be.
~Kamala Harris

Hey ya'll, it's me.

Yep. Still here. Fighting. Showing Up.

Fixing meals and kissing "boo-boos". Doing holy work.

Resisting with joy and confidence, taking pride in rest.

Loving my husband, gathering knowledge, you know, those "regular" things.

Passionately creating spaces that are safe and warm and life-giving.

Looking into the eyes of my children, wondering what the world will be like for them.

Will they know peace? Will they finally get the chance to live as a human being, not as a construct determined and defined by others?

Yes, we are Black. Black is beautiful. It glistens. It warms, it comforts.

But it also draws attention, attention of which it never asks.

So, I must weep and pray. Teach and tell of the horrors from which our Blackness has come.

Yet, joy is there too. Happiness. Connection. Culture. Community.

Identity. I sprinkle joy around like confetti.

I am a Black woman. Sophisticated, educated, and melanated.

My sons are young kings who have brilliance in their veins. They rise like the sun on the horizon.

My daughter is a little queen who commands respect with the corners of her smile and the smooth glide in her gait.

My husband is the rock and cornerstone of our home, the strength and virtue of our family. His presence is not a threat. It is safety and peace.

We hold space as equals. We hold space as experts in our fields. We laugh and we love.

We are image bearers — holding up the light of truth and the banner of justice.

That's my introduction.

I'm still here, slaying giants and making it plain.

Holding hands and crossing intersections of racism, sexism, and everything else.

Advocating for a better life that rushes like a waterfall, splashing drops of value and equity everywhere.

Taking time to smell the roses, all while reminding folk why thorns have purpose.

Yep. Hey ya'll.

It's me. Unbroken, unwavering, and unapologetic.

— Quantrilla Ard —

39

Surviving and Thriving

Education is transformational. It changes lives...
the force that erases arbitrary divisions of race
and class and culture and unlocks
every person's God-given potential.
~Condoleezza Rice

The first day at my new elementary school finally arrived, but I wasn't quite sure if I was ready. Mom drove me to school and escorted me to my third-grade classroom. Standing together just outside the classroom door, Mom held my hand very tightly while giving me a reassuring look.

"You're going to be fine," Mom said. I nodded my head in agreement to appease her. But I just wanted to go back to my old school. She reached for the door and knocked, and my third-grade teacher soon appeared to meet me.

"You must be Mrs. Langston with our new student, Billie," Mrs. Smith said, with a warm smile. She was young, pretty, and wore attractive eyeglasses. These attributes helped me feel more comfortable as I walked into the classroom. It also helped that Mrs. Smith didn't identify me as the new, sole Black child in the school's only third-grade class.

Mom and I stood at the front of the classroom as Mrs. Smith introduced me to my classmates. My young mindset and vision needed time to adjust to new Caucasian faces staring at me versus familiar

African American faces at my former segregated school.

Looking up at Mom, I asked, "Do I have to stay?"

"Yes, you have to stay," she said. She placed her arm around my shoulders and whispered words I'd never forget... "Be brave, strong, and courageous."

From the front of the room, I saw an empty desk near the window. Mrs. Smith had placed me between classmates who turned out to be really nice, friendly kids. Mom stayed in the classroom as I took my seat and settled in at my desk.

Then, the dreaded time for Mom to leave came. I wanted to cry but managed to hold back the tears. I just kept repeating her words to myself... "Be brave, strong, and courageous."

It was September 1965, during the height of the civil rights movement, institutional busing, and the desegregation of public schools in coastal Virginia. My sister Denise and I were the first Black children to integrate this school. My family had worked hard to advocate for us to make this happen for us. My father had filled out forms and advocated for us to go to this better school.

My interaction with my Caucasian classmates was surprising. When I smiled at them, they smiled back. Our lunchroom was housed in a separate building, so we walked in a straight line to get there. While in route, no one intentionally spaced their body away from mine. During lunch, I always had someone to eat with. At recess, we played on the monkey bars... together. After a few weeks, I began to feel comfortable, like a regular kid again. But not everyone felt that way. There were always a few kids who'd give me a snarky look or who wouldn't speak to me.

Regardless of what I faced, I was a determined eight-year-old girl who wanted to learn, grow, and make good grades. I learned how to stand on my own, and the next year I helped the new Black kids adjust.

Fifty-five years have passed since I met Mrs. Smith and entered her third-grade classroom. My experience on that September day in 1965 has been etched forever in my memory. Being the eight-year-old Black student who sat in that classroom without anyone who looked like me was challenging, difficult, and sometimes uncomfortable. It served as my first lesson in being independent.

The kindness of a few good kids who were willing to treat me like a friend made my early interracial experience easier. Looking back, it could have been much worse. I didn't receive extremely harsh, overtly prejudice remarks. And no one called me ugly names, at least not directly to my face. I knew I was different, but I didn't allow myself to feel different.

To my surprise, one of my classmates who sat in my row near the window gave me a Christmas present at the end of my first term. I remember that moment with gratitude. It made me feel like I belonged.

The elementary school integration experience was the beginning of an education that prepared me to be an honor student in high school. My parents then sent me to Howard University, where I graduated with undergraduate and graduate degrees in anthropology/journalism and education. I'll always be grateful to my family for their advocacy, and for the rewards that came from following my mother's advice to hang in there and be "brave, strong, and courageous."

— Billie Joy Langston —

From One Hood to Another

People don't think to ask for anything.
They don't want to be told no.
~Sophfronia Scott, Unforgivable Love

I've always had dreams bigger than myself, or at least bigger than where I was raised. For twenty-three years, I called a particular housing project off Pennsylvania Avenue in Washington, D.C. my home. It was surrounded by tall wrought iron gates, and I can't say if that was to keep us in, or others out. But I walked past them every day, sometimes squeezing through the bars as a shortcut, and sometimes climbing over the top if they were chained closed.

"School girl" is what they called me because I was smart. But no matter how much I accomplished, I felt a shadow over me because of where I lived. Nothing good comes from the projects — at least that's what they said. The projects are supposed to be full of crime and poverty and a collection of lazy people who rely on government assistance or work low wage food service or caretaking jobs.

But that wasn't us. We had to make the best of our situation even though everything around us was a constant reminder that we had nothing. We weren't supposed to have hope or envision a future, but we did.

My mother had four children and never married. We were certainly a stereotypical low-income Black family on the surface. But the thing about stereotypes is that they are steeped in prejudice. Those stereotypes didn't include my mother's sacrifices, grit and determination, and how hard we children worked. We had passions, knowledge and skills.

We all had dreams bigger than the projects, and we all left to pursue our educational and professional dreams. My mom had to stay, but no amount of darkness could dim her joy at seeing all her children go off to college. We all finished our undergraduate degrees, too.

My dreams didn't stop there. Since high school I'd told people that I wanted to get my Ph.D. in English. I had an English teacher who told me I could do it, and I believed it.

After finishing my undergraduate degree in English, I applied to two graduate programs, but I was denied. I felt like a failure. I was afraid to try again because I thought I would be rejected, but then I found another program. Before I pushed Submit on the application, I prayed the most specific prayer I've ever prayed in life: "Lord, you know my heart and my dreams. I desire to get into graduate school. Lord, just get my foot in the door, and I'll do the rest. And Lord, we both know I don't have the funds, but I know that if I am accepted, I won't have to pay for anything. Amen."

Submit.

A month or so later I received an e-mail from the graduate program stating that I would be admitted into the program provisionally. I would need to maintain a certain grade point average. Oh my god, I was in! The following semester I began working at the Writing Studio on campus, which provided a tuition stipend. I didn't have to pay for a single class. Thank you, God. Fear of rejection had almost cost me my dream.

Sometimes I thought maybe a master's degree was enough. Not many people in my immediate circle or family had one and there was no way I could actually afford a doctoral program. But I was so close to my dream. Just a few more years of school and that would be it for my formal educational journey.

But how was I going to pay for it? Why go through the trouble of even applying without knowing how I would finance it? I had some crazy faith. If I did it once, I was hopeful that I could do it again.

I found one school. Just one. The odds of me getting into this one program were astronomical, but I applied to the Ph.D. in Writing and Rhetoric program with an assistantship.

Three months after applying I received an e-mail from the director of the program: "Congratulations new student and Teaching Assistant."

— Ronada Dominique —

Pretty Brown Girl

The most alluring thing a woman
can have is confidence.
~Beyoncé Knowles

I pressed my face to the window. My vision was blurred by the waterfall of tears I could not seem to control. The school bus came to a halt and kids got off, but I refused to let them see my face. "Oreo cookie, Oreo cookie, Oreo cookie!" was still ringing in my ears.

The embarrassment of being dark-skinned was pouring right through my ten-year-old body. I wished I could hide but the best I could do was to burrow into the oversized red hoodie I was wearing.

Four years later, I was staring into the bathroom mirror. Phrases like "you're pretty for a dark skin girl," "if only you were two shades lighter," and "the blacker the berry the sweeter the juice" made me scream "I hate you" into the mirror. "I hate you, I hate you… I hate you!" I melted to the bathroom floor breathless and sobbing. I was barely through my freshman year of high school and the only person who had ever told me I was beautiful had died a few months ago. My grandfather meant it, too. At the time, I didn't believe him.

Ten years later, I picked up *People* magazine as I stood at the counter to pay for my groceries. Lupita Nyong'o graced the cover as "People's Most Beautiful Person." I squealed with excitement but was quickly reminded of where I was as I felt the stares of the people around me. I paid for my stuff, including the magazine, and rushed home.

"Mom, look!" Barely able to contain my excitement I pushed the magazine at her. "She is dark-skinned like me!" I ran to the bathroom mirror, the same mirror that reduced me to tears ten years earlier, and ran my fingers through my hair. Just like Nyong'o, I'd cut my hair short and natural and I never felt more beautiful.

And now, the natural light coming through the stunning wooden windows gives the studio good vibes. I place my colorful yoga mat on the floor and watch beautiful women of color fill the space. The sense of belonging overwhelms me as we flow through the vinyasa sequence. As I take warrior II pose, I reflect on the years when I felt angry, sad and weak because of what I believed to be a deformity. My brown skin was the target of relentless bullying.

Things have changed. Today, my brown skin is complimented more often. I see women like Lupita Nyong'o, Michelle Obama, my yoga teacher, and my mom being recognized for their dark-skinned beauty. And I realize anyway that the essence of my beauty is not just my smile, my brown eyes, or my hair…. It is the self-confidence on the inside that generates beauty. I am a pretty brown girl.

— Aerial Perkins-Good —

The Shack

*If we have had no past, it is well for us to look
hopefully to the future — for the shadows bear
the promise of a brighter coming day.*
~Frances Ellen Watkins Harper

I was eight or nine when I first saw the old shack on one of the many strolls I took with my grandmother. We were often silent as we took in the beauty of the flowers and magnolia trees that lined the sidewalks of our small, southern town. I don't remember ever caring where we were headed; it was just nice to feel her soft, warm hand wrapped around mine.

My grandmother Louisa was approaching her late seventies when I lived with her. She suffered from a leg wound that I never understood, so I accepted the thick wrap of bandages that always covered her entire leg. The crudely fashioned walking stick that she used (and seemed to love) accompanied us on every trip, near or far, as it tapped along to the rhythm of our pace. As a side benefit; the walking stick discouraged an occasional dog or two from even thinking about coming near us.

Sometimes we headed for the market; on other days we visited a sick relative or one of my grandmother's friends. House visits were my favorite because I usually ended up stuffing down a slice of pound cake followed by a tall glass of lemonade. I was always happy and content as I quietly learned from the old, wise adults. In their opinion, people in my mother's age group knew absolutely nothing—especially the ones who lived "up north."

On the evenings when we ended up at a weekly prayer meeting, I struggled to hide my disappointment. The services were long and ended far beyond my bedtime. Even the loud singing and praying couldn't keep me awake. To make matters worse, we had to pass the "white cemetery" during our walk home. It stretched nearly two city blocks and the huge tombstones rising out of the total darkness looked like ghosts to me. The crickets, owls, and lightning bugs seemed to conspire with the dead for my soul. Even the moss hanging from the twisted branches far above my head appeared lower and sinister on those nights. Only the tapping of my grandmother's walking stick reminded me that I was still in loving hands.

On this particular day we started out earlier but I was as eager as ever. Being an only child with no brothers or sisters to play with, a walk with a grandparent was a treat. This was Georgetown, South Carolina in the early 1950s; there was little for me to do. Asthma usually prevented me from running, jumping, and doing all things fun.

We walked several blocks down Cannon Street before turning left. At some point I thought we were going to visit someone in Back Landing. The neighborhood was exactly what it sounds like, a swampy area near the river that flooded whenever a bad storm came to town. Boats and piers were damaged, but the tiny, shotgun houses that many families lived in miraculously survived. They stood in defiance as they waited for the next storm. The town itself, one of the oldest in the state, was one of many that dotted the southeastern coast along the Atlantic Ocean.

Segregation was still the rule, but the town had its own peculiar separation policy that most likely developed from convenience or necessity. Rather than white and Black neighborhoods in the main part of town, there were white and Black streets, and even white and Black sides of the street. One side of the street would have large colonial homes owned by white families, while small, well-kept homes owned by Black families stood directly opposite them. On this day we walked along the white side of the street, when suddenly my grandmother came to a complete stop.

She continued holding my hand as she guided me a few steps toward the driveway of a large, stately home. The vast yard behind the house was filled with flower beds and giant trees. Hidden several yards beyond them was an old, abandoned shack that begged to be torn down and put out of its misery. The wood was gray and splintery, nails protruded through the sides, and a rusted padlock barely held the door in place. My grandmother carefully balanced herself with her walking stick before speaking quietly.

"You see that old shack back there?"

"Yes, ma'm," I replied quickly.

"That's where I washed and ironed clothes six days a week for fifty cents, sometimes a quarter if that's what they decided to pay me. I worked from sunup to sundown." Her eyes seemed to travel years into her past. "Sometimes I scrubbed floors in the big house until my knees gave out." She cleared her throat.

"I want you to do better. You have to promise me you'll do better."

I knew that I lived in a segregated world and that I couldn't drink from the "whites only" water fountain. I also knew that people like me couldn't try on clothes or shoes before buying them. But all of that paled with my new revelation. It was different because the person I loved so much had been so mistreated by the way of life that she tried so hard to shield me from.

The sight of the shack that my grandmother once labored in for pennies forced me to begin the process of growing up. Soon I would grasp the concept of "live-in" domestic work, which my mother resorted to in New York. Questions began to flood my thoughts daily. My new hero, the woman who raised my mother and my uncle, plus her deceased sister's children, had suffered a life that she didn't want me to live. After several minutes I was finally able to say, "I promise" before we turned in silence to go back home.

No, I didn't become a rocket scientist, but I did well. I never forgot my promise to the woman who worked her entire life for pennies. From that day forward she became my role model and my hero. In time I grew to understand how much I owed the mothers and grandmothers in my community and around the world who climbed mountains before I even learned how to walk. How did they do it? I still wonder.

— Debra L. Brown —

Paying the Poll Tax

We all have the same dream, my grandmother says.
To live equal in a country that's supposed to be the
land of the free. She lets out a long breath,
deep remembering.
~Jacqueline Woodson, Brown Girl Dreaming

M y earliest recollection of politics, elections, and voting goes back to 1952 or 1953. I was six or seven years old when I accompanied my mom to the place where people who lived in our rural farm area in Jefferson County, Arkansas, were required to register to vote.

My mom drove us to Tucker, Arkansas, an unincorporated community in Jefferson County, located approximately five miles from our farm. Tucker's notoriety came from being located along a major north/south railroad track. It provided the closest station stop for in/outbound passengers bound for/from one of Arkansas's oldest prison farms for white inmates during that time.

Beyond the prison, a post office, one major mercantile store, a cotton gin, one gas station, and the Julius Rosenwald School for Negroes formed Tucker's local metropolis. The mercantile store is where everybody from our area registered and voted.

To register to vote, Negroes or "colored folks" (as we were often called) were required to pay a "poll tax." As a tenth or eleventh grade American History student, I learned that the tax emerged in some states within the United States in the late 1800s as part of the Jim Crow laws.

Election officials used the tax to restrict voting rights. Payment of the tax, plus unfairly implemented literacy tests and overt intimidation, achieved the desired effect — disenfranchising African Americans, Native Americans, and poor white voters. Congress finally abolished the poll tax through the 24th Amendment to the Constitution in 1964.

Many families in our area could not afford this tax. The night before our trip to Tucker, I had overheard my parents discussing that they would have to pay three dollars each. This was a hardship.

There were two entrances at the mercantile store. The main entrance was on the east side. All registration and voting activities took place from a second entrance located along the building's north side.

As my mom and I climbed the stairway to the north side entrance, we could hear women laughing and talking. But all fell silent as we opened the door and entered the room. Three middle-aged white women were present. Their faces turned slightly red, and their body language made them appear as though they were somewhat angry and agitated that they had been interrupted. Two women sat at a table, while the other sat nearby with her arms folded.

Again, fear surged inside me because face-to-face contact with white people was infrequent. I always felt safer when I watched white people from a distance, rather than dealing with them face-to-face.

Before we left our car, I thought it was odd when my mom removed two bills from her purse — a five and a one. When we walked through the door, she visibly held the money firmly in her hand, with her purse on her arm. Later, when I asked why she did this, she explained that our neighbors had warned her that these white women had yelled at them as they entered the room, asking, "Do you have the money on ya today? If you don't, you can't register to vote, so you can just go on back out."

Mom was determined to register to vote that day. As she entered the door, she wanted to clearly show them that she was ready to pay the poll tax.

One of the ladies sitting at the table began asking questions and preparing the paperwork needed to register my mom and dad. Mom held a tight grip and did not release the six-dollar payment until she received two poll tax receipts. She and my dad would be required to present these when they returned later, as this same room would serve as the polling location to vote on Election Day.

As my mom took the receipts and held them firmly in her hand, the white lady sitting on the sidelines spoke for the first and only time, in a loud and stern voice, "I do not see why y'all want to vote!" Immediately, I felt a knot form in my stomach, and I started to shake a little.

My mom never looked toward this white woman. Instead, she dropped her head, looked at the floor, and firmly gripped the receipts and my hand. We walked out of the door and quickly down the tall stairs.

As we were heading back to our farm, passing the prison compound again, I felt myself breathing a sigh of relief, and I was able to let the fear go. Why? I do not know. There were no words to describe my fear, confusion, and other emotions felt back then.

Mom gave my dad the receipt when we arrived home. He placed it in his fireproof safe.

The thing that confused me about the white women's behavior was that the poll tax was a hardship for poor whites as well. But I could only assume that their overall treatment was not the same as my mom's. Poor white women may have been disrespected, but I doubt they suffered from fear.

By the time I reached late adolescence, knowing more about the world around me, including the murder of Emmett Till, school desegregation in Little Rock, and discovering the KKK, I had formed what I thought was my profound worldview. My mantra had become, "White People Are Not Human!"

I held firmly to this belief until 1964, ironically the same year in which the poll tax was abolished across the United States. I graduated from high school that year and was attending college. I was reading a newspaper that recounted events that had occurred surrounding the death, during the summer, of my fourteen-year-old cousin, Debra Baker. I suddenly realized that the mantra that I lived by, which started with my mom's poll tax experience, was no longer entirely true. Thus, my new mantra became, "Some White People are Human After All." And my fear subsided, a little.

— Edna Faye Moorehead Briggs —

Birthin

*Every day, pregnant women walk into their doctor's
office for checkups, advice and treatment; but that
experience is very different for Black women.*
~Kamala Harris

"**M**aydell, if you don't stop screaming, they'll never let another colored person in here again." Race relations was the last thing on my mother's mind that day in October 1952. By coincidence, my mother and Aunt Claudine had been admitted within hours of each other to the colored maternity ward at the Alexandria, Virginia hospital. They were best friends, married to brothers, and both pregnant with their second child… my mother, Maydell Belk, with me. She was twenty years old, loud-mouthed, fearless and proud. She had a low threshold for both physical pain and the emotional pain of being ignored in the understaffed and poorly equipped ward that was reserved for Negro mothers-to-be.

According to Aunt Claudine, every time a contraction hit, my mother yelled at the top of her lungs, cursing the nurses, my father, and the white patients that she had a clear view of in an updated ward across the hall.

"Oh, shit. I need pain medicine now. Now goddammit! Can anybody hear me? I need something now. Where the hell is our nurse?"

As she saw the nurses ignoring her to meet the needs of the white mothers across the hall, she became even more agitated.

"Hey, hey… what about us over here? How about fluffing our pillows? How about giving us some water?" Another contraction hit. "Oh, shit. Forget the water, give me some drugs now!"

Aunt Claudine, who was in the very early stages of labor, was petrified and knew all too well what could happen to uppity colored folks. She was convinced that she and my mother would be thrown out of the hospital before either one of them delivered.

Finally, one of the Black cleaning ladies came by to ask Mom to calm down. She said that everyone in the hospital could hear her, including my father and Uncle Milton who were on baby alert in the waiting room.

"You can tell Lonnie and Milton to kiss my pregnant ass. When was the last time they had a baby?" Another contraction hit and my mother started screaming, this time louder than before, "Oh, shit. Oh, shit. Oh, shit."

Aunt Claudine, clearly embarrassed, whispered, "Maydell, you got to stop acting the fool. Those white people are looking at us like we're heathens. Just do your breathing like they told us and shut up."

"No, Dee… I really do have to shit… and I think the baby is coming! Call somebody. Oh my God!"

The nurse arrived with the bedpan just as I entered the world… literally full of shit.

To make matters worse, the hospital got the fathers confused. In the nursery, after cleaning me up, they showed me off to Uncle Milton. He left the hospital, leaving my Dad "to wait" for my birth, which, of course, had already occurred. Later, when Aunt Claudine had given birth to my cousin, Connie, and the babies had been sorted out, the hospital called to congratulate Uncle Milton on the birth of his daughter. He replied, "Yes, I know, thank you." He went back to work and didn't see his real daughter until the next day. It was all a little confusing and over the years generated a lot of teasing about me being born in a bedpan and the Belk family's baby-swapping shenanigans.

While my mother never disputed Aunt Claudine's version of my birth, Mom did note that once my prim and proper Aunt Claudine went into labor, she yelled so loudly that Mom couldn't resist teasing her. "Now Claudine, you really do need to lower your voice. What will the white folks think?"

Aunt Claudine's response, "Oh, shut up. Just shut up Maydell. I need some damn drugs!"

In fact, Mom's and Aunt Claudine's yelling did little to move race relations forward in Alexandria. Each returned to that hospital three more times to give birth in the separate but "equal" colored ward.

Finally, Mom had enough. For the birth of my two youngest siblings, she chose freedom over convenience. She traveled across the Potomac to Howard University's Black run Freeman Hospital in Washington, D.C. to bring them into the world. According to her, at Freeman, she got the respect and dignity she deserved, and no one gave a shit about how loud she yelled.

— Judy Belk —

Don't You Wish You Were White?

We're here for a reason. I believe a bit of the reason
is to throw little torches out to lead people
through the dark.
~Whoopi Goldberg

I can't remember my little friend's name but I really liked her. She was the friend my parents allowed me to visit independently like a big girl. I think I understood that my playmate was white but that had no meaning to me.

In 1957, five-year-olds didn't know what prejudice was, but I was about to find out. As we were playing one day, my friend looked at me with the biggest smile and said, "Don't you wish you were white?" I felt confused, puzzled and somewhat shocked. I remember thinking, *Why would I want to be white?*

I remember the conversation I had with myself. I concluded I would not want to change who I was. I liked my life better than I liked hers. At five years old, I loved my life. There was nothing missing, nothing broken, not that I knew how to communicate that at age five.

Fast forward to September 1970, my first day at Eastern Michigan University. It was an impossible dream come true. I had the proudest parents in the whole wide world as we walked down the dormitory hallway to my room.

When my dad and Uncle Andrew brought my things in my new

roommate was already unpacked and off on an adventure somewhere. She returned later, we introduced ourselves, and she was gone again. She knew lots of people in our dorm, which was great because I knew no one. Zero!

I was like a fish out of water, but at least I had a nice person to room with. She sometimes returned to the room with her friends, who also seemed nice.

Every dorm had a Room Freeze, meaning you couldn't change roommates for the first six weeks of the school year. That roommate who I got along with came into our room one day and said very casually, "Terri, my father doesn't like the idea of me living with a Black girl so we are not going to be able to stay roommates." I kid you not. The same feeling, the same bewilderment that took me by surprise at age five, swallowed me up at age eighteen, only this time I had language.

With the same casual attitude as my sweet little roommate, I delivered my response. With no judgment or malice toward this precious young soul, I said, "Oh that's fine, when are you moving?" I never changed how I acted toward her. And I saw her almost daily because we still lived in the same dorm. I knew all her friends there, too, so I continued to greet them as well. There were a few Black girls in the dorm who I'd gotten to know by then so getting a new roommate was simple.

After successfully completing the first year of college I saw my former roommate on campus as everyone was heading home. She said hello and we chatted. I saw her all the time, so I expected this brief conversation to be like our former ones. Then she asked, "Are you coming back to school this fall?" I said yes. She asked, "Do you have a roommate?" I told her I wasn't sure. Then she said, "Well I'm coming back in the fall and I don't have a roommate. If you are looking for one, I would love to be your roommate this fall."

That was fifty years ago, and I do not remember if my former roommate returned. What I do remember is a valuable lesson in the power of love.

— Terri Redwine —

46

Good Enough

> *Our parents taught us, quite matter-of-factly,*
> *that we needed to be twice as good as the next*
> *(white) kid, because that is what it would take*
> *to be considered almost equal.*
> ~Susan Rice

Growing up I'd always been told that I had to be twice as good as white people to be seen as just as good. This was the rule, simply because I was a Black girl. However, I attended a diverse elementary and high school for gifted and talented students in Chicago, and this never proved true. Each of us was judged on our own merits.

As I ventured through undergrad in Michigan, I still didn't witness that unfair treatment I'd heard about. I was surrounded by white people and hadn't met any slackers who achieved greatness by doing half as much as I had. We worked hard and our productivity and accomplishments seemed to equal the effort we put into them. Studying through the night meant success like As and Bs. Doing less resulted in attaining less, such as probation for poor grades.

This continued with the graduate work I did at a predominantly white institution in the South and ultimately with my doctorate at a university with similar demographics.

It seemed like that truism about needing to work twice as hard was false. It must've been a message passed on during the pre-civil rights movement when my grandmother had to prove herself worthy even in a menial desk job. Perhaps it was an outdated concept that ended in the 1960s when my father's all-city athleticism was overshadowed by underqualified white men chosen to play with the Chicago Bears. Maybe it died in the 1970s with my aunt's affirmative action admission to a university. My ancestors had paved the way. Family stories were now folklore. I believed everyone around me worked just as hard and we were on equal footing.

But the truth was revealed when I sought my dream job at a research university in 2012.

He was a charismatic, bearded, white male, whose over six-foot stature commanded attention every time he entered the room. I'd applied for his job three times. Even though I was more qualified because I'd been an assistant professor somewhere else for two years, and even though he didn't have the specific type of doctorate they'd asked for, the department hired him for the tenure-track position. The following year, I was hired as a visiting professor. Our different titles meant he ranked higher, had a permanent position, and made about twelve thousand dollars more than I did.

He was a talker, the kind who has a story for every situation. The guy who's like, "Yeah that reminds me of the time when…"

He was perfect in every way except he didn't know what he was doing. And as it turned out, he had a story for that as well. He told the program coordinator and me about his experiences one day as the three of us met in her tiny square office.

"So, the professor kept talking about some theory that he thought I should know," he started.

The program coordinator sat in her brown, leather chair, glancing every so often at her monitor, then up at him, and back to me.

"And, you know. I had no idea what he was talking about. I just nodded along, and you know… I was just faking it 'til I made it," he laughed.

The program coordinator looked at me and offered an eyeroll.

"You know? That's how I got through," he said.

I didn't know.

I'd never met anyone like him in the twelve post-secondary years

I'd spent working hard to attain all things academic. I had no idea what he meant when he said he faked it 'til he made it. Did he mean he faked it to where we stood... side-by-side? Surely, that couldn't be true.

It wasn't until the following semester when he had to teach methodology for a British literature course that the curtain of my naiveté was raised.

He knocked on my door.

"Got a minute?" he asked.

"Sure."

He pulled up a chair. Even sitting down, we weren't equal. I had to look up at him.

"How do you teach this?" he asked.

Although I hated the wordiness of British literature, I still remembered memorizing and reciting the first fourteen lines of Chaucer's *The Canterbury Tales* for an undergrad assignment. I'd read and analyzed at least six of Shakespeare's tragedies and comedies in another course and written about how the Brontë sisters presented women in their novels. Later, I taught what I'd learned to bored high school students.

He didn't have this background. He had a Ph.D., just like me; however, he wanted me to cram four years of undergrad, eight years of grad school, and ten years of teaching into thirty minutes so he could do the job for which he'd been hired, the one for which I couldn't secure an interview.

So, I explained it to him.

That semester, we shared the same students, who often bragged about completing his assignments. They researched authors via Google and relied on SparkNotes per his directions.

I seethed with resentment for several months. Up until that moment, I'd only *studied* systemic racism and structural inequality; *living it* was different. It was hard. White privilege and patriarchy were more than theories and hashtags; the two merged and manifested into a living breathing man, who sat two doors down the hall and made more money than I, while knowing far less.

That year, the department offered me a tenure track position after they saw what a "hard worker" I was and after the only tenured African

American woman in the department happened to die from cardiac failure. She, ironically, was an affirmative action hire in the late 1980s.

I accepted the position; however, I only remained two more years. I traded that job for one at a community college.

Every semester, I wonder if leaving was a big mistake. Did I squander my giftedness for comfort? Each time, I arrive at the same conclusion. Although my family tried to prepare me, being twice as knowledgeable just to work alongside a less than capable white male was too much for me to ignore. Every time I arrived on campus, I felt as if a dose of twenty-first century racism slapped me in the face. And the sting of it was too much to endure.

— K E Garland —

47

Back Home

Your willingness to look at your darkness is what
empowers you to change.
~Iyanla Vanzant

We arrived a day before the family homecoming began in the quaint, southern town of Pantego, North Carolina. I'd only volunteered to drive because I retired early and was available. With Dad's COPD, I knew driving was out of the question for him.

He was curious why so many of his cousins made the trip to this town annually. Following breakfast, he said, "Let's go for a ride."

As the chauffeur, I got the car, anticipating a casual sightseeing trip through the local town and the surrounding area of 200 residents. I was relieved of that notion quickly. Dad directed me away from town. I was curious where we were headed. After several miles, he told me to stop.

"Why are we stopping here?" I asked.

As far as I could see, there were fields that extended to the horizon. I knew nothing about estimating acreage, but this farm was huge. The only sign of human life was far in the distance. About a half-mile from the road, standing alone, was a huge mansion with white pillars. In its earlier years, it might have been lovely, exquisite even. But today, the brightness of the sunlight exposed the weariness of the property. It was worn.

Without answering my question, Dad slowly opened the car door and got out. Our relatives had been attending this homecoming for more than forty years but this was his first time. He lifted his video camera and began filming. I watched him. He wore his white sneakers and traditional white cap that covered his head full of silver hair. Like hundreds of his peers, his suspenders raised over his stomach and crisscrossed in the back with the imprint visible through his shirt.

He filmed the old place, the surrounding fields to the east and west, then turned his back to the house and placed the video camera on the ground.

"Get the camera out of the car and take a picture of me," he instructed.

I silently did as I was told and got the camera, swung it in front of my face and aimed. But the expression I saw on his face was not the one I expected. It was not a smile. It was not even neutral, although something about it was familiar. A hint of discomfort surfaced. I hesitated for a few moments, waiting for his expression to change. When it didn't, I snapped the picture.

"Okay. Now tell me what this was about," I said.

Much slower than I had noticed before, he bent over, picked up the video camera and silently walked back to the car.

I was still puzzled about why we had stopped here. Why a picture of this old place? Why film these fields? What significance did they hold for him?

I studied the house again for clues, staring more closely at the brick pillars on both sides of the long driveway where he had stood for his picture to be taken. The pillars were at least three feet high and had been painted white some time ago. In the column on the left, where Dad had leaned, was a gray metal nameplate. Recessed below the top row of bricks was the name "Wilkinson."

Snatches of old conversations, fragments of exchanges between my aunts and uncles, returned to me. As if whispered by the ancestors, I recalled the name. This land was the property worked by my biological family. This is where Dad had spent untold hours of his youth. This is where my aunts and uncles spent hours bent over in the fields, from the time the sun came up until it went down. How many backs had ached here? How many thighs and knees strained for hours in the sweltering heat?

I realized we were on the land that robbed my dad of his youth. He probably spent many a day out of school picking crops and doing a man's job while still a boy. This type of abuse is seldom acknowledged. No recovery groups were ever formed for the men and women who were forced into the hard life of sharecropping.

We were on land he'd once called home.

I didn't ask any more questions as we got in the car and drove away to await the official opening of homecoming. The pain, agony, and uneasiness of those memories remained unspoken between us. It was enough for me that he chose not to say one more word about it. I think I understood why he had not joined the pilgrimage-like return to this area that his other family members had made annually. It would be like returning to the scene of the crime.

— Sharon Moore —

48

Doing It Alone

You don't make progress by standing on the sidelines,
whimpering and complaining. You make progress
by implementing ideas.
~Shirley Chisholm

I t was August 1965. My seventeen-year-old sister, thirteen-year-old brother, and I made the quarter-mile walk to the bus stop to start my first day as a high school sophomore. We would be among the first students to be a part of voluntary desegregation in Cherokee County, South Carolina.

A family member had convinced me the only chance I had at a better life was to get a different education than my high school offered. I wanted a home where I didn't have to go outside to use the bathroom or have to draw water from a well. In the winter I wanted to sleep in a warm room and not see the stars through the roof. If that meant attending a white high school, I would.

When the bus pulled up, so did a South Carolina Highway Patrol car. I was confused. What was going on? As we boarded, we weren't told where to sit, but it was obvious from the driver's eyes. We sat directly behind him.

When other students boarded, they looked at us with disgust or quickly looked away pretending we weren't there. My heart raced. I remembered the patrol car behind us and felt safer. I couldn't wait to get to school to be with my friends!

My heart sank during the opening assembly. I was the only person of color in the sophomore class. Where was everybody? I couldn't believe my friends had all backed out. I was alone and frightened but determined not to let my fear show.

Some of the girls talked to me in the bathroom, but never in the hall or at lunch. My sister was on a different lunch shift. My books were my only companions. I immersed myself in them to survive the isolation.

I worked hard to get the best education I could. I made all A's on my report card, but the teacher gave me a B for my semester grade in biology. I knew the playing field was not equal, so I didn't challenge her. My parents didn't say anything either. After all, what was a poor Black man with a fifth-grade education who worked in a cotton mill going to do?

My sister didn't return to school after Christmas break. I never asked her or our parents why. I felt the pressure was too much for her. The exclusion was getting to me also. I was a true outsider the rest of that year. How I ached to be in my old high school!

When I returned to my old school in the fall I was greeted warmly and quickly became one of the popular kids. I was elected to the homecoming court and made the basketball team, but there was something missing. I couldn't put my feelings into words. Was I where I was supposed to be? I was no longer satisfied with the status quo for Black females. I felt like an outsider in my once-safe happy world. I had to find out where I fit in.

After graduation I ended-up exactly where I didn't want to be — the cotton mill. I had let myself down. I had been through too much to stay there. Somehow, I had to get out.

A year passed, and then a girlfriend at church told me of a nursing program that we should attend together. A door opened and I applied; she didn't. History was repeating itself. I was in school alone again. But this time I had a different outlook. When things got tough, I remembered trying to stay awake as I worked third shift in the cotton mill. I graduated and became a licensed practical nurse. I was elated. I wanted a job in a doctor's office, but a Black nurse in the 1970s was unheard of. I took a second-shift position at a hospital.

Finally, my family was able to have the dream house with running water and an inside bathroom. I no longer had to sleep in a cold room. But I knew there had to be more to life.

A charge nurse position came open in the emergency room. A Black nurse had never worked at that level. I applied. After several anxious days, I got it! There was a lot of rumbling in the hospital around the promotion. I had to prove to others, and myself, I was worthy and capable. I had not been given the opportunity because of affirmative action. I had earned it.

After a few years the familiar unrest raised its head, I started looking into obtaining a registered nursing license. Every door I tried to open shut. When I was about to give up, the RN shortage at my hospital became so severe it was in danger of losing its certificate of need. They started a registered nurse program. The door I had waited on opened in 1989. I would have to make the one-hundred-mile round trip daily and work every weekend so the hospital would pay my tuition. As a wife and mother of two teenage children, I was ready for the challenge.

The graduating class of 1993 was one of the largest for the York Technical College program: sixty-three nurses from an original class of one hundred and twenty. I was the only Black. Afterwards doors started opening for me as never before.

I landed a job with one of the largest manufacturing companies in the world, and quickly learned how to maneuver with leadership. I was given a private parking space and a company credit card. I was privileged to fly to a safety meeting in the owner's private plane. During the conference a division president approached me and said, "You are a pioneer." I didn't know what to make of his statement until I surveyed the room. I was the only Black female there, but I didn't feel like an outsider.

Others may not be able to go with you, but you can leave a trail for them to tread. To my surprise, one day I received confirmation from a former Girl Scout, who said, "I became a nurse because of you." Later, I received the 2001 Occupational Health Nurse of the Year.

Don't wait for a leader to arrive. Become one.

— Mae Frances Sarratt —

Everyday Struggles

Clear and In Plain Sight

Grab the broom of anger and drive off the beast of fear.
~Zora Neale Hurston

Morning drive down 78
Sun's high and bright, not a cloud in the sky
Fastlane ridin', I look in my rear view
Deep breath… Hands 10 and 2
Make sure they're clear and in plain sight
Slow down, five miles below the speed limit
I didn't call my friend back Sunday
She probably still needs me
It can't be today
Turn down the volume
I'm probably too loud
Why the hell am I blasting NWA right now
Hands clear and in plain sight
I didn't say I love you to my mom last night
It just cannot be today
I wonder if he knows how I feel about them
Someone strange sat outside my house the other day
I didn't do anything… Just on my way to work
But why do I need to have my
Hands, 10 and 2, Clear and in plain sight

Should I just pull over?
No, wait, I'll merge right
Go 'head and pass me
I didn't say my prayers last night
God please let him pass me
He merged right
Heart beating outside my chest
Okay what was it my dad taught me?
Keep your hands clear of anything and in plain sight
Speak slowly and clearly. Only speak when spoken to
Yes, sir. No, sir. No sudden movements
If he pulls me over, drive to a well-lit highly populated area
I'm scared
I didn't do anything
My hands are clear and in plain sight
Why is he following me?
Are my genetics that suspicious?
Sweating, shaking. He merges left
I exhale, not guilty
I was scared
Because the way I was born is a threat
I'm tired. I park my car. I walk into work
"Good morning. How was your weekend?"
"Well… I didn't really do anything."

— Chenelle Williams —

A Mask in Terminal C

*We may encounter many defeats
but we must not be defeated.*
~Maya Angelou

We were navigating the double pandemics of COVID-19 and racism in May 2020 when I traveled to New York City and New Jersey. I saw more masks in use at airports, on the plane, in taxis and hotels, more so than what I'd seen in Colorado. I was thankful for the mask requirement, not only for the primary reasons of health and safety, but because it protected me at a much deeper level. Sitting masked in Newark Airport the morning I waited for my flight back to Colorado, I experienced a harsh reality. The reality is that no matter how palpable or justifiable my emotional pain, I am more comfortable masking that pain for my own self-protection than releasing it for my own healing.

I was sipping my over-priced chai tea latte in Terminal C and watching the nearby television screen showing CNN's video footage of the protests and riots taking place across America in the aftermath of the George Floyd murder. A news segment was announced highlighting the stories of African American men. I eagerly awaited this story because the African American male newscaster sounded excited as he prepared the viewers for the upcoming segment.

The segment was about coming-of-age stories, but not the ones about a first kiss or first dance, first job or first car. The survey was taken on social media and the question that was posed was, "How old were you when you had your first encounter with the police?" The question was not phrased, "have you ever," but "how old were you when...?"

Immediately, I found myself reminiscing about the experiences of the men in my family. I recalled in vivid detail my brothers sharing their stories of being stopped as teenagers and as grown men by the police while driving, or in our neighborhood and sometimes in front of our home.

The newscaster read the stories, one after another, of young African American men being held at gunpoint, being searched and frisked, or being detained in front of their homes. These were heartbreaking stories of unimaginable terror at the initiation of rogue police officers; and these African American boys were between the ages of fourteen and seventeen when they had their first police encounters. I listened intently to the common themes of misidentification and harassment as the stories were read.

The newscaster's voice broke as he read story after story. He almost begged the videographer to go back to the screen displaying the written stories and not have the camera focus on his face so he could have a moment to regroup. Nevertheless, the camera remained locked on his face, and the brother had to swiftly pull it together on live television. My eyes filled with tears because I wanted to protect this newscaster from his personal grief as he undoubtedly remembered his own story, and yet I had no power to maintain my composure sitting in Terminal C.

Drinking a chai tea latte in the airport required that I remove my mask. Before I realized what was happening, the tears were flowing down my exposed and unmasked cheeks, and all the painful history of my brothers — known and unknown — became a rallying cry in my heart. I sat in the airport in physical isolation because of social distancing, but in great emotional isolation because of years of racialized distancing. My memories were embedded so deep within, and yet they began bubbling to the surface as I locked arms with the CNN journalist on the television screen who struggled to contain his emotion.

I have grown weary of watching my brothers weep during television interviews. Not because the tears are unwarranted or a sign of weakness, but because the tears are an indicator of hopelessness, a desperate cry for justice that seems to be perpetually ignored. Not only are everyday African American men being interviewed on the streets during protests, but also African American college professors, attorneys, judges, politicians, physicians, authors, research analysts and corporate CEOs are weeping during news interviews as they discuss the murder of George Floyd and the historical racism that has haunted this country for 400 years.

So, as I sat crying in Terminal C, trying desperately to hide my emotions and my vulnerability, I wiped my eyes and remembered my mask. I was thankful that the required mask became my shield in the midst of private pain as I strategically placed it back onto my face. While my face remained covered, my eyes displayed the grief my heart could not contain.

— Wanda G. Anderson —

50

Wake Up, America

*So while once we asked, how could we possibly
prevail over catastrophe, now we assert,
how could catastrophe possibly prevail over us?*
~Amanda Gorman, The Hill We Climb

It was January 6, 2021, and this had to be a nightmare. After a peaceful, quarantined holiday with family in Atlanta I was driving home to Ohio alone. For those who know me, this was nothing new. Driving is my therapy. I spend so much time in my car it has become my safe space, I even call it my sanctuary. In this nightmare, however, even in my sanctuary I didn't feel safe.

I was an African American woman driving alone from the South to the North. Although I was on a familiar route, this time felt different. You see, America had reverted back to a country that I had only experienced in history books. The narrative in my dream was one of a country where not only were we plagued by a pandemic, but the racial division was such that African Americans were being hunted and killed. In this nightmare, at a rate that mimicked southern bounty hunters of the past, white police in America were shooting Black and brown bodies as though they were chasing runaway slaves. To make it worse, there had been a special election in Georgia the day before my trip that had completely divided the country. It might have been called a political split, but I knew it was racial.

To keep up with the election results I listened to National Public Radio. In a breaking news report, the reporters were obviously shaken.

They spoke with terror as they shared the unbelievable scene happening in the most developed nation in the world. I listened as the terrified reporters shared that rioters had entered the nation's Capitol where government leaders and employees were running for their lives and taking cover!

Could this be real? This had to be a nightmare, and all I wanted was to wake up, but I couldn't! To make it worse, friends and family started calling and texting to make sure I was alright. One friend called quite disturbed, asking, "Has the next Civil War started?"

I usually stopped two or three times on the nine-hour drive to Ohio. This time, I was too afraid. I only stopped once, when I had to. I just wanted to get home. Never in all my forty years had I been so uncomfortable driving anywhere in America. Never had I felt such overt racial tension, and that was after months of racially incited killings, riots, and political unrest. This all made driving while Black quite intimidating.

With all the progress, how could I be living the same fear of driving in America that my parents and grandparents had experienced way back then. How could anyone in America be afraid to get gas and use the restroom in 2021?

This had to be a nightmare, right? *Lord, please wake me up, this can't be really happening!* As I got closer to my destination, the adrenaline from listening to the media and the phone calls from people checking on me made it feel like some kind of war movie. I felt that if I could just cross the border between Kentucky and Ohio, I could exhale. Instead of running on foot to escape to the North, I was driving it.

When I hit Ohio, though, I still didn't feel safe. I passed by Cincinnati, and with the gas gauge dropping toward Empty, drove two more hours to my home.

When I finally made it home safely, the nightmare continued on every TV channel. It really was the year 2021, and everyone was having the same waking nightmare. It's time to wake up, America. Please!

— Angelle M. Jones —

51

A Pleasant Black Woman

*It's not about asking, it's about demanding. It's not
about convincing those who are currently in power,
it's about changing the very face of power itself.*
~Kimberle Williams Crenshaw

I don't remember when the resting face I present to the world became one with a semi-permanent smile regardless of what I'm feeling inside. It started out because I had suffered through braces for years and thought I should at least show off the results. Then, sometime in my early twenties, a photographer told me to make sure I had a "pleasant" Black woman face. This led to a "perplexed" Black woman face from me. He further explained to me that as a brown-skinned Black woman, I had to be extra careful to appear "pleasant" to make people more comfortable around me.

Years later, I realized I never stopped smiling. Now, I realize that that "pleasant" Black woman face really is a kind of armor because, as in the case of Dr. Susan Moore, who recently passed, letting it slip can kill you.

It sounds hyperbolic until you hear more of Dr. Moore's story. She tested positive for COVID-19 on November 29, 2020. While hospitalized, she shared on social media her experiences, which involved what she believed was disparate treatment based on her race — she was a Black woman. Studies back up this belief, showing that health care providers are less likely to deliver effective treatment to people of color when compared to their white counterparts.

This medical doctor's assertions of pain were dismissed. This was until a CT scan showed the distressing state of her lungs. Only then was she prescribed narcotics as treatment for pain. Still, she was discharged. When she needed to go back into a hospital, she chose a different one where she received more compassionate care and was ultimately diagnosed with pneumonia. Tragically, she died on December 20, 2020.

After reports of her death and her complaints were made public, leadership at the first hospital implied that she intimidated the staff. This of course placed the onus back on Dr. Susan Moore for the dismissive care she received. This woman, while suffering and in pain, apparently should have pasted on a "pleasant" Black woman face so that health care providers would fulfill their oath of taking care of the sick. If Black women have to be pleasant in order to deserve competent care while suffering from this virus, we are in serious trouble.

I recently published a book addressing the dismissive treatment Black women are subjected to when interacting with the U.S. health care system, *EmpowHERed Health: Reforming a Dismissive Health Care System*. In the book I detail years of being ignored when expressing that I was in pain. My most vivid memory involved crawling on the floor to grab a remote control because I could not stand up due to unbearable pain.

The day I decided that I would no longer accept the doctors dismissing my pain was the day I took what has (somewhat ironically) become my favorite picture. It was an unseasonably warm day in early 2018. I was wearing a burnt orange sundress under a button-down denim shirt and a camouflage print jacket. My curls were crisp, the sun hit the bronzer on my face, highlighting my cheekbones. And, as my mother would say, I showed every single one of my teeth with a dazzling smile.

I look so happy in the picture , but inside my body screamed in pain. Looking at that picture, no one would ever know that I left the doctor's office and spent hours Googling my symptoms.

I wondered why I didn't remain in the doctor's office so that she knew how serious this was for me. And the answer is, I didn't want to inconvenience her.

That night I knew, and later a specialist confirmed, that I had been living with thirty fibroids — benign tumors that grow in the uterus and would need surgery. Saving the doctor from the inconvenience of having to go further in diagnosing me ended up inconveniencing me.

As I think about the conversation I had about making a "pleasant" Black woman face so that everyone could feel comfortable around me — the big bad and angry Black woman — I think about how that immediately put the onus on me to address the implicit biases of everyone around me. Why should we continue to accept a world where someone's unreasonable assumptions based on tropes and systemic racism are somehow the problem of the oppressed?

I started to think of the case of Anjanette Young, a Chicago woman, handcuffed naked while police officers milled about her home as she screamed at them that they were in the wrong house. As it turned out, they were in the wrong house. I wonder whether a "pleasant" Black woman face would have saved her from being treated as less than human while having her rights violated. She was never given the opportunity to put on a "pleasant" Black woman face.

The bias, the dehumanization and the victim blaming are all having a devastating impact on Black women's health. There is substantial research linking healthcare provider beliefs and implicit biases about Black women to racial disparities in health and healthcare.

I am an attorney. Dr. Susan Moore was a doctor. Anjanette Young is a social worker. Success, education, money, even fame will lose in the face of unchecked racism. And while it will take years to fix systemic racism, we can decide that starting now we will not place the burden on the victims. We will not blame Black women for a system that often fails them.

Most importantly, we will not force them to adopt a "pleasant" face in the face of racism.

— S. Mayumi "Umi" Grigsby —

52

Equipped, Qualified & Black

When I hear about negative and false attacks,
I really don't invest any energy in them,
because I know who I am.
~Michelle Obama

N o matter how many times you've been disrespected or treated "less than" because of your skin color, it hurts. The day a patient's husband told me that they weren't seeing "my kind" was no exception. It cut a little deeper given the raw wound I was already carrying given the murders of George Floyd and Breonna Taylor, among others.

When he said this to me, I felt so many emotions: anger, sadness, humiliation, frustration, and numbness. Yet, I couldn't fully "feel" any of them because I don't have that liberty. My next patient was waiting, and the one after that, and the one after that. No matter what happens, as a Black professional woman, I must continue to give my best at all times no matter what is happening with me. I wear my professionalism as a badge and my mask like freshly applied make-up in the morning. Best face and foot forward is how I approach each day.

To be honest, it had been a while since I'd dealt with such "in your face" racism in the workplace. Oncology is already challenging, for the medical professionals and the patients. There should be no room for racism. To think that people who are literally fighting for their lives could also hate you for living yours. Befuddling!

Then there are those who want to have complex discussions that do not pertain to their illness. "What's wrong with me saying All Lives Matter?" a patient says to me. *Oh Lord, I can't have this discussion with you* is what I am screaming to myself.

The patient asks again, as I'd hesitated to respond. I am fairly certain that I am one of the few Black people this person can talk to about this. I do my best to be diplomatic; after all this is a hematology and oncology practice and I am the nurse practitioner.

I say, "It's all about the context in which the phrase is being used. Saying Black Lives Matter doesn't mean that all lives don't." The patient looks confused, and I am immediately tired even though it's only the beginning of my clinic day. I kindly say we need to get to the treatment room. I'm thinking *I don't have time for this, Lord. Help me.* Best wishes are extended to my family and I do the same. Before parting though, the patient says, "I would like to discuss more when you have time." I smile and get ready for my next patient.

I once had a child come in with a patient and announce, "Look, she's brown!" Talk about awkward. The encounter overall went well. However, it solidifies that even if I wanted too, (and I don't), I can't forget my race or the color of my skin. Then, there have been the silent encounters in which I can tell that the patient has an issue with me being Black. He or she is at least "nice" enough not to acknowledge it openly. They just give off vibes that scream, "I really don't like people like you."

While my white counterparts move freely through this world without a second thought, I think about everything. *How would it look if I did this? What would they think if I did that? How would my words be interpreted if I really told you how I feel?* I've always known how many in the world would view me. My parents made sure I could navigate in certain spaces and climates. They prepared me for the challenges of being Black in America. Sometimes, it's more difficult than I ever thought it would be. I love my Blackness though, from my melanin-rich skin to the incomparable rich heritage. I am resilient. I am an overcomer. I am persistent. I am determined.

I suppress my emotions and extend my devotion to those I serve. It's my calling to help people even if there are some people who don't truly want my help. I compartmentalize how I'm feeling in my heart and in my head and do what I must do for the patients I serve. I admit that it is getting harder and that sometimes I want to give racists (covert and overt) a piece of my mind.

I have been caring for others in some sort of nursing capacity for well over a decade now and I have seen my share of racist antics. The demeaning smile. The condescending look. The one-word responses that really say, "I am only talking to you because I have to." The refusal to look me in my eyes. The insistence on talking to the white person who is with me despite me being the one leading the conversation. I could go on and on. Unfortunately, to some, it does not matter that you are equipped and qualified to help them. They only see your skin color, and that is their loss.

To cope, I rely heavily on my faith, my family and my friends. Good support systems are critical. I limit my social media. I rarely watch the news. I exercise (walk mostly), listen to music and read/ listen to books that allow momentary escape from the foolishness of the world and uplift my soul and spirit. I know that I was put on this earth for a purpose and that purpose will be fulfilled according to God's plan for me no matter what.

— Coretta Collins —

53

COVID-19 During the Black Lives Pandemic

There is no room around me in which to be still,
to examine and explore what pain is mine alone —
no device to separate my struggle within from my
fury at the outside world's viciousness, the stupid,
brutal lack of consciousness or concern
that passes for the way things are.
~Audre Lorde, The Cancer Journals

I walk up to the reception desk at Albany Medical and say, "I have COVID." I do not say, "I think I have COVID," because at this point I am certain.

Earlier that evening my heart rate spiked to 122, 138 then 148; my temperature shot up to 104. I don't really think the ER can help me, but I need a witness other than my husband, Lee, to what's happening to me. Maybe I'm hoping they will magically restore my weakened will to survive.

They send me to a quarantine room and the waiting begins. After the first hour, a deep chill sets in. This room with its refrigerated air feels like a slow death. I can feel my fever going back up. It takes two blankets for my body to stop shaking. I stand up and do my breathing exercises as I've been doing these past ten days.

**

I had spent most of quarantine sheltering-in-place as suggested, but two weeks prior to my trip to Albany Medical, on the Sunday after George Floyd's murder, I attended a Black Lives Matter congregation in Poughkeepsie, New York. I was invited by the event organizers to facilitate one of the breakout circles that explored the question, "What would change for you if Black Lives Mattered?"

We created a wide spacious circle but were still not the recommended six feet apart. During my active facilitation, I removed my mask and put it back on when listening. Later that week, I attended a large rally across the Hudson River in Kingston, New York. Everyone wore masks but social distancing was impossible. On Saturday, driving through an unfamiliar part of Columbia County, I stopped and asked a woman for directions. She came ridiculously close to me and began speaking. I turned my face away but did not move away. I wish I had.

The following Sunday, I woke with a high fever and knew I was in trouble. I texted Isa Coffey, an herbalist, friend, and partner in a COVID wellness initiative we'd been working on together, to get resources into the Black and brown communities in and around the Hudson and Kingston areas. I wasn't anticipating being a recipient of these services.

Isa responded immediately, meeting Lee with a kit containing important elements such as a thermometer, an oximeter to measure the levels of oxygen in my blood, and herbal tinctures to support my breathing and heart health.

I had no idea, no precedent in my life, for the frightening journey I was about to embark on, through the strange terrain of a COVID infection. Unlike many of the illnesses we are accustomed to, COVID does not progress in a linear fashion. One day the temperature and oxygen levels are good and you believe you are getting better. The next day there are strange pains pulsing through your body and your fever goes up while the oxygen in your body declines. Because COVID has the ability to access ninety percent of our cells, it is a highly flexible entity—one that can evade our frontline attempts to put it down. Before this day when my will to survive seemed to be slipping through my fingers, I thought I had been improving.

***

Now, in this frigid hospital room, I breathe and raise my arms, just as I learned to do in Aunt Peggy's ballet class when I was little, opening the space in my chest, releasing the oxygen I no longer need. Hold and open. Hold and open. Hold and open a little more, until something releases, places in my lungs that were starting to close down, go to sleep, gradually numbing off into death. My breath says, "NO! Wake up. I won't have this!"

By the third and fourth hours of waiting, I'm exhausted and then desperate. They won't give me any Tylenol for my rising fever. Fortunately, I've brought my own water.

I wait five hours to be admitted into the inner sanctum of the hospital where a nurse administers an IV to hydrate me. I lie on an examining table plugged into a large monitor that I'm unaware of until it suddenly begins beeping. I turn to see the red display showing my oxygen levels dropping to 86, then 79, far below the acceptable level of 95. I watch my heart rate spike again. Lee tells me to calm down and I breathe, willing myself into calm. The numbers stabilize and the beeping stops.

Waiting and more waiting. Nothing but time to reflect on this illness and the place where I most likely contracted it. I can't stop thinking about the glaringly obvious irony—in a space of Black folks gathering, yet again, to reaffirm that Black Lives Do Matter, where we were repeating the words of Eric Garner and George Floyd, "I can't breathe," I might have exposed myself to the virus that is now stealing my breath.

COVID-19 and white supremacy are both stealthy and cruel diseases. COVID-19 doesn't just mess with your respiratory system; it attacks your heart, brain, and other organs. White supremacy enters our bodies carrying a diseased set of subconscious beliefs and unless you are acutely aware of what you are truly feeling and thinking, you will never notice its presence as it silently infiltrates your heart and mind.

COVID-19 is new to me but I've been long aware that I carry the disease of white supremacy in my body. I know because I have been paying close attention. So many liberal and progressive white people bristle at the idea they might be racist. They say, "I don't have a racist bone in my body," or "I'm the least racist person in the world." For so many years, I too lacked the language and concepts to help me understand what I was experiencing, but that did not inoculate me from the disease.

Many years ago, walking up the street in my old Upper West Side neighborhood I passed two teenage Black girls from the projects. For some reason, on this particular day, I caught a soundtrack that had probably played out unnoticed hundreds of times in the past. I heard myself thinking, "These girls in their big earrings, tight jeans, popping gum as they talk, are going to grow up to be baby-mothers on welfare and never make anything of their lives." I was horrified by the level of racism and self-betrayal implicit in this judgment. I was disgusted with what I heard myself thinking but there it was — my own unadorned racism and I had to deal with it.

It's taken me years to understand the mechanics of how I became so alienated from my own identity. There are so many stories along this path, and I see how they stretch all the way back to my Jamaican great-grandparents, and grandparents passed on to me by my American-born mother.

I see the long path of those first ancestors emerging from the slave ship into a world fraught with new rules that needed to be grasped quickly because survival depended on it.

My great-grandmother, Isabel Turner, was an acknowledged daughter of an Irish plantation owner and his "mulatto mistress." This was an important marker. I can see how, from the slave ship to this moment in the nineteenth century, my family line had progressed steadily along a path that would erase as much of its African origins as possible. I see myself at a crossroads on this path, in the late twentieth century, when, as my aunt once said, "If you were to have children with a white man, those children would be seen as white."

**

Eight hours of waiting in these freezing hospital rooms and I finally have to stand up. I can't deal with being prone and plugged in any longer. I work my way around the IV tube and monitor line attached to my finger and stand by the examining table. The nurse comes in.

"I want to go home," I say.

"I'm so sorry," the nurse says as she detaches the IV drip. "I can't do anything."

Outside, in another room a man is bellowing, "I'm in pain! I'm in pain!" He sounds angry. I've tried to stay away from anger because it drains my energy and sets my heart rate into an uneasy pattern. Despite my best efforts, I have felt the roiling in my blood, my own impulse to shout, "I'm in pain. I'm furious. Fuck this shit."

I have been carrying this impulse for most of my life — sometimes venting it, but mostly suppressing it — understanding that an angry Black woman is perceived as a threat. I understood the price of the white privilege extended to me was my silence, or at best, a voice muted in academic tones of reason when speaking about my experience. It meant never shouting, "I'm in pain!"

Now, I feel a wave of petulant anger emerging. I want others, the doctors and nurses, to feel my discomfort. One part of my brain understands they are working hard but another part says, "Fuck it. I've been here for eight hours and need to go home. I need you to care about me!"

I recognize my voice of white privilege; a voice formed early from the belief that the world should/would/must care about me. I have moved through my life alternately expecting and demanding that the world care about me. Unlike so many Black people in this country, I have not lived a life where my daily survival is a question. Until contracting COVID-19 and having to turn my entire focus to survival, I have not known a life where "I can't breathe" is my truth. It has been a frightening and strange new reality for me.

I have been fortunate. People, society, and circumstance have extended much grace to me throughout my life. I felt that grace walking out of the ER, twelve hours after checking in, with Lee by my side, steadfast and loving. As we walked down the hospital ramp to find our car, I felt we were walking away from the scene of a battle. Gazing at the sunrise, I felt gratitude knowing that I would have a chance to heal.

**

It is impossible for me to imagine the lives of Black people who have lived with the daily struggle to breathe easy whether because of daily microaggressions or outright violence experienced in white spaces, systemic oppression, harsh working conditions, fear, anxiety, high blood pressure, PTSD and so many conditions common to the Black experience in this country. I cannot imagine these lives, but I now have a real corollary: like the disproportionate number of other Black people experiencing COVID-19, I understand what it means to struggle to breathe, to feel my entire body overtaken by an invisible force that desires only to crush my will.

COVID-19. White supremacy. They both attack the hearts, minds and bodies of all whom they enter.

On the day that my fever spiked to 104, Isa said to me "I truly believe that this virus carries fear into the body." A little while later, as I immersed myself in the soothing bath she recommended, I felt the essence of my fear emerge from behind the heat and confusion of my fever. I understood what my body had been feeling. The presence of an invasive intelligence that, having gained entry, was now attempting to rewrite the very language in which my body functioned.

As I named this fear to myself, I felt a burst of coherence, a simple determination that would carry me through the next twelve hours in the ER and beyond to the following days where my body would begin the slow process of healing.

There is great power in the naming of a thing. In myth, fairytales, and fantasy these words, incantations or codes hold the key to truths that have been intentionally hidden, truths that are needed for the survival of a people, sometimes their very planet.

We are at the convergence of many crossroads now, a place where magic words need to be spoken by each one of us. We must be willing to listen with deep honesty to the words we've been speaking to ourselves all along and acknowledge the fears and judgments we hold against ourselves and others. We must be willing to stand, as I did many years ago on the Upper West Side, in astonishment and shame, and resolve to do better. And we must learn to care for ourselves in the process because, like COVID-19, white supremacy is a shape-shifting disease that has worked its way into the deepest recesses of our beings.

Each one of us must become willing to name our hidden words and move forward with intention and with gratitude for this opportunity to heal.

— Dara Joyce Lurie —

The Price of Living the White Life

*It's important to me that youth everywhere,
no matter their race, religion, or gender,
know that anything is possible with perseverance.*
~Ibtihaj Muhammad

I pay $2,340 a month in rent. This is just one of the prices we pay in the Black middle class to escape the Black and brown communities we're from. The idea of raising my brown children on the Southside of Chicago scared me. Not only would I have to constantly worry about their physical safety, I had to worry about the quality of education in our zip code.

Our area wasn't terrible. We lived less than a mile from one of Chicago's prestigious universities, and just barely over a mile from the Obamas' Southside home. Yet, the school district in this area was one no white parent would send their children to, and one I rejected as well.

My academic experience, especially in my formative years, was in the private school system. My middle-class parents could afford that luxury. We did for a while, sending three children to the same private school. But the $10,000 price tag for preschool for my three-and-a-half-year-old was the last straw. We decided to leave our African American community and head west to the suburbs.

The tree lined streets, the big houses, the starry nights, the quiet. Wow, did it seem worth it. Until the daylight came, and we got the look. We all know the look: "Oh, the new neighbors are Black." Then came the probing conversations: "So, what do you do for a living?" "Where did you move from?' And my favorite: "Are you renters or buyer?" Yep. Always protecting their investment.

Now, all the neighbors weren't like this. They just never engaged. They watched but didn't speak. I was okay with that. I got used to the looks and the subtle interrogations. I was here for the safety and the education and could deal with the colonized mentality of the suburbs.

My family and I lived with the challenges of being in a white community. My children were getting the education I desired them to have, without the onerous sticker price. It was a sacrifice my husband and I were willing to make. We saw the stories on the news about the ever-increasing inner-city violence. *Not my kids*, I thought. *They will be able to walk to school, ride their bikes and even go to our downtown area coffee house with their friends.* This is exactly what I wanted for my children. So, I thought.

As the years went by, my kids got to do all the things they could never do in our Chicago neighborhood. They hung out at the park and went to the small movie theater with friends. I was even able to accompany my daughter to Wisconsin to see her favorite artist while my thirteen-year-old and my nine-year-old boys took in a movie and lunch solo in our downtown.

I was never worried about their physical safety, but the trauma of being Black in America was ever present. My husband and I admittedly had some regrets. We began to miss being in black and brown communities. My kids didn't have friends who looked like them. My daughter didn't have peers that rocked the long knotless braids that had become the style of her generation. My boys wouldn't have loud, social interactions with others in black and brown bodies who understood the physical and cultural challenges of being darker skinned in America. There was no cultural counterpart to help them understand the challenges they would face once they left the bubble of this affluent suburb.

My children became the "face of the race" in social studies classes when the Civil War and civil rights were on the agenda. My daughter talked about how uncomfortable the looks made her feel. Again, I thought it was a sacrifice for safety. The sacrifice became too great when my first-grader, the only brown body in the class, was told by a classmate, "I don't play with brown people. They smell."

I wept. I took to the community's Facebook page to express my heartache and received the "I'm surprised" or "I'm so sorry that happened" responses. The meeting with the school staff only served to take valuable time from my day and introduce me to white-washed responses.

Then there was the depression. The isolation of being the darker of their friends, not to mention the genetics of being of African descent. The feelings of being "too much" all while "not being good enough." Then came the acknowledgement that shook me to my core. My daughter told me, "I don't like being Black. None of my friends look like me."

What had I done? My kids may have been physically safe, but emotionally and socially they were wounded. This is the price of living in a Black body while wanting the white life.

I began to deposit affirming concepts of Blackness into my children. When the world began to shake from the chants of "I Can't Breathe" and "Say Her Name," my children began to have the true Black experience. They were able to identify with the black and brown bodies that had been slayed by those in white bodies, and the protesters fighting for change.

My thirteen-year-old daughter took to social media and found her voice, using her platform to decolonize her peer's mindset on race and body image as well as being an ally for LGBTQ+. My sons are able to advocate for their rights to be in brown bodies without carrying the burden of white folk's comfort. There is still growth happening, and I can see that our investment in living the white life has yielded something: resiliency.

— Casandra Townsel —

55

Shopping While Black

I am followed in department stores. I have walked in
dressed professionally or dressed in jeans...
and instantly, security is on my back.
~Tamron Hall

My due date had come and gone. I was huge, miserable, and tired of people asking if I were having twins! Yet, I couldn't resist going into the nursery several times a day to imagine my baby finally living there. *Come on, baby!* I thought, as I waddled around the room, hoping that my next trip to the doctor would be to deliver Baby H.

During my nine-month checkup, the doctor said, "No worries, I just delivered a fourteen-pound baby the other day. Naturally. You'll be fine." My heart skipped a few beats.

"Wait, you're saying my baby will be fourteen pounds at birth?" I asked in disbelief and dread.

He laughed. "No, the mother was diabetic. That's not your case. I would say your baby is about nine pounds so far. He or she is just very comfortable and in no hurry to come out." He reached out his hand so that I could pull up from the examining table. "Just continue to eat well, but don't diet at this stage. Go for walks and think positive thoughts. Pretty soon we will celebrate the birth of your baby."

With those words, I began a more rigorous walking regimen.

One day my friend Audrey called. She was a former co-worker and we'd become close because we were the only two women of color in the place where we worked. Our personalities clicked and we remained friends even after she left to pursue other interests. "Have you been walking?" Audrey asked.

"Yes."

"Did you walk today?"

"Not yet."

"Okay, get dressed, I'm coming to pick you up. We're going to walk around the mall."

"Audrey, the mall is the last place I want to be in my condition."

"But you'll be with me, and we're going at a time when not too many people will be there. And when you say you've had enough, I can take you home. I'll be there in twenty minutes. Be ready." Audrey disconnected before I could protest.

Once we arrived at the mall, I asked if she needed to buy anything. "No, I figured we'd dream shop."

Dream-shopping is something we did pre-pregnancy. We would pick a group of stores to window shop at or walk into a department store and pick out items that we'd like to have — if we had the money.

Frankly, I appreciated her efforts, but I wasn't feeling the notion of dream-shopping today. All I could concentrate on were the stares I received from passersby and the weight of the baby. And it was discouraging to window shop for clothing that wouldn't fit me again for months, if ever.

Audrey must have felt my pain because she suggested we walk into a department store and look at their home furnishings. We browsed several sections before I realized that a Caucasian woman was following us at a distance. She pretended to browse but was clearly focused on our activities. I didn't immediately say anything to Audrey.

Finally, we reached the living room and bedroom sections. I opened the drawers of a nightstand and noted their depth. I could place quite a few items in them, I thought. Nice!

To test my suspicion, I walked over to a dresser and picked up a small decorative piece to admire. I looked from the corner of my eye, and sure enough, she was watching me. I walked over to Audrey, who was feeling a comforter's texture.

"I like this one. I wouldn't mind having this on my bed," she said.

"Don't look now, but we're being followed." Audrey turned her head slightly to see what I was talking about.

"No, don't look! She's pretending to admire something in the corner, but she's been trailing us for a while."

"Why?"

"Undercover security," I told her.

"She thinks we're stealing?"

"I don't know, but let's try to lose her."

Audrey looked at my girth and smiled. "I don't think it'll be hard for her to find us."

We both smiled and walked around to another department. Sure enough, our "friend" appeared.

Already feeling cranky from the heaviness of advanced pregnancy, I didn't need this to add to my aggravation. "I'm ready to go," I announced.

"You sure? I wouldn't let her annoy you."

"Nah, I'm done! There could be a hundred people shopping, but they choose to follow the specs in the rice. It happens frequently and it's irksome!"

We headed toward an exit. I looked around. Our "friend" was about ten feet behind us. When she saw me watching her, she quickly turned her head and pretended to be looking for something. Frustrated, I yelled out, "Come on, Audrey, I don't know how much longer I can hide this nightstand under my blouse!"

We left the store giggling like two schoolgirls.

—Robin D. Hamilton—

56

Colored, Negro, Black, African American, Other...

You may not control all the events that happen to you,
but you can decide not to be reduced by them.
~Maya Angelou

Where are you from? It took me years to understand that my long curly hair, light skin color and facial features confused many people. I was "colored" when I was six and my grandmother told me I could not use the bathroom of the many gas stations we drove by on our way to our "country" home in Virginia. "I don't understand," I repeated as we passed each one. "I have to pee!" She always told me we couldn't stop, and that we were almost there. I would understand later how dangerous that time was for our family when I learned to read the "No Colored" signs.

In the 1960s, I was "Negro" when I rode with my parents, house hunting in Washington, D.C. It had become a weekend routine. My parents were so excited about being able to afford their own home. It became a game, finding the "For Sale" signs. I remember my mother asked my father to stop at what she called the perfect house. We got out of the car with wild anticipation, but my father seemed hesitant.

When we approached the front door, it was immediately opened by a tall white man. He stared at us angrily, blocked the door, and said, "We don't sell to Negroes."

My parents decided later to buy an empty lot and build their first home.

Later, I was "Black" when four of us were accepted into a private Catholic school. We quickly bonded, meeting often at each other's homes, since none of us were in a class together. Experiencing daily racist remarks and other insults was the norm. As we shared our experiences, I decided to write to the Archbishop to complain that our experiences did not reflect the teachings of Christ. My mother was shocked when his office called to arrange a visit to our home. He sat quietly in our living room as I described our painful situations, but nothing changed. My high school years taught me that because of the color of my skin I would be treated unfairly and judged harshly.

As the first woman accepted into a previously all male college, I battled many preconceived ideas and resentment. Most of the priests did not want female or non-white students. I became a founding member of the Black Student Union and was the spokesperson during our "sit in" at the president's office. My push for equality became a priority during my college years as I experienced discrimination at a new level, on and off campus. When I answered ads for off-campus housing, I was told it was "just rented" when I showed up within minutes of my phone inquiry.

Graduating with degrees in psychology and drama, I moved to New York to pursue acting. I was fortunate to get enough work to support myself as an actress and model. My ambiguous looks put me on many movie and commercial sets. I became a member of the Screen Actors Guild. Defined as "African American," I joined the committee that wrote the document "Window Dressing on the Set," which exposed the fact that film crews often shot two versions of commercials. One with white actors, which would air, creating residual income for the actors, and the second one with African American actors. That one would not air. We would wait and watch the white actors perform the identical script, then replace them at the end of the day for a one-take shoot.

This practice allowed them to claim they had hired a certain number of minorities to meet a quota. Quota became a familiar word. As a model and actress, several agencies told me they had already signed an African American, so I freelanced for seventeen different agencies. I was called when "their girl" was not available. Many of my bookings came from me going to open casting calls.

I changed careers after marriage. Working for several corporations, I saw how differently I was treated. Twice, I trained someone younger and less experienced, only to have them offered the next promotion or become my supervisor. My accomplishments, and skills were ignored. James Baldwin said, "To be African American is to be African without any memory and American without any privilege." That quote defined my life. "Affirmative Action" laws had opened the doors but had not prevented discrimination. Anger, pain, and disappointment became my daily emotional companions. After twenty years of generating millions of dollars for several corporations, without equal compensation, I quit.

Months later, I got a call from a young former co-worker whom I had mentored. She tearfully told me of her experience at work. I advised her to see a lawyer. Weeks later, she told me, the lawyer wanted to meet with me. He explained I was the strongest example of discrimination, and he'd only take the case if I agreed to be the lead plaintiff in the class action lawsuit. Two years later, we settled out of court the day before the trial.

Years later, I started learning my true history, beyond the limited American version. I traveled to West and East Africa. Learning about the ancient kings, queens and the many Black American geniuses empowered me to heal from the daily impact of living in a hostile society. Slowly I began learning to transform the anger and allow love in.

Recently, I took a DNA test and discovered I am sixty percent African and forty percent European.

I cannot deny the entirety of who I am; and I won't limit myself to a classification determined in the seventeenth century. I learned the word "race" is a human invented term and not a biological concept. It is simply a social construct that bestows or denies benefits and privileges.

I am much more than the color of my skin, my country or my culture. So now, when I see that little box asking for my race, I check "Other."

— Sheila L. Quarles —

57

The Elephant in the Room

Nobody's free until everybody's free.
~Fannie Lou Hamer

I am a Black woman. I am a Black woman whose significant other is a police officer. I am a Black woman whose significant other is a white police officer... plot twist!

Every day I watch the love of my life get ready for work, a career he decided to pursue nearly seventeen years ago. I quite like watching him get ready for work. For one, the man looks amazing in his uniform. But mostly, I'm proud of him. I'm proud of the man he is, and I love that he chose to become a police officer because he wants to serve our community.

However, I also get a twinge of anxiety when he's dressing for work. I hear the clicks of him attaching his equipment to his belt, which is quite heavy, but what sticks with me the most is the sound of the Velcro as he's putting on and adjusting his bullet proof vest. For me, that's when I remember the enormity of his job. That's when it sets in — the dangers associated with his line of work. That's when I think about his fellow officers who have died in the line of duty. That's when I say a little prayer that he comes home after his shift. Not long after I hear those sounds, we kiss, say "I love you," and out the door he goes.

Then I wait for him to come home.

You know who isn't coming home? Sandra Bland. Philando Castile.

Alton Sterling. Atatiana Jefferson. Tamir Rice. Eric Garner. Elijah McClain. Amadou Diallo. Breonna Taylor. George Floyd. #SayTheirNames

The first time I remember seeing video of police brutality was when Rodney King was beaten by white police officers in 1991. I was in elementary school watching the grainy video footage of Mr. King being kicked and beaten. Guess what? Those officers were acquitted.

What happened to the officers who fired forty-one shots that killed an unarmed Amadou Diallo in New York City? They were acquitted.

How about the officer who shot and killed twelve-year-old Tamir Rice within two seconds of arriving on the scene? Charges were never brought against him. Tamir should be a thriving eighteen-year-old today.

History has shown us time and time again that Black lives do not matter. We cannot look at birds in Central Park while Black. We cannot play video games in our houses while Black. We cannot drive while Black. We cannot sleep in our own beds while Black. Where can we feel safe being Black?

Unfortunately, George Floyd's death was the tipping point for many people in this country. I can still hear the cries of him calling out for his mother as the life was being drained from his body. His death forced my partner and me to address the elephant in the room. We could no longer have surface level conversations about the injustices that continue to happen to Black people in this country. We had to have a candid conversation about the constant anger and frustration I feel as a Black woman because of the disparity in treatment of Black people in America.

As I write this, I feel myself growing upset because I think about the Black lives cut short at the hands of police. I ponder what amazing things those individuals could have accomplished if they were still here. I'm tired of turning on the television or scrolling through social media and seeing yet another instance of a Black life lost.

I also wait for my partner to return home from his shift. I look forward to the sound of him unclipping his utility belt. I especially, listen for the sound of that Velcro. That's when I can breathe a sigh relief.

I just want Black people to be able to breathe.

— Crystal E. Newby —

Raising Our Children

Curating

I'd tried everything to protect my children's innocence
and shield them from harm, even subconsciously
curating their appearance to make them more
palatable to even the most inhumane individuals in
our society. I bought them skinny jeans instead of
comfortable baggy ones and made sure
they wore bright colors.
~Doreen Oliver
Sunday Review
The New York Times

i.
"Curating" is a curious term as a Black mother's reference
to buying her teenage sons' fashion. But let's not get down
on the mother here. She only wanted her sons —
one with autism even — to be able
to shop unhassled with a sitter —
a white sitter even — who talked the cops,
goaded by store employees,
down from coarsely interrogating the sons.
This is why people say "Abolish Police" — from weapons practice on
15-year-old wanted posters of Black men to a knee on the neck until
death.

ii.
One poster interrogates the sky: *"How Many Weren't Filmed?"*
In Detroit the three murdered at the Algiers Motel[1]
The three murdered in Orangeburg at South Carolina State.[2]
All this was way before a franchise popped up on every corner
in suburban and urban New Jersey
and autism became a coveted diagnosis.

— Cheryl Clarke —

[1] The Algiers Motel murders of Carl Cooper, Fred Temple, and Aubrey Pollard, three teenage black men, occurred in Detroit during the racial uprisings of 1967. The motel, black-owned and reputed to be a site of illegal activity, was rushed by members of the Detroit Police Department, the Michigan National Guard, and the Michigan State Police after reports of gunmen on its premises. This resulted in not only the three murders, which included a valet to the popular singing group the Dramatics, but also the beating and abuse of nine other guests. In 1968, investigative journalist John Hersey wrote a searing account of the murders in his book *The Algiers Motel Incident.*

[2] On February 8, 1968, in Orangeburg, South Carolina, Samuel Ephesians Hammond, Jr., Delano Herman Middleton and Henry Ezekial Smith were shot and killed by police who fired on student demonstrators at the South Carolina State College campus.

58

Hand-Me Down Blues

One is a mother in order to understand the
inexplicable. One is a mother to lighten the darkness.
~Mariama Bâ

The Summer of 2020 was remarkable in many ways, including an increase in support for the Black Lives Matter movement. My younger son and I decided to attend one of the protests planned in response to the horrific murders of George Floyd, Breonna Taylor and countless others at the hands of the police. "I need a T-shirt" he told me. Understandably, he wanted suitable attire — something that expressed his anger and frustration. He wanted people to know what he felt and where he stood just by looking at him.

In typical teenage boy fashion, this request was made only days before the event. We immediately searched for and found a Black-owned company that offered a T-shirt with the message he wanted, and equally important, all proceeds supported the Black Lives Matter movement. Unfortunately, the shirt would not arrive in time for the demonstration. My son was disappointed.

As he searched for another shirt to wear, I remembered that I purchased one for my older son when Eric Garner, another unarmed Black man, died by the hands of the police. That was six years earlier. The shirt bore the three words that Eric Garner whispered in his final moments, the same words as George Floyd when a policeman had his knee on Mr. Floyd's neck: "I Can't Breathe." I thought it would be perfect for my younger son if I could find it.

I started looking through the bins where I kept hand-me-downs as I have done countless times before for other items. Digging through the pile was always a walk down memory lane as I recalled when one item or another was worn or purchased. I remembered when I bought the shirt, and my older son's frustration and despair at the death of Eric Garner.

I remembered that I could not offer him any real words of consolation. Not for Eric Garner. Not for Trayvon Martin. Not for twelve-year-old Tamir Rice or any of the other murdered Black people killed by those sworn to protect them. He wanted a T-shirt too. He wanted some outward expression of the inward confusion and pain he was experiencing at the realization that he was considered expendable and a threat — not a teenage boy.

The fact that the same T-shirt with the same message was still relevant six years later filled me with overwhelming sadness until I stopped digging and started weeping into the bins of clothes.

I thought of everything that happened and everything that had not happened in the six years since I bought that shirt. Six years of watching videos of unarmed Black men and women die at the hands of the police. Six years of mothers losing sons and daughters, children losing fathers and mothers, communities being robbed of the unknown promise and potential of so many futures. Six plus over four hundred years of fear and frustration.

I. Can't. Breathe.

The words on the T-shirt were the same ones Eric Garner whispered in New York. We had marched before. We protested before. We stood against police tyranny before. Six years later, we were still dying. When would it end?

My younger son only had a vague recollection of the murder of Eric Garner, but he will never forget George Floyd. No matter how much he may want to erase the horrific image of his face smashed against the blacktop and the smirk on the face of the police officer. He will never forget watching him die on that video, and neither will I. Neither will any of us.

I still don't have many words of comfort or consolation. I just hope this time will be different. I hope this time the words turned to action will lead to lasting change. I hope the senseless killing of Black men and women at the hands of the police will cease. I hope we will dismantle systemic racism once and for all. I hope that my sons will eventually feel safe in their own country and in their own skin. I hope that one day Black lives will finally, fully and completely matter. Most of all, I hope that in another six years I will not be searching for that T-shirt because we still can't breathe.

— Sharisse Kimbro —

Crowning Their Beauty

I feel that the kinks, curls, or tight coils in Afro hair is beautiful and unique. No other race on this planet has hair like ours — that makes me proud.
~Monica Millner

As I stared at my daughter's hair seemingly going in every direction, I inhaled deeply, ready to take on this challenge. Hours earlier, while visiting a friend out of town, I was unexpectedly taught how to braid hair into cornrows. On my way back home, I visualized my fingers separating and then weaving the sections of Kennedi's hair in and out, forming a perfect cornrow.

My daughter was two years old, but I had never learned how to braid her hair. Now was the moment of truth. Could I really do this? I had tried many times before but just couldn't get my fingers to work together and manipulate her hair into the seemingly complicated style.

But that night was different. I parted her hair into sections with my comb, and my fingers moved exactly how I wanted them. I braided a beautiful cornrow into my daughter's hair, and then another. And another. Soon, all her hair was neatly braided back in straight rows. I leaned back in awe as my husband complimented my work. My heart was bursting with pride as I considered this a major feat as a relatively new mom.

Braided hair was like a rite of passage in my community. Didn't almost every little Black girl wear her hair braided at some point during her childhood? I did, along with my three sisters. Our mother washed and styled four heads every Saturday night so our hair would look new and fresh for church the next day, and the following week.

As a child, I didn't look forward to those Saturday nights, with the tugging and pulling of my hair, and sitting on the floor between my mother's knees while she watched something on TV that I had no interest in. When I had my daughter, I wanted "hair time" to be different — a special time for mother-daughter bonding, with fewer tears and more smiles.

When I had my second daughter, Kassadi, I noticed her hair was different than Kennedi's. When I was growing up, African-American hair was generally placed in two categories — good hair or nappy hair — as if those words were antonyms. This categorization usually came from within the Black community, and measures of beauty were often based on hair texture and length. Even though my two daughters had very different hair textures, I saw no reason why they both couldn't be considered "good" hair.

I implemented an alternating schedule for styling their hair. It usually took me about two hours to complete their braided styles, so we always picked a movie that both mom and daughter wanted to watch. That made the time go faster and took their mind off the discomfort they might have felt during the process. If styling took longer than expected and the movie was over, whining and complaining would soon follow.

I lovingly cared for their hair, using products and styling techniques to ensure it was healthy and strong. I was determined to be the one to define beauty in my household. Because African-American hair is so versatile, I was able to style each of them uniquely, giving them a hairdo that complemented their facial features, hair texture and length. After I finished, I would gush and tell my daughters how beautiful they looked.

I truly cherished our hair time together. I painstakingly washed, detangled, and styled their hair, knowing they would see it in their reflection each day as they looked in the mirror. Their hair was my art canvas, and I wanted to create a masterpiece. It was important to me that they liked what they saw, as I knew their self-image would follow them into their teenage and adult years. I would always hold my breath as they looked into the mirror, watching them stare at their reflections and wait for a smile and verbal approval.

I rarely did their hair the same way, not just because they had different textures and lengths, but more importantly, I didn't want them to compare styles or think that one looked better than the other. As they grew older, my daughters would send me pictures of styles they wanted, some of which looked complicated. Most of the time they came out well, but there were a few disasters.

My daughters are now teenagers. They no longer need me to wash their hair. My older daughter taught herself how to braid, and occasionally tries out new styles. I only get the honor of braiding or twisting her hair a couple of times a year. My younger daughter decided to loc her hair, so that was yet another styling technique that I had to learn.

I still do her locs regularly (sometimes referred to as dreadlocks), and occasionally watch videos to learn new ways to style them. When I look at the finished product, I'm still amazed that I was able to create such a work of art to complement Kassadi's beauty.

I'm often asked why I don't just pay someone to do their hair, instead of spending so much time doing it myself. I always felt privileged to have the ability to do their hair. I knew every section, the areas that were always tangled, and the curve of their heads. This was always a labor of love for me, and I've never regretted the time I've spent on their hair.

One day they will be off to college and then living their own lives. I pray that they have daughters of their own so they can define and create beauty for my grandchildren. I hope they find their own way to ensure "hair time" is their own unique experience of spending quality time together and bonding while tending to one of the most important physical features of a Black female, regardless of age — her crown.

But if not, they can bring them over to Grandmom's house. I'm sure these fingers will still be able to work their magic.

— Tonya May Avent —

60

Destined to Teach

They say to serve is to love.
I think to serve is to heal, too.
~Viola Davis

I don't know exactly how it started. All I know is my grand-mother would bring pencils and carbon paper home from her job. They were being thrown away at work, but they still had some use left in them. I would take the pencils and carbon paper and use them to create worksheets for my two brothers and three cousins. By the age of six, I was their teacher every weekend. I created their work (mainly math), and I taught them how to do it.

I should have known that I had the heart of a teacher in me, but I didn't because in real life I was not treated well at school. I lived in the west end of the city, but I was bussed to the far south end for elementary school. There were no Black teachers. My white teachers made me feel inferior.

For example, I was ostracized when I did not memorize my multiplication table. Well, I didn't want to memorize multiplication. I wanted to understand it.

Then, I was expected to write in cursive just like the handwriting book. Who does that? I knew that everyone's handwriting should be unique, so in my mind, I didn't feel a need to copy someone else's handwriting.

My wish to do things differently led to me repeating fourth grade. The following school year, I had a desire to learn to play the flute, so

I went to the music room. The music teacher began to examine each person's tongue, teeth, and lips. Then, he told us what instrument to play. Based on my anatomy (possibly my full lips), I was directed to play the clarinet. But I had fallen in love with the melodious sound of the flute. My mother sacrificed and purchased the clarinet but the desire to play an instrument quickly waned.

Skip ahead to middle school. There, I was a compliant student for the most part. I was frequently on the honor roll, and often finished my work ahead of others, so I was allowed to go to the special education classroom to help teach students. This, again, sparked my desire to become an educator.

That spark soon died out, though. The last straw was when the assistant principal pulled me and several other Black students into his office after a food fight in the cafeteria. I was not involved in it, but I was presumed guilty. He said, "Well, you all, excuse the expression, acted like a bunch of niggas in there today." Although I didn't really understand, at the time, why it felt like a theft of my soul, I knew that I wouldn't become a teacher.

I was admitted into Central High School's first magnet program, and I chose computer technology as my area of in-depth study. Although my only Black teacher at Central was my gym teacher, my experiences there were positive. When I graduated from Central with a four-year academic scholarship, I still did not know what I wanted to do. I began taking general classes in college, and eventually decided to major in humanities. Actually, I think an advisor looked at my transcript and determined that humanities seemed to be an area of interest. During the majority of my college time, I worked at a daycare because I wanted to be with my sons, and then, I went into banking.

After I earned my MBA, it was hard to find work, and anyway my sons were school age and I wanted to stay home to take care of them. But my household income didn't give me such options. In order to be on the same schedule with them, I decided to take a job as a substitute teacher. It wasn't too many days after this decision that a sixth grader picked me up and moved me out of the way, so that he could cut class. My husband was livid and wanted me to quit, but I became a regular sub at one of the most challenging schools in the district.

The students called me names and rejected me, but I knew why they were putting up those walls. So many teachers had left them that they didn't want to embrace a teacher who would then abandon them. These at-risk students, with their promise, reignited my long-lost desire to become an educator.

I went back to school and obtained the necessary credentials to become a teacher. I stayed at the lowest achieving schools because those students needed quality teachers. I loved those students as if I had given birth to them.

One day, some superintendents from another district were doing walkthroughs, and one of them stopped me to say, "Your class is an oasis in the middle of chaos." Still today, those words make me proud of my students.

It is almost two decades later, and I am still trying to be the best teacher for every student whose life I touch, especially for those students who may need to see just one teacher who looks like them.

— Kimberly Mucker-Johnson —

61

White Dolls Need Not Apply

It's time to write our own story.
~Misty Copeland

"Come! Let me comb that picky hair of yours!" That stopped me dead in my tracks. I watched from afar as my partner's niece wrangled the Afro on my daughter's Black Barbie into a high puff. She was not gentle; this was an arduous task she was performing.

I assumed this was a reenactment of her own hair combing adventures at home. The venom in the words stung. I was rendered speechless. I just sat there for a while watching her and my daughter play with my daughter's dolls.

"My dolls have pretty hair," she said. "It's straight!"

At six, it's likely that she did not see the irony of her statements. The doll's hair she was struggling to style looked exactly like her own. It was soft and pillowy, Afro-textured hair.

This was just one more validation of the choice I had made for my own daughter years prior. All her dolls were Black with curly or kinky textured hair. This was not happenstance, it was by design — intentional, fever-pitched parental design.

Long before my daughter was born, I decided that her room would be adorned with dolls, art, and storybooks filled with little brown faces that looked like hers. I put everyone in our village on notice that there'd be no white dolls or books with white characters. This was a bone of contention between my partner and I as the baby's due date drew near.

You see, growing up in a predominantly Black and brown society here in Trinidad, he did not see the need to reassure our unborn child of who she was in every inch of our home. This, to him, was a uniquely American mindset and despite my dual citizenship, I was clearly the insolent Black American in this scenario.

If I'm honest, I wore that — insolence — as a badge of honor because my gut, my experience, my having grown up in a white society had taught me how to keenly assess spaces and places for equitable representation. I noticed while browsing in local bookstores that I'd see only one or two children's books that had Black characters in even a supporting role. I noticed that we imported children's programming from America and the U.K. — where there are documented histories of ignoring Black lived experience. *Sesame Street* would not be enough to prepare my little Black girl for the world.

I found Black girl renderings on Etsy and framed them, handmade Black baby dolls, and Black Barbies. I ordered every book I could find with Black protagonists. This was part of my new-mom prep alongside sterilizing bottles, birthing class, and picking baby clothes.

It was just one more thing to be checked off on my list. I don't think I ever wondered if any of the white moms I knew ever had to consciously or intentionally make sure that their kids' spaces validated their existence. I just knew what had to be done for my child.

On a visit to my midwife, we got to talking about my baby prep and I told her about my rule and how I'd been stocking up on art, books, and toys that represented my unborn daughter.

My midwife turned to me and said "Good! That's what you should be doing." She went on to say that the one thing her daughter — now a young woman in her early twenties — thanked her for was providing an environment that validated her beauty. She too had surrounded her daughter with art, books, and toys that echoed her Blackness.

One day, toward the end of my pregnancy, my partner came home looking a bit shell-shocked and said something to the effect of

"I get it now."

He then told me about a co-worker whose child admitted to hating her skin and her hair, to wanting to be lighter and have "better hair." She was five years old.

Her mother was caught off-guard and scrambling to find ways to validate her beauty.

After that day, we never debated my methods again. Our daughter will be five in a few months.

It hasn't always been easy. Not everyone in our village has understood our stance and therefore it has been an uphill battle.

One of my daughter's aunties went so far as to purchase a Disney Princess doll with blond hair and blue eyes and give it to my daughter for Christmas one year. Needless to say, it was discarded. I was livid. It felt like a slap in the face.

And then there are the teachers at preschool who give out *Frozen* stickers and coloring books as prizes when the kids do well. They even watch Disney princess movies in aftercare. I don't have the luxury of discarding or shielding her from it all. Sometimes, it can feel like an all-out assault on my parenting, but then I remember that this is why I have curated our home to reflect my daughter's beauty. The outside world is filled with examples of beauty and favor that do not include her.

I've still needed to have heart-to-hearts about why she doesn't need hair like Elsa's because she has beautiful hair of her own. I've had to reinforce the visuals, books, and toys that surround her, by being an example of a Black woman with natural hair who embraces my natural beauty. I have even authored a series of children's books that are based on her.

Her dad and I split all parenting duties fifty-fifty at our house. He can't really comb her hair, but he does wash and detangle it. He will sit with us and take out her braids or sit with her for hours playing with her Black Barbies.

He regularly tells us we are beautiful and he is extremely affectionate. Girls of all races need that reassurance from their fathers, but I'd be remiss if I didn't acknowledge that deep down there is something that makes my heart smile when I see a Black father doing that for his daughter. Perhaps, it's because it is something that is rarely seen or acknowledged in mainstream media, even in predominantly Black and brown societies.

Dolls have never been my thing, but my baby loves them. They have provided an invaluable opportunity for me to teach her how to love herself, care for her hair, and be a fanciful Black girl. She knows that blackness comes in many shades, hair textures, cultures, and shapes, and that they are all beautiful.

I expected this would be an uphill battle, but I wonder how much more painful or difficult it might be for my baby girl had I not taken my Black-dolls-only stance.

— Melissa A. Matthews —

62

A Love Letter to My Unborn Black Daughter

*There's always something to suggest that you'll
never be who you wanted to be. Your choice
is to take it or keep on moving.*
~Phylicia Rashad

I t is difficult to imagine that my life has led me to this point because, honestly, I was not supposed to make it this far. And unfortunately, darling, neither are you.

By the time we meet, I will have earned my law degree from Georgetown University Law Center and joined the ranks of the most educated group in the country, Black women. At the same time, I will have invited you into the same world where Black girls are criminalized, under protected, and overlooked in schools.

Thoughts of what can happen to you during school hours when I am not there to physically, emotionally and psychologically protect you keep me up at night. Black girls represent sixteen percent of the female student population, but nearly one-third of all girls referred to law enforcement and more than one-third of all school-based arrests.

Like Salecia Johnson, at six years old, you may throw a tantrum during story time and be physically restrained in handcuffs to "calm you down" because your teacher is trained to call the police instead of de-escalating situations in the classroom. At ten years old, you may overhear your dad and me arguing and are unable to focus in class the next day, which agitates your teacher who gives you detention for being withdrawn. Or like Kiera Wilmot, at sixteen years old your interest in science may lead you to conduct a science experiment that results in a small explosion and, even though no one is hurt, felony charges.

What frightens me most is that your teachers may not take an interest in your educational aspirations, passions and general wellbeing. Research has shown that Black girls' attachment and sense of belonging in school can be undermined if their achievements are undervalued. Unfortunately, as a Black girl you may get less attention than your male counterparts early in your educational career because you are perceived as more socially mature or self-reliant.

I solemnly swear to encourage, support and assist you in realizing each and every one of your dreams, from being a fairy princess to one of the few Black women to argue before the Supreme Court of the United States. However, there is no doubt in my mind that your teachers' support of your dreams and aspirations are as equally, if not more, important as the support you receive from me and your dad.

There is no doubt in my mind that my life would have turned out differently had Mr. Gillenwater and Mr. Post not shown interest in me as a student and a person. What is unfortunate is that it took eleven years of schooling in the New York City public-school system to finally be exposed to teachers who had a passion for teaching and genuinely cared about their students.

I pray that I have the wisdom and insight necessary to weed out all the potential issues with teacher-to-student engagement through all the research I complete, interviews I conduct, and schools I visit when your dad and I choose a school for you.

I want to be perfectly clear. I am not saying any of this to scare you. I am telling you this out of love. Your grandmother came to this country from Jamaica in the West Indies with nothing other than a middle-school education and all the hope in the world that your aunts and I would have better educational opportunities. However, the research I presented to you here suggests that educational opportunities are not equally accessible to Black girls.

And as for you, sweetheart, I request that you help me show the world how beautiful and magical you truly are. Because only then will the world be able to see you for all that you are and can be.

— Taifha Natalee Alexander —

I Am Not the Nanny

*In your life, if you're lucky enough, you are born
during a moment in time when the world
is ready for the change you're bringing.*
~Jacqueline Woodson

There she was again. The mirror in the women's section of the store reflected the blond middle-aged white woman I was actively avoiding. She was lurking at the end of the aisle, pacing the floor and glancing from side to side in search of her quarry. Ignoring the approaching saleswoman, I pushed my cart around quickly and ducked out of sight behind a display. When the woman stopped to speak with the salesclerk, I breathed a sigh of relief.

Barely a half-hour earlier in another part of the store, Baby Girl had been sleeping in her car seat, which I had placed in our cart. Strands of light gold hair were peeking out from around her furry pink and white hat when this same white woman first approached us.

"Oh, she looks just like a little doll, She's beautiful." gushed the woman. She was short and plump, weighed down with double strands of pearls, and smelled of Chanel No. 5.

"Thank you," I said and continued down the store aisle to finish grocery shopping.

The woman moved to block our path and I quickly responded by positioning myself between her and my sleeping child. The woman started to step aside and then quickly moved to sneak a feel of Baby

Girl's hair. "Oh, it's smooth and soft, just like mine."

Once more I moved between her and my cart. "Don't. Touch. Her." I glared at the woman and pushed the cart in the opposite direction when the commotion woke up the baby and she stared up at me with sleepy eyes.

"Oh, her eyes are blue just like mine. She has blond hair and blue eyes just like me. She's my baby. Yes, she's my baby."

I sped off in the opposite direction at a pace that was fast enough to get us out of there and yet not so fast as to imply that I was fleeing the scene of a crime. And that is how we ended up looking at women's clothing instead of shopping for groceries.

From my hiding place, it seemed the woman had left the clothing area. I took several deep breaths. Should I try to finish shopping? I only had a few more items to get and I didn't relish another shopping trip that week. I pushed the cart back into the grocery section and bent down by the shelf, looking for peaches. Suddenly there was the smell of Chanel No. 5 and a familiar voice. I stiffened as I heard her insistent plea.

"Let me see her. Let me just hold her," she said with outstretched arms.

I rose to a standing position and placed myself between the woman and my cart.

"My baby, she could be my baby. I lost my baby. She looked just like that baby!"

She pointed at Baby Girl, who by this time had decided to stretch and wake up. Oh, please stay asleep I thought, but instead she yawned and opened her eyes and gazed at me with a little smile.

My thoughts drifted to her father, a pale white man from Europe, and how I expected my genes would dominate my husband's and that we would have a caramel-colored baby. Instead, we had a beautiful pink baby who we loved dearly. My mama said Baby Girl took after her high yellow relations. Who knew those recessive genes would win the gene pool lottery?

"She could be my baby," I heard the woman wailing. Warning lights started flashing in my head. Quickly I made my way toward the escalator. The woman was following us, muttering about that Black woman with a baby in the cart. Now she was saying, "That's my nanny with my baby."

We needed to get away from her. My mind began to work overtime. Two scenarios came to mind.

I envisioned the security officers approaching me and telling me to hand over the child, demanding proof that I was her mother. What proof did I have? Would he take the ravings of a crazed and lonely white woman over the protestations of a Black woman? I saw my child ripped from my arms.

Or I could take defensive action and ask a salesperson to call security because this woman was harassing us. Would they also be put off by the fact that my daughter's complexion and coloring were so light? I realized how vulnerable we were. This crazy white woman had the power to interrupt our lives and put my daughter at risk because she judged my daughter's appearance to be more white than Black.

I made my way along the aisle closest to the wall, heading toward the elevator. Darting out of the aisle, I pressed the "Down" button, then dashed back and waited with Baby Girl in the cart. We could check out on the bottom floor. But as I turned around I saw the blond woman coming into the aisle.

She was too close. The last thing I needed was for this delusional woman to get in the elevator with us and play the "She's the nanny" card with the security guards. Lord knows I had gone through this before and it was tiresome when strangers assumed that I was the nanny of my own child.

I picked up my daughter and her car seat, abandoned the cart, and pounded down the stairs. On the bottom floor we exited the stairwell and I saw the blond woman at the top of the second-floor escalator, surveying the store and clutching my abandoned cart by her side.

We slipped out the side door and into the parking lot. Baby Girl miraculously went back to sleep, totally unaware of the dangerous situation we had just escaped.

The next day I applied for a passport for us, one with my daughter and me together in the photo. I got official proof from the United States government that Baby Girl is my child and I am her parent — proof that I am not the nanny.

— Cora Cooper —

The Jig Is Up

We all think there is a formula; as long as we
love our children, that's really the only solid
thing I know that works across the board.
~Jada Pinkett Smith

"**B**ut I want it loooong," my four-year-old whined, rubbing her tiny hand across the two coily puffs in her hair. I pinched the bridge of my nose in frustration.

"You're wearing it like this," I proclaimed. "I'm tired and still have to wash my own. It's bedtime anyway."

It was wash night: the evening in a Black household carefully scheduled to get through the lengthy process of washing, conditioning and styling our hair for the days ahead. We had made it to the styling portion of our evening, and as any Black mother and daughter can attest, wash night can be a stressful ordeal when opinions clash and skill is limited. My daughter frowned as I tied a silk scarf around her hair to keep it neat for the morning.

"I just want it to be like yours," she pouted.

It's hard raising young girls. They are bombarded with messages of who they should be and what they should look like from the moment the first seedling of self-acknowledgement begins to sprout. What the world perceives to be beautiful versus what isn't seeps in like a poison far earlier than I realized before becoming a mother.

"I don't like my short, puffy hair. Will it be like yours when I'm big?" she asked. I peered over the top of her head at my reflection in the bathroom mirror, seeing my smooth strands spilling across my shoulders, the product of blow dryers and flat irons.

"I don't know sweetie. Everyone has different hair. If everyone looked the same, wouldn't that be boring? I love your hair just the way it is." It broke my heart to see her saddened by the beautifully kinky curls that sprouted from her head.

In bits and pieces over my lifetime, I had been conditioned to associate the straightened version of my hair with professionalism and beauty. No one ever said it outright. The education was constant and subtle, punctuated by the harsh moments that burn into our memories. I remembered the feeling when a white playmate told me her mother said we couldn't be friends because I was Black. I grew up with books and movies where the princesses were fair with long golden hair, but I didn't realize how that contributed to the way I saw myself.

By the time I was an adult, for every job interview and every occasion of merit, my knee-jerk reaction was to ensure I'd have enough time to freshly straighten my hair. Working in corporate America continued to tether me to the subconscious notion that the texture of my hair was somehow an extension of my suitability for my position. I frequently saw the differences in the way that Black women were regarded depending on where they fell in a range of "More Black" to "Less Black" and it seemed I had begun to act accordingly. And yet, I believed I loved my Blackness. My skin. My soul. My body. My hair.

I thought I loved all the pieces of me, but I found myself actively participating in the narrative that my Blackness needed to be altered to be acceptable. How could I teach my daughter to love herself and every characteristic of who she was when I was not exhibiting that to her in my own actions?

I wanted her to embrace her short, kinky mane. I hoped she'd be proud of her deep brown skin. I wanted her to appreciate her full lips and every Black feature she possesses as a part of loving herself completely. After putting her to bed, I stepped into the shower with the image of her downtrodden face flashing through my mind. The realization had dawned on me that straightening my own hair to feel like I belonged when I walked into the office wasn't doing my own daughter any favors.

I let the water run over my hair. The mass thickened. The strands twisted and coiled. I recalled a corporate team-building event I had opted out of merely because I didn't want my work team to see my wet, kinky hair after the planned rafting activity at Harpers Ferry. I felt ashamed of the way I had been complicit in continuing the devaluation of Black women by acting as if the texture of my hair was an ugly mark to be hidden away from the delicate sensibilities of my white counterparts.

We all know I'm Black! What was I trying to hide? It was ridiculous, and there's no better place to start with change than in one's own home. I'd start showing her the versatility of our hair and the beauty of our natural crown by embracing it for myself in any setting. I could only expect her to know how to love herself if I showed her how it's done.

I woke the next morning excited. I fluffed my natural, tightly coiled mane into neat order before heading to wake my little muse. Her eyes fluttered open as recognition of a new day sunk in and she regarded me curiously.

"Now we're just like each other," I declared and kissed her small nose. She smiled at me and patted my hair. Moments later, as my own mother arrived to spend the day with her granddaughter, she took in the state of my hair.

"Aren't you going to work today?"

"I am," I answered lightly.

She looked puzzled. "With your hair like… that?"

I smiled, "The jig is up, Mom. They know I'm Black."

— Rachel R. Perkins —

Interracial Adoption for Beginners

I really don't think life is about the I-could-have-beens.
Life is only about the I-tried-to-do. I don't mind
the failure but I can't imagine that
I'd forgive myself if I didn't try.
~Nikki Giovanni

I was raised in Boulder, Colorado in its granola munching hey-day of hippiedom. I was adopted at seven, by a white mother and a Black father. The story I want to tell you, though, is not of then but of now.

I was a scared, scrawny little Black girl then. Now I'm all grown up, a singer/songwriter poet, living in Italy. In love with an Italian pianist Marco and with my life as an artist.

Just before it became impossible in early 2020, Marco and I were in Austria performing. We took an extra three days to turn it into a work-cation and were enjoying those glorious mountains. At dinner before a show one evening, a family of three were seated next to us. They were two white Italian parents with their little adopted Belgian girl, who is Black. I had my usual conflict when coming across such a combination. As I sat making polite conversation with these pleasant people while simultaneously trying to engage the child, on the inside, I started fussing. My brain went into overdrive, wondering how quickly I could bring up my own experiences without being rude, or if I even

Raising Our Children | 239

ought to.

My left brain said reasonably, *It's pretty damn nosy*, because Lefty just speaks that way, *and downright rude to poke your nose with no invitation into the lives of a family you've just met.*

Then the right brain just had to have her say with, *But, don't you owe it to that baby girl?* and coyly continued with, *You know you should give her parents at least some food for thought; what they then do with it is outta your hands.*

Lefty calmly interjected, *None of your business, besides which, we live in different times now; there is all kinds of information available. Interracial adoptions are taken much more seriously today; progress has been made in assuring children are properly looked after.*

Righty responded, *Ha! Sure! Just look at her hair, doesn't look to me like the mother is availing herself of all that available information! Humph!*

Lefty admonished, *Those butterfly clips she's put in it are tots adorbs, just stop it.*

Righty said, *Yes, but uh, have you seen HER HAIR?*

As is so often the case when debating with myself, the result was... I choked, said nothing. Lefty rejoiced, yet I felt like it was unresolved, like I hadn't done my best.

But what are you going to do? Five minutes after meeting them, stress the importance of these parents' extra responsibility since they chose to adopt a child of color? Encourage them in a few seconds to be vigilant in helping that beautiful baby to know, to really know, she is gorgeous? Prevail upon them to celebrate her color and compel them to instill a fierce, robust, and stable sense of self? Warn them of the arduous road ahead raising a Black girl in a predominately white society? Slip them the link to the article "What White Parents Should Know About Adopting Black Children" on Huffington Post, perhaps? Or the Times' thoughtful commentary on the subject?

Er, no — out of the question. Dinner was over, and it was time to begin. So off we went to the piano in the bar.

The girl and her family came to listen, along with a remarkable number of other children. I can't remember another gig, ever, with so many teeny tykes in attendance. Mom and her baby started dancing gleefully, and before you knew it, the floor was covered with little kids flinging their bodies about. Marco and I had a wonderful time entertaining them, both sides of my brain were in agreement this was the best thing to do. Encourage joy, spread love, be present, give freely and joyfully of everything I had to offer.

Despite the happiness of that moment, the all-around pleasure of that performance, my brain was back at it the second we were done.

Righty, sobbing inconsolably, admonished Lefty, telling her a teachable moment was within her grasp, and she just let it disappear, like the unfeeling, relentlessly logical creature she is.

After a restless night spent thinking of what acceptable method I might have used to broach the topic with her parents…what that might have looked like, Marco said, "Give them a CD and your e-mail at breakfast."

I stared at him, "Oh... uh, oh yeah... There's an idea!"

So simple. Why had I been fretting so?

As soon as we stepped into the dining room, we met the family on their way out. I handed over the CD, told the mother I was adopted and that my adoptive mother is white. She was lovely, thanking me profusely, telling me she had been told to seek out successful transracial adoptees.

(*Yikes!* screamed Righty inside. *I dunno how successful our adoption was, but yeah whatever…* while Lefty hissed, *Don't listen to Righty; keep smiling!*)

She continued, telling me that the hair was standing up on her arms (which would be the Italian equivalent of the hairs on the back of your neck...) because of our fortuitous encounter and said she had many questions. My relief was absolute while Lefty and Righty both cheered.

— Lisa Marie Simmons —

Unworthy

Your self-worth is determined by you. You don't have to
depend on someone telling you who you are.
~Beyoncé Knowles

The parent who raised me gave me the nickname "Ugly." I learned in my teens that I was in fact quite pretty, but the damage had been done. I had moved around in the world believing that not only was I tragically unattractive, but I also felt unloved and unworthy. One parent wanted absolutely nothing to do with me and the other never called me smart, beautiful, or used any of the other positive words that most parents heap on their children on a regular basis.

Once I was old enough for hormones to kick in, I did what anyone in my situation would do — I went searching for love. I became boy crazy. If any guy said anything to me, like "hi" or "your friend's cute — hook me up," I swooned. I did everything in my power to make him believe I was exactly what he wanted and needed in his life. This usually didn't work. So, I took it a step further and began to have sex, hoping that if I did this he (any he) would have no choice but to love me. My heart was broken many times.

I'm not sure if you're aware of this, but one of the consequences of sex is *gasp* pregnancy. That's in fact what happened to me. I literally sat up in bed one December morning and said to myself, "Oh my God, I'm pregnant." I just somehow knew. I was a senior in high school and terrified out of my mind. I called the father and he... well let me put it this way. The term "ghosting" was created just for me. Not only did he change his phone number and pager number, the dude MOVED! Yeah, that lonely feeling I'd always felt was just multiplied by a trillion.

So… I hid it. I hid my pregnancy from everyone except a very close friend. I went to doctor's appointments alone. I went to ultrasounds and heard a heartbeat all alone. I had morning, afternoon, and evening sickness every day throughout the entire pregnancy — alone. At about six and a half months, I couldn't hide my belly anymore, so I told my parent, who immediately scheduled an abortion and took me to a clinic to begin the process, even though I was entirely too far along. (That was another reason I chose to hide the pregnancy).

On a bright and sunny August morning, I realized that the feeling of needing to go to the bathroom was, in fact, labor. A friend drove me to the hospital and my son arrived quickly. Two days later, I left the hospital in one direction and my son was carried out in the other. You see, I just knew I'd be worthless as a mother. I mean, my parents didn't like me, boys used me, and the baby's father was absent. How was I, someone with the ink on my high school diploma still wet, going to be a good parent?

I decided that adoption would be the best thing for my son. During my pregnancy, I secretly went to an adoption agency and found an amazing couple to be the parents for my child. They were worthy even if I was not. They were smart and fun and gorgeous, and they loved each other. That's the type of household my child deserved.

My son is now twenty years old. While I know that adoption is one of the best decisions I've ever made in my life, there's also a piece of me that wonders. Had I just realized back then what I know now — then maybe things could have been different. Now I know how worthy I am, how worthy I have always been. Maybe that knowledge could have been enough all those years ago.

— Courtney Tierra —

Taking Care of Me

Strong Black Woman

I am a strong woman with or without
this other person, with or without this job,
and with or without these tight pants.
~Queen Latifah

My skin is Black,
My body is female
I am told I am pretty but more often I am told; "You are strong"
In a world filled with misogyny and racism that I face,
How does that bring birth to a strong Black woman in my place?
They say "support is not for you"
You are not seen as vulnerable, you are not seen as weak.
Yet, the scars on my left arm would refute that fact.
They tell a story that is both sad and gory.
A story no one wants to be told.
I'm not ashamed, I lived it,
I was broken, now that part of me is lifted.
I know underneath the mangled skin and the grief that was been
    buried deep within,
Another me emerged,
I call her by her name, I call her… Brave.
She's forever tattooed on my left hand, to show the world how I am
    now made.
Yet when my strength falters, like it often does these days,
My scars awake from their sleepy slumber,

They call me to sing, they tempt me to dance,
To join them once again in the misery of their pain
I do not succumb, as I know how it will end… it will all be in vain.
I make a daily resolve.
I cannot choose that path again,
I will not let that be my fate.
I question myself, maybe I am really strong?
To keep on going when you want to give in,
To persist, to endure as you know that there is a shining light within.
Yet I know being strong does not get you much support,
The people remind me
"You're a strong Black woman, that is what you have become.
What good is support to you, if you were born strong?"
As you know how to make it, you know you can take it.
I reply,
"Yet sometimes I need support and I know that wanting it doesn't
    make me wrong.
It makes me human and that is what really enables me to be STRONG."

— Rebecca Olayinka —

Naturally Me

Nothing natural can be wholly unworthy.
~Anna Julia Cooper

At the age of thirty I was taking a weight-loss pill which made me lose about twenty pounds in two weeks. I was looking good but not feeling good. Then the weight began to come back although I was still taking the pills. I became very ill and my grandmother told me to go to the doctor; she suspected that I had a thyroid issue.

I went to my doctor and told him I was feeling very drained and lethargic. I'd gained those twenty pounds back, plus some more. I told him that my grandmother told me to get my thyroid tested. I was sent to the endocrinologist who confirmed that I had hypothyroidism.

To this day, I have no idea how my grandmother knew, because hypothyroidism doesn't run in my family. I had never heard of such a thing. The endocrinologist explained to me that my thyroid was underactive and that could be the cause of my weight gain. I began taking Levothyroxine and as months went by, I began to experience all the symptoms of hypothyroidism: fatigue, sensitivity to cold, dry skin, unexplained weight gain, and hair loss.

One evening I washed and dried my hair. Then, as I combed it, my hair began to shed by the handful. I remember sitting on the floor crying. I took pride in my hair. Growing up I had long, thick, shoulder length hair. I wore my hair long until the 1980s when the rap group Salt-N-Pepa came out. I begged my mother to cut my hair in an asymmetrical bob so that I could look like them.

I lost hair from all over my head but especially on the top where I had a huge bald spot. I was devastated. How could I go out in public with a bald spot? What would people say? I was in a panic because my friend was having her birthday bash that evening and I was supposed to attend. I called her and with tears in my eyes told her I wouldn't be able to attend her party.

Tonya wasn't having it. She showed up at my house about an hour later and took me to the wig store. I purchased the first of what would become many wigs of all styles and colors. From short hair to long weave to braids — you name it, I had it.

There were times when I wore a different wig every day depending on my mood. I bought wigs for birthdays and special occasions. Yes, I have a Thanksgiving and a Christmas wig. If I bought a new outfit, I had to buy a new wig too. I truly became obsessed with wearing wigs.

One day I was on social media taking a quiz, and one of the questions asked whose hair I wished I had. My answer was nobody's, because I already had every kind of hair.

My hair has a mind of its own; sometimes it grows back and sometimes it doesn't. In the summer of 2010, my hair was growing and my bald spot was filling in nicely. I decided to wear a short natural hairstyle for the entire summer. I received so many compliments. Actually, I received more compliments about my natural look than I did when I wore my wigs.

Years went by and I kept up my routine of wearing wigs when it was cold and wearing my natural hair in the summer. Then, in September of 2020, I was looking for a wig and couldn't seem to find anything that satisfied my taste. I went to the three beauty supply stores that I normally frequent but none of them had what I was looking for.

That evening I was whining to my husband about it and he looked at me, smiled and said, "Baby, just wear your hair, I like your natural hair."

I looked at him for a moment, thought about what he said.

"Are you telling me that you like my hair better than the wigs?" I asked.

"I like them both, but I don't like to see you stressing out about wigs. You have a million wigs in the closet; pick one of those."

I opened the closet door and began to rummage through my wigs. Some I'd worn multiple times, some only once. I had no idea how many wigs I actually owned.

That night I was on the phone with a friend and told her about my wig quandary and she said, "Cassie I love your natural look, I get to see how beautiful you are."

She went on to tell me that when you wear wigs, you can be anybody, but when you're natural you have no choice but to be yourself.

After we ended the call, I began to think about what she'd said.

Was I hiding behind my wig?

Was I trying to be someone else?

I decided to go natural.

The next day I contacted my cousin who owns a barbershop and set an appointment to get my hair cut. I got my cut and stopped by the beauty supply store to purchase some dye — just to add a little color to my hair.

It feels good to get up each day and not worry about what hair to wear. I feel free, and I can honestly say that I don't miss wearing those wigs. I'm embracing my natural hair and I absolutely love it!

— CaSandra McLaughlin —

An Abundance of Love

We all must live our lives always feeling,
always thinking the moment has arrived.
~Tracy Chapman

The year 2015 was quite special for me, a multi-hyphenate artist. What is a multi-hyphenate artist? That's someone who works in all different sectors of the arts.

That year, I was accepted into the Lincoln Center Directors Lab, an intensive program for directors, writers, and others involved in the performing arts. It was exciting; for three weeks our days were filled with practical application, panels, seminars, interviews, live theatre and lots of networking.

At the end of the three weeks, I was exhausted but filled with ideas. On our last day, June 27th, the stage manager for our group asked me what I was doing for the summer. Please understand, during the three weeks of the program we could not work, which meant I was now abundant in knowledge yet bereft financially. I literally brought my lunch every day and kept breakfast to a minimum.

So back to the stage manager. I told her I didn't know but I would love to visit my bestie Cherish who had moved to Los Angeles earlier that year to pursue our vocation. I didn't have the money to get myself from New York to LA, so I said I would leave it in God's hands.

One of the things that brought Cherish and me together is our faith. She is a preacher's kid, and my mother kept her Bible awfully close. Cherish is a heterosexual Christian, and I am a Bisexual queer

Christian. I am fortunate that I came to my sexuality with truly little fanfare. I came out in college and my announcement was met with… "Good for you girl but we suspected already!"

The next day, on June 28th, I went to the Village to watch the pride parade. As I was viewing the parade, I wasn't getting the same love I normally get from the drag queens. I was worried I had lost my "Black girl mojo" which was a little disappointing. Normally at Pride there is ton of swag given out, from key chains, to socks, to LOTS of condoms, bags, T-shirts.

After more than two decades of viewing these parades, I felt no inclination to jump up for the items that were thrown into the crowd. I just stood back and let the younger, more eager participants try to catch the swag.

As the faith portion of the parade was coming down West 3rd Street, I saw churches of every denomination, synagogues, temples, etc. They were all showing their love and acceptance for the LGBTQ community. I was about to take some photos and post this affirmation on Facebook and Instagram — to let people know that God's love is for everybody. Just as this thought crossed my mind, a man came up to me and said, "Do you have a Twitter account?"

I replied "Of course, who doesn't."

He said "Take a picture with me, post it and I will give you a round-trip ticket anywhere in the U.S." I was stunned for a moment; all I can remember was mumbling "God bless you" over and over.

It was all of five minutes and I had a roundtrip ticket on Jet Blue (ironically one of my favorite airlines). I was amazed that just the day before I had voiced my wish and placed it in God's hands. This stands as one of my favorite and most powerful testimonies.

— Mia Y. Anderson —

The Day I Got Pulled Over by a Cop for No Reason

Challenges are gifts that force us to search
for a new center of gravity. Don't fight them.
Just find a new way to stand.
~Oprah Winfrey

I laughed and talked with my friend as I drove southwest of Philadelphia in my red Hyundai Scoupe. Flashing lights in my rearview mirror gave me pause. I checked my speedometer. Under the speed limit. I panicked, thinking perhaps I'd exceeded it while we were chatting. I flicked on my right signal and pulled over.

I was nervous as I watched the white cop approaching the car. With two Black females sitting in the front seat, what could go wrong? I placed both hands on the steering wheel and asked my friend to stay quiet and not make any sudden moves.

When the cop stood outside my door, I waited for him to speak. "Is your vehicle registered?"

"Yes, sir."

"I didn't see the sticker on your windshield."

"It's right there, sir," I said, gesturing with my head toward the lower left corner in front of me.

He took a step and bent forward, removing his shades to check out the sticker prominently displayed on the windshield. "Must have been the tinted glass," he said.

I wanted so much to say, "Or perhaps the super dark shades you're wearing, sir," but I didn't dare.

He asked for my license and registration, which I promptly gave to him. I waited while he checked everything out on his computer. A few minutes later, he strolled back to my car and handed my registration and license back to me. "Everything checks out," he said and continued to stand next to my door.

I waited in vain for the "You're free to go." My gut clenched. I didn't want my friend and me to be another statistic. Two attractive women of color shackled and hauled off.

"Do you need anything else, sir?" I asked.

He shook his head but kept standing there.

At a loss for what else to do, I invited him to church. With a nervous smile, he declined, backed away from the car, and sent us on our way.

I should have invited him to church sooner. It would have saved me all the anxiety coursing through my body.

— Cassandra Ulrich —

The Young and the Rested

It is so liberating to really know what I want,
what truly makes me happy, what I will not tolerate.
I have learned that it is no one else's job
to take care of me but me.
~Beyoncé Knowles

Napping is new to me. I'm usually the mover, the shaker, the restless soul who can't stay still. Now I retreat to my room for midday naps and press pause on the COVID-19 and Black Lives Matter posts that infiltrate my newsfeed. If I'm going to make it through a global health crisis and achieve social justice for all, I need my rest. Rest is a form of resistance and I am a well-rested revolutionary ready to take on the world.

I used to stuff my thumbs into the crowded pockets of my jeans to keep them from twiddling. I'd think of errands to run, like picking up odds and ends from the dollar store, or take on new hobbies like letter writing and yoga — anything to help me escape the boredom of a blank agenda.

Then, the pandemic hit, followed by store closures and shelter-in-place orders that forced me to spend more time with myself. I thought of creative things to do — virtual karaoke parties with family and friends, scavenger hunts in the garden, photography assignments — but they were quickly replaced by meaningless meetings and Zoom calls as I navigated the waters of working from home.

When my self-assigned lunch break finally arrives, I look for the two-year-old first. "You want to go to the park?" I ask eagerly, competing with Elmo and Big Bird for his attention.

"Not today, Mommy!" he responds with such clarity. But I refuse to be deterred and move on to the seven-year-old. "How about a walk in the park?" I ask enthusiastically.

"I'm busy," she responds curtly as she retreats to designing clothes out of old T-shirts for her dolls. Finally, I approach my husband, my last chance for lunchtime companionship. He is finishing up a work proposal as I softly massage his shoulders.

"Huh?" he responds, barely looking up from the dim glow of his laptop.

"Wanna go on a romantic walk around the neighborhood?" I whisper in my most seductive afternoon voice.

"And who's going to watch the kids?" he retorts, deflating my blissful balloon of daily adventures.

"I'm taking a nap!" I announce and stomp straight into the bedroom. I snuggle under the covers fully clothed and frustrated. The curve of my growing belly pushes against my pillow. The kids knock on the door not even five minutes into my nap, making false claims of starvation and bloody boo-boos. Luckily, I remember to lock the door to protect myself from their terrorist attacks. "Tell Daddy!" I bellow groggily.

My eyes close and I float between dreams of day cruises to the Bahamas and starring as the lead actress in a daytime soap opera. It's like binge watching my favorite TV shows, but far less strain on the eyes.

My alarm pressures me to wake up at the twenty-minute mark. At first, I resist and then I give in, remembering the series of scheduled meetings and deadlines before the end of my work-at-home day. The only escape I have besides grocery store runs and the occasional take-out order are my trips to the doctor. My OB/GYN reports that I am now in the second trimester and stresses the importance of eating balanced meals and getting daily exercise. "It's recommended that you get at least thirty minutes of exercise a day. Is this something you have been doing?" she asks as if reading from a script.

"Yes," I lie with a smile. It's hard for me to lie without smiling, but luckily, she can't see it from behind my mask.

"Great to hear. What is your preferred form of exercise?"

"Na... natal... prenatal yoga."

I correct my course quickly. Sometimes it's hard to commit to a lie. I mean it isn't a complete lie since I did do yoga throughout my last two pregnancies. This one was just proving to be different. A surprise baby during a pandemic doesn't always allow for business as usual. I greet the alien figure on my sonogram photo and pack it neatly into my purse, making my way back into the world. I would usually treat myself to ice cream or a Target run, but this time I just want to go home. Not to take a walk or join an imaginary yoga class, but to engage in my new favorite form of exercise. My nap lasts two solid hours and I cherish every moment.

— Aja Moore-Ramos —

71

Traveling Abroad to Heal Within

I don't like to gamble, but if there's one thing
I'm willing to bet on, it's myself.
~Beyoncé Knowles

In the Summer of 2016, I decided to run off to Italy. I was a thirty-five-year-old overworked, divorced mother of two who needed a break and had PTO to burn. I loved my life then and I love my life now, but I was spiritually and emotionally depleted. I often went through my journey feeling as though my purpose was solely tied to what I supported: my kids and my work. There was nothing left for and tied to just me.

So, I made the decision that while my kids were visiting their dad for the summer, I would spend a week in Italy in communion with myself and God; it would be the ultimate "Eat, Pray, Love" experience.

I had no real plans outside of catching my favorite diva on stage, and I had no travel companion. I was going to live "Una Bella Vita" and take in the lessons that were meant for me.

Well, "Una Bella Vita" started off real ugly. I missed my flight. I lost a day and had to spend the night sulking in Chicago after spending a vital organ's worth on a new ticket. I had come too far not to get to Italy even though I was only ninety miles from my house. Going back home was not an option.

The very next day I boarded my flight and landed in Milan.

Apparently, I am directionally challenged because I ended up in Casarile, which is twenty-three miles and a $99 cab ride from the airport. The hotel was dirt cheap, but it was clean and the staff treated me as if they weren't quite sure whether I was Beyoncé or not, so it felt very five-star. The staff would randomly play Whitney's version of "The Star-Spangled Banner" wherever I happened to be. Besides being masters of flattery, they were warm, hospitable and always eager to feed the frazzled American.

For two days I did nothing but lie around my quaint room, sleep, sunbathe, and talk with complete strangers who would ask to join me in whatever mundane thing I might be doing. It was truly beautiful.

It was this first part of the trip when I got *Lezione* (Lesson) #1: You don't have to be busy to be entertained! God will place you where and with whom you need to be to get what you need!

On day three it was time to meet my best friend who was coming from Spain where she lived at the time. We were attending the Beyoncé concert. My friend was to meet me at the concert, but her flight was late so we only got to see the end together and most of our time was spent being in awe that the two little Black girls who met in sixth grade and grew up in 53206 were finally traveling like they dreamed of. Beyoncé was wonderful by the way.

The next day my friend went back home and I was solo again. I finally decided to go into Milan and visit Duomo di Milano. This fourteenth-century cathedral was captivating. I've never been Catholic a day in my life, but I felt so at peace in the sanctuary. I took the liberty of praying at the altars, and I lit candles to the saints and put some of that holy water on my forehead; I could use all the help I could get. I laid all the burdens and concerns of my heart on those altars. Jesus and the Saints had their work cut out for them.

When I got up I knew my prayers had been answered because it felt like the weight had been lifted from me. That's when I received *Lezione* #2: God dwells everywhere, knows no language barriers, and has no borders.

After that I knew it was time for me to move on. I chose to go to Verona for no other reason than it was an hour train ride and was where *Romeo and Juliet* was set. I didn't have great expectations for the little town and planned it to be a day trip. Of all the things I'd been wrong about in Italy this was the biggest. The moment I set foot there, I knew I was "home" for the rest of my stay.

Forget Rome; forget coliseums; forget air conditioning! I had cobblestoned streets, swanky shops, operas, plays, and *osterias* on every corner. I had found my utopia! I had to quickly find lodging and decide how I'd fill my time.

It was just my luck that I arrived when *Romeo and Juliet* was being performed every night on stage. It was an experience I'll never forget. I sat there with my self-taught, broken Italian and was able to follow the story. I shared laughs with my adopted "Nonna" who insisted that I join her and her family. I sat under the moonlight in the outdoor, mountainside theater and enjoyed a classic love story while being served light snacks.

That revealed *Lezione #3*: Things don't always happen as planned, but they always happen as they should!

I spent the next two days wandering around the tiny town, eating everything that wasn't nailed down, and sitting on Ponte Pietra bridge over the Adige river. It made me focus on what I was grateful for instead of all that I had to worry about. For the time being I was going to enjoy being in a foreign land where no one knew who I was or what I did for a living. All that mattered was that I was open to experience what I'd never known before. I ate, prayed, and thought hard about love.

That's when I got the greatest lesson of all, *Lezione #4*: You owe it to yourself to honor your heart and your soul, not just your obligations and roles. Give yourself the space and opportunity wherever you may be in the world to just be. You deserve it. You'll emerge better for it.

— Sharonda Hunter —

72

Finding Peace and Comfort in My Closet

If you don't like something, change it.
If you can't change it, change your attitude.
~Maya Angelou

I have a space in my home where I go to reflect, meditate and pray. It is my calming place where I can be sure to find a few moments of me time without interruption.

This space is my closet. Growing up, my dad would refer to this space as a prayer closet; the place where I could connect with myself and the Creator. My closet is where I have found peace in the midst of my personal storms.

One hot summer day, I sat cross-legged in the middle of my closet positioned right underneath the vent, allowing the air to blow down on me. I sat there panting and trembling from an anxiety attack I experienced shortly after having a conversation with someone who told me she wanted our relationship to go to the next level. She was in love with me. What should have been an emotionally gratifying conversation that ended in celebration, turned out for me to be absolutely terrifying.

I was not ready. I thought I was, but at that moment I realized that I was far from it. I was still healing from another relationship and needed more time. My heart wanted to love and feel loved again, but I was afraid. I lived in fear of being hurt and steered away from getting too close to anyone who could possibly break my heart.

As I sat there calming myself down, I began to think of all of the affirmations I would say whenever I struggled with fear or doubt. I started to visualize all the little Post-it notes my dear sister wrote and placed throughout my home, reminding me who I was and what I was capable of. I realized that in order for me to move forward in my life and to no longer be bound by fear in any relationship, I needed to reconcile and recover from my past relationship. I needed to uncover it and to stop burying it so deep within.

Why was I so afraid? My last relationship was riddled with emotional and verbal abuse. He would do and say the most horrific things that would leave me feeling broken and confused. According to him, I was stupid, unattractive, a horrible parent, and was just not good enough. He would end mostly every assault with "I knew I never should have married you... you were the biggest mistake I ever made; I want a divorce!"

To the world, we were a strong couple. We went out socially, entertained in our home and had developed a very positive reputation in our neighborhood. We looked happy. But I was lying; I wanted to be happy and tried to appear as though I was in hopes that it would actually happen.

It took me years to leave, but when I did, I immediately began to fill my time with everything but dealing with the abuse I had endured. Not only was I ashamed of admitting that I had been the victim of abuse, I was also in denial that I had suffered greatly as a result of that abuse. I desperately wanted to believe that I was unaffected by his words and lack of emotion. But as I sat there in my closet, I realized that it was because of those words that I felt like I was not good enough and un-deserving of love.

Needless to say, I got out of that closet, stood up tall and called a therapist. I began to work on me. I needed to restore myself and heal from the hurt and damage that I had endured. More importantly, I needed to acknowledge what placed me in a destructive relationship and uncover the childhood experiences that influenced my behavior.

The closet continues to be the space where I seek solace in times of distress and confusion. It is also the place where I celebrate the accomplishments made in my own journey. It provides me with a sense of safety when I need a moment of self-reflection. I am grateful for this space and the moments of clarity that I have received because of it. It has allowed me to engage with myself and to engage in my healing. It is because of this space that I am where I am today.

I did the work, and I am continuing to work on me. The same person who expressed love for me, that caused me to retreat into my closet is also still standing by my side. It is that love that has caused me to experience what true love feels like, what true love looks like. Not just outwardly but within.

I am strong, I am enough, and I deserve to be loved in a healthy way.

—TAH—

Who Is Listening?

Don't wait around for other people
to be happy for you. Any happiness
you get you've got to make yourself.
~Alice Walker

One Sunday in 2018, my pastor played a video clip of an amazing young musician with God-given talents who attempted suicide after a breakup with his girlfriend. Although he'd shot himself, he didn't pass right away. His sister and parents were able to minister to him, and he repented before he died.

Shortly after that, I learned a teenage nephew of one of our church members committed suicide. Months later, another family in our congregation suffered the same blow.

What was going on?

After that third loss, my pastor made an appeal from the pulpit. "If any of you are struggling with depression, come to the altar for prayer." A hush swept across the sanctuary. "Come on. Don't worry about who is watching you. This is about you! Let's pray, saints, for your brothers and sisters."

The number of members who responded surprised me. Some who I thought appeared to have it all together, with no cares in the world, were struggling.

I petitioned Jesus, along with the congregation, for them to receive deliverance, strength to overcome, and restoration. The magnitude of the moment left me grieving for my brothers- and sisters-in Christ.

Witnessing this was groundbreaking. Our Black churches and our Black families don't acknowledge depression as an illness. We usually brush it off. We say, "You need rest!" or, "Treat yourself!" or, "Go on a vacation. You'll be fine!"

How many times have we uttered those sentiments without much thought?

My pastor wouldn't let the subject go another Sunday. This time, he called the demon out. "If anyone has been contemplating suicide," he said, "I want you to come to the altar for prayer."

What was God telling him?

The urgency in his appeal was concerning. More members flocked to the front, including a good friend of mine. I'll call him "Clyde."

I blinked, holding my breath and wondering if I were dreaming. With Clyde at the altar, it was becoming real. He was my husband's high school friend, a groomsman in our wedding, and redeemed by the Blood of Jesus.

Every Sunday, Clyde and his wife sat in the pew behind my family. How could it be? Clyde was a quiet man, yet strong in the Lord. Depression — okay… maybe — but suicide? It never crossed my mind — until it did.

For real? Suicide? Shock didn't begin to describe my emotions. Had Clyde been trying to speak to us about his woes with his job and finances, and we just weren't listening?

I recalled one night after Bible class when Clyde sought prayer from the pastor. Was he planning his death then? I saw that he was wiping away tears that night and alerted my husband to check on him. Clyde just said he was stressed. "My truck keeps breaking down. All the overtime on the job, money is tight… It's too much to handle."

Too much too handle.

Not knowing the hopelessness Clyde was experiencing, Kerry did his best to encourage him, especially after Elder Johnson prayed for him. Clyde was back on track — or so we thought.

One Sunday, while Kerry and I were driving back from out of town, we listened to the church broadcast. The message was powerful.

God commanded His people to stretch out on faith. Our cousin, who is also a member, said the spirit that day was high and Clyde rejoiced like they had never seen before.

We thought this was a good sign.

Not long after that day, one of our assistant pastors called Kerry, my husband, with news about Clyde's suicide attempt.

Two days before Clyde's suicide, he was rushed to the hospital for an apparent stroke. The stress had mimicked the symptoms — loss of movement and speech. By the time I visited him that evening he could talk and move again, unlike when my husband visited him earlier. His wife was in the room with him, along with a nurse who sat quietly nearby, tapping on her computer.

While we praised the Lord he didn't suffer a stroke, Clyde had the oddest expression, almost disappointment.

We learned a hospital psychiatrist assigned a nurse to his room after asking Clyde a series of questions, including, "Are you having any thoughts of suicide?"

"Yes," Clyde had answered.

"Do you know how you're going to do it?" he asked in a clinical tone, lacking compassion, according to his wife. What kind of question was that?

The physician followed up and felt Clyde wasn't at risk. The discharge papers were signed because Clyde — a quiet man — didn't seem in mental distress.

Was the doctor listening to Clyde?

Two days later, Clyde hung himself in his garage. His wife remembered later that Clyde had been in there building or banging on something. She didn't think anything of it. As Clyde lay in the ER not responding, we prayed and let our thoughts drift: What did we miss?

Devastated, family, friends, and the church couldn't equate the man rejoicing in the aisle less than a month earlier with the one who killed himself.

Kerry said God knew Clyde was sick, because he would never have taken his own life otherwise.

Ephesians 6:10 came to mind, "Be strong in the Lord, and in the power of His might," so why were Christians committing suicide? I cried out to the Lord. If Clyde, who we thought was strong in the Lord, couldn't make it, where was our hope?

God removed the anxiety about my own salvation but gave me no comfort about losing Clyde.

I replayed my husband's statement and wondered, Were all suicide victims sick?

What defines sick? When I suffered a seizure, decades earlier, one medication, Zonegran caused me to experience suicidal actions — not thoughts — but an aggressive and physical urge to jump out of my skin, which would have led me out of a second-floor window. Praise God, the doctor weaned me off that drug, but what if... what if my husband hadn't listened when I said, "Something is wrong with me. I'm freaking out."

It's by God's grace and will I didn't yield to the medication's urges. I wonder if medication would have saved Clyde's life. In hindsight, a prescription from the doctor and prayer from the pastor might have helped him overcome his darkness.

Suicide, depression, and mental illness victims are speaking within our churches, families, and Black communities. We must stop what we're doing, look, and more importantly, listen.

— Pat Simmons —

74

The Power of "No"

The most common way people give up their power is
by thinking they don't have any.
~Alice Walker

As a child, I couldn't wait to be grown. I saw "getting to twenty-one" as freedom, unbounded by anybody's rules. Life would be a wonderful marathon of doing whatever I wanted, when I wanted, and how I wanted.

The reality? Winter, spring, summer, fall. No matter what the weather, I had to get up five days a week and go to work. The big reward was supposed to be payday, but payday often meant paying bills with only a few dollars left for a new pair of shoes or something special for dinner.

A few things changed in my life around the age of forty: my 20/20 vision began to slip, my low blood pressure began to rise, and I discovered the power of "No." What is the power of "No?" It's turning down requests that require you to "go that extra mile," requests that are just not a good fit for you. The first time I said "no" I was shocked, and so was the other person, who'd never heard me say "no" before. But guess what? We survived it.

Time passed and I found myself saying "no" to someone else, a big someone — my mainstream publisher. I turned down the deal they offered me and walked away with no book contract, publishing house or agent in sight. It was a crazy move in some folk's eyes, but my spirit said it was the only move to make. "No" had now become a part of my vocabulary.

It was scary and it left me with deep anxiety. Some of my fellow authors marveled at my bravery. After all, this was a major publishing house and I wasn't that big of an author yet. I hadn't gotten close to making the New York Times Bestsellers list. But I left anyway, and a year later, I had a new agent, a new publishing house, a twenty-eight-city book tour and a six-figure book deal. For me, that illustrated the power of "No."

Since that time I've used the power of "No" often. I've abandoned lucrative business arrangements because I realized proceeding wasn't in my best interest. I've turned down business contracts for the same reason. At the end of the day, "No" protects me and I've come to respect its call when I feel it. But the most interesting example happened just recently. I told myself "no."

I'm an independent author now and there are times when I work seven days a week, hardly taking any time off. I had a major literary event coming up and I had been working hard on it for months. One day something said: *Don't do any work today.* Of course, my business mind immediately ran down the list of things that needed to be done and balked at the very idea. But that voice inside me was insistent. *Take some time off. No work today. No work tomorrow and no work the next day.* Three days of no work? That was crazy.

I was saying "no" to myself and it felt very strange. But the little voice wouldn't go away, so I yielded, striking a bargain where I would compromise by relaxing for a few hours in front of the TV. I popped some popcorn, eased into my recliner and watched a few shows. Afterward, I got back on my computer and tried to do some work. I couldn't.

The next day it was the same thing—I didn't feel like working at all, so I didn't. By day three I knew exactly what I was doing, I was giving myself a "stay-cation"—away from work. I enjoyed it fully, but more important, I was giving my mind, body and spirit a much needed and long overdue break. I was recharging myself.

I didn't understand that part until after five days of no work, I got back to work and it flowed real smooth. Things that had perplexed me suddenly made all the sense in the world. Glitches that I was having with my website totally disappeared, and uploading my video on YouTube was a piece of cake. Not only that, new and fresh ideas started coming to me in a steady stream and the writing for my next book was effortless. It was then that I knew that as a result of walking away from work, telling my own self "no," the heavens had opened on all my creative fronts.

— Margaret Johnson-Hodge —

75

Naturally, Powerfully Me

It was when I realized I needed to stop trying to be somebody else and be myself, I actually started to own, accept and love what I had.
~Tracee Ellis Ross

O h. My. Goodness. They are right. I AM beautiful. These words rang through my head one sunny day in June as I looked in the mirror after successfully styling my curly hair. It was 2013, and at this point I'd had natural hair for about six months.

I always felt a sense of dread when looking in the mirror, so I usually approached the task tentatively. I have many less than fond memories of sitting in a chair as my mom wrestled and tugged my coarse, thick hair into four neat braids with barrettes. That style seemed to follow me throughout grade school, until the sixth grade. The struggle of maintaining my natural hair weighed heavily on me, and my mom's hands, and always made me feel that something about me was... off.

Shortly before getting my sixth-grade class picture taken, my uncle walked in the house and said to my mom, "One of my friends is a hair stylist; she said she can do her hair." I watched as she sat in silence for a few moments, looking both relieved and concerned.

After what seemed like hours, my mom said, "Okay, let's go ahead and try it." She turned to me and said, "Cassie, you're going to get a relaxer. Remember when I used to get my hair straightened? That's what we're going to do for you. This will make your hair a lot easier to manage!" Easier to manage? That sounded more than good to me! My mom proceeded to tell me more about what to expect, and we set an appointment to see my uncle's friend at the salon.

After sitting in that salon chair, my hair was no longer a hassle, unless you count having to make appointments every few weeks to maintain the relaxer before, God forbid my hair got "nappy" again. Taking care of my hair did get a bit easier; however, having a new look did not change how I felt about myself. It did nothing to build my confidence. I was still the same self-conscious little girl, now with straight hair (and bangs, ugh). My lack of self-confidence stuck with me as I transitioned into adolescence and young adulthood.

After ten years, I decided I had enough of "the creamy crack," keeping up with hair appointments, and finding someone I could trust to relax my hair. I wondered what it would be like to let my hair be… free. I sat at my desk in my college dorm thinking about how I would look with natural hair. Would I be able to pull it off? Could I commit to learning a whole new way of doing my hair from YouTube?

I graduated from college in May 2011 — and that was also the last month I got my hair relaxed, as attempting to go natural right before my graduation day felt a bit risky. I transitioned back to my natural curls slowly instead of doing the "big chop." After about thirteen months of transitioning — buying hair products I didn't know how to use and wrestling with my combination of straight and curly hair, I started to feel that I made the wrong decision. I almost went to get my hair relaxed again, but decided to stick it out. It all made sense when I finally cut the relaxed ends off my new curly hair.

After I unraveled the two-strand twists in my natural hair that day in June, I watched the curls frame my chubby cheeks and felt like I was meeting someone new for the first time. Before that fateful moment, I never saw this young woman who looked like she had just experienced the best day of her life. Indeed, I was witnessing the birth of a new version of myself in front of that mirror.

I stood there for another ten minutes, turning my head from left to right, up and down. Years of doubt and low self-esteem melted away as I looked in that mirror. I had felt more confidence in those ten minutes than I had in all my twenty-three years of life. I lifted my head high, stuck my chest out, and walked out of my graduate dorm room like a goddess floating on a cloud.

Returning to my natural hair texture helped me get more acquainted with my personal power and strengths. Making the decision to go natural may not be a big deal to some, but it has been a monumental change for me; it changed my view of how I fit in this world. After that summer day, I found myself speaking up a little louder. I stood a little taller. I smiled a little wider. I really started to believe in myself.

Since that day, I have continued to build my confidence and encourage myself to live in my truth, and I continue using my natural hair as an outlet for self-expression and creativity as unapologetically as possible. I've become more creative with my natural hair; I experiment with hairstyles I never thought I would wear.

In that moment in the mirror, I found who I wanted to be, twenty-four hours a day, seven days a week. I am incredibly grateful that I had the opportunity to welcome my true self into the world that day.

— Cassandra L. Tavaras —

76

Confronting My Rapist

Each time a woman stands up for herself,
without knowing it possibly, without claiming it,
she stands up for all women.
~Maya Angelou

I don't know why I dreamed about R the first week of quarantine. But I did. I woke up in the early hours of the morning filled with rage. Apparently, many of us were having vivid dreams as we lived in collective fear and anxiety and asked, "What's next?"

R was the man who sexually assaulted me the summer before, a situation I hadn't actively or fully acknowledged. But my sleeping mind seemed to want me to wake up and do something. It screamed at me to protect us.

I'd been in Paris, France for forty-eight hours when R and I met up on one of the city's many bridges for our date. This would be my first date in the city of love. I was there on a month-long work trip. R was Scottish and had been living there for a few months. I got off the bus and spotted him approaching with a grin. He had milky pale skin, dark hair, and light brown eyes.

We built an instant rapport and bonded over our shared religious background and the fact we were both middle children and English speakers navigating French language and culture. Our attraction to each other was palpable as we sidled up to a Canada-themed bar (yes, this is a thing) near the Seine River. We spent the next few hours flirting and drinking white wine and then gin and tonics. He loved those. I'd never tried one before. I told him I wasn't a heavy drinker and he regaled me with tales of drinking culture in Scotland and encouraged me to have a bit more. I did.

He layered on the compliments all night, telling me how gorgeous my skin was and asking me questions about my experiences being Black in the U.S. I'd later come to realize he was fetishizing me (and would continue to do so all night) but my inexperience with dating made me eager to receive any and all compliments from a man like R.

I stumbled out of the bar with his arm around my shoulder. He took my bag and supported me as I walked. Suddenly, his hand reached for my breast. I took it and held it in my hand instead. We kissed in front of Notre Dame and he suggested we ride Lime scooters around the city.

"Which way do you want to go?" R asked, pointing to either side of the bridge. I pointed back and he said, "Perfect, that's the way to mine."

I asked him then if he just wanted to hook up with me, because if so, I wasn't interested. He kept saying no each time I asked but continued to grab at my breasts and my butt as we went in search of our scooter.

When we got to his room, he threw me on the bed. I'd already told him on our elevator ride up I didn't want to do anything beyond making out. He seemed to have other plans, playfully taking off my clothes and sticking his hands in places I didn't want them. I put my clothes back on and tried to get off the bed. This cycle went on for what felt like hours until finally I asked if he had a condom. I was ovulating and trying to hide my fear of what could happen if he grew angry at my continued resistance.

I stopped resisting. Then we cuddled. Then he asked for more sex. I asked him to order me an Uber. I left. I was dissociating so I don't remember exactly what happened, which makes me think if I was asked to testify in a court, I'd be seen as unreliable, a liar. Some days, I still believe I am those things because I don't remember — and because I went to see him again.

He called me the next day to say he was smitten with me and

wanted to see me again for a movie and a sleepover at his apartment. I agreed. I thought maybe he'd be my first boyfriend.

Our sleepover turned out to be far from what I'd imagined. He'd been out partying the night before and was hungover from taking half an ecstasy pill. He fetishized me and distanced himself emotionally. He gave me a yellow T-shirt to wear and sang the Wiz Khalifa song "Black and Yellow" as I put it on. I fell asleep next to him, shivering as he hogged the whole blanket and a bedside fan blew on me. I left in the morning feeling anxious and used. Most of all, I felt disappointed I didn't get the control back I'd unknowingly been grasping for.

Now, more than half a year later, I had the dream. I sat up in bed and let the words flow in a fit of concentrated rage into the WhatsApp text box. I told him coercion is not consent, that he fetishized my Blackness and sexually assaulted me. I told him how he used our shared religious beliefs to gain my trust and manipulate me. I told him how he made me feel like a whore, like I was nothing. I told him I went to see him again because I liked him and wanted to believe he was a good person — it was easier than believing something bad had happened to me. I told him he better not treat another woman this way again. And I closed with a very satisfying "good fucking riddance."

I wasn't looking for a response when I confronted him, but I got one. It was everything I'd feared it would be — some variation of "I'm sorry you feel that way" said without taking any responsibility for what he'd done to me.

My boyfriend at the time asked me if I'd reported it, said no, tried to leave or fight him off. No. Yes. Yes. No. You can't report something you're in denial about. I know now the answers to these questions don't matter. In the aftermath, I learned about the concept of "tend and befriend" from Julie Peters' book *Want: 8 Steps to Recovering Desire, Passion, and Pleasure After Sexual Assault*. It's a stress response common in female mammals.

"Overwhelmingly, sexualized violence happens with someone the survivor already knows and trusts — someone they already see as an ally," Julie said in an interview with Bridgitte Jackson-Buckley. "So when they are being attacked, rather than fight or flee, they might try to calm down their perpetrator, placate him, and give him whatever he wants so the violence doesn't escalate… Tend and befriend helps us understand that because we stopped struggling, participated, and/or checked out so that we could get it over with, we survived. Whatever we did to get through it, we survived. That's not shameful, it's powerful."

Looking at my story through this lens, I've managed to move out of shame and into self-love and compassion. I did what I needed to do in the moment to survive and I dissociated from and numbed the experience in the months following until my mind was ready to process it. Like Julie says, "that's pretty powerful."

Dr. Nicole LePera shared an Instagram post recently which stated, "Anger is a calling to honor the needs that have gone ignored, unmet and unseen."

Working with an embodiment coach has taught me we store our trauma in the body and when we repress memories or refuse to process things, the trauma is still there and will keep resurfacing until we face it. I'm thankful to be at a place in my journey where I can recognize the pain and anger sitting in my body and, instead of ignoring it, I know how to honor and release it. It is no longer my burden to carry. That belongs to him now.

My great-great-grandmother was also raped by a white man in the early years of the twentieth century. She was ovulating. She got pregnant. Her family disowned her. Her husband left her. She was alone until she gave birth to my great-grandma. I've been thinking of her often over the last few weeks as our country begins to process the white supremacy that has ravaged us for centuries.

Though I don't know the details of her rape, I can't help but see the similarities in our attacks. We were both ovulating. We were fetishized and abused by white men in racist societies that told them they have a right to Black bodies. I can't help but think she must've been in his room with me, protecting my body in a way she wasn't able to her own as I asked for a condom. I can't help but think she was with me during the months I dissociated from the pain with alcohol, clubbing, and a new boyfriend. And she was there with me the morning I woke up in a fit of rage and stood up for myself to the man who thought it was okay to violate me.

I feel her with me as I write this. She is proud.

—Alexa Goins—

77

Tracks

My belief is that communication is the best way
to create strong relationships.
~Jada Pinkett Smith

owels and swimsuits crowd the table upstairs, waiting. I stand in front of my laptop watching lines spread across the southern United States. There is no mistaking it. We will drive into the path of Hurricane Irma on our trip.

"So, we're just supposed to die trying to make the beach trip this year?" I say to my husband, who is pacing the living room.

Kevin shrugs. "I think we'll be fine. I've been keeping an eye on it."

I nod and then shrink into the couch to hide the weather updates that are scrolling across my phone screen. Kevin is determined for us to make the annual trip to Virginia Beach to see his mother Lucy. I am determined not to get us killed. There's also the other part of me that is tired of this tradition and wants to start making our own.

We usually pack our luggage each autumn, fly to Virginia, then caravan to the beach with Lucy and Kevin's sister and her family. Kevin and I punctuate the drive with stories about our lives before we met. I often recall my eight-year-old-self trying to hear my parents' whispers from the back seat as we drove to our vacation spots. I want to travel the open road with my own children the way my parents shared those experiences with me. I want my children to giggle as they wonder about their parents' secrets. When I share this with Kevin, he smiles and says, "I want that too."

During the trips to Virginia Beach, our unrest typically begins in small ways. We leave the caravan to follow winding paths. We slow down to discuss groves and cemeteries. We veer off course to Colonial Williamsburg, delighting in the hours-long retreat. We sample Americana.

This year, we want to drive to the beach instead of flying. The road trip serves as ballast to our independence. However, with the looming hurricane, Kevin and I look to Irma to provide an excuse for us to go our own way. The news is a swell of misery detailing the aftermath of Hurricane Harvey and predicting the devastation of Irma.

We imagine ourselves braving swirling winds and rising flood-waters for the sake of a family vacation. Neither of us can stand that pressure weighing on our conscience. Neither of us wants to endanger our daughter Halaina. We wait for co-workers and friends to shout us down. We hope our mothers will wring their hands, their voices shaking as they call, begging us to cancel our trip. No one gives us what we want — permission to say no.

This hurricane, powerful and unforgiving, uproots our desires and throws them right at our feet. We want to be respectful of Lucy and all that she has done for us. Yet, we have outgrown the beach tradition.

We pray (and I fast) for clarity. The days drift by and the devastation grows before we find our resolution. We cannot cast away the beach tradition altogether, but we also have to set boundaries. We agree to journey to Virginia Beach, stopping in Alabama to visit my grandaunts. While there we will assess the weather ahead to determine if we should continue or travel to a different destination — just the three of us. We also decide that we should visit the beach every other year, reserving the off years for our own travels.

We load my SUV with luggage and emergency supplies, then journey a day behind Irma's path. When the road ahead is clear, we drive through the Natchez Trace, a parkway lacquered in shades of green, to Virginia. We are the last to arrive at After Ours, our beach house for the week.

On the third day of our stay, the Atlantic climbs closer to the house — another hurricane churns toward us. Lucy, Halaina, and I take our last walk on the beach before the storm hits. We are three generations signaling the start of a new era. I lift Halaina up, her toes leaping over cord grass that carpets the shore. Our steps deepen; our heads bend lower as we march. The wind snatches our words.

Lucy clears her throat. "Do you think you guys will come back next year, or not? We have to reserve a house in the next day or two and we want a good one like this."

I pause and search for the right way to say what must be said. Lucy did not give birth to me, but she is still my mother. She sends cards to thank me for raising her granddaughter and for the way I love her son. She sends gifts that anticipate our needs and to say she is thinking of us. She deserves kindness and not rebellion.

Yet, as my own daughter bucks in my arms and stretches away from me so that she can walk on her own, I know that independence is inevitable. My life is changing in ways that I am just beginning to understand. It is leading me on a course that does not mirror my mother-in-law's. Lucy's life is changing too. She is holding onto familiarity with her traditions, but these fine grains of sand are slipping through her fingers. We need to let go of her hand and find a path that fits us all the best.

I inhale and blink back the tides cresting my eyes. "No, we probably won't. We want to do something on our own next year."

Lucy smiles and nods her head. "I get it," she says. "Don't worry about it." She gazes down at Halaina and smiles. "Come on! Let Grandma hold you so Mommy can get a break."

Her response surprises me. I expected Lucy to be upset or to challenge me. I know now that this is the way of mothers — to lead their children as they forge the way ahead, to know when to let their children go so that they may lead instead.

As we crest the dunes, I gaze at our footprints trailing to and from the beach, mine crossing over Lucy's, Halaina's prints in the middle of mine. Realization crashes over me as I study our tracks. The present parallels the past; the future merges with the present. Lucy has been this way before with her mother — leaving behind old traditions to create her own and merging them when needed. I will take what I need to create new traditions with Halaina. My daughter will do the same until our paths diverge and we go our own way. Until then, we will all enjoy the intersection.

I am thankful for the traditions that have been given to us. I will take the parts that I love and in turn replicate them to delight future generations. By watching the steps of my mother-in-law, I've also learned how to be gracious when my own children approach me one day and announce that they want to go their own way. I will tell them that we cannot leave behind the traditions that laid the way for us. We cannot abandon what formed us. But we can take pieces of the past and make them like new.

— DW McKinney —

Sisters, Friends

Seen and Heard

For there is always light, if only we're brave enough
to see it. If only we're brave enough to be it.
~Amanda Gorman
The Hill We Climb

in my world
little Black girls
are born
to be seen
and heard
to defy docility
and look up
and see themselves
in the face of the moon
in the mystery, magic and
mysticism of night
to climb trees and
break glass ceilings
to open doors and
walk in light
and not shadows
because little Black girls
are l i g h t
little Black girls
are l i g h t

Black girls
are l i g h t
girls are l i g h t
are l i g h t
l i g h t

—Liseli A. Fitzpatrick—

The Same Block

I know now that what is tragic isn't the moment.
It is the memory.
~Jacqueline Woodson, Another Brooklyn

I shared a love of the Beatles with a girl who lived two doors away from me on the same block of rowhouses. We were BFFs. In the late fifties, we sang to 45 records in my cool as a cucumber basement on some days, and on others, we played in her toy-filled bedroom. She had every doll there was. I dreamed that I could have her bedroom.

My parents said that she had so many toys because she had no sister or brother. She insisted that her dog, Betty, was her sister. I scoffed at this. Betty was a fat, middle-aged, mixed-breed dog like most of the dogs of our childhood. She had no specific breed identity, nothing you would recognize as being a Shepherd, a Beagle, a Pug, or a Poodle. She was not the sort of dog with a ruff you'd want to bury your face in, except that I remember that my friend often did.

I look back and think how cruel it was of me to ridicule this animal who was so important to my friend. The truth was I was jealous of her dog. We had a cat and I wanted a dog.

I didn't realize that things occurred at her house that should not have — that her parents were alcoholic and her father a monster. I'd like to think the things I later found out were not happening then. Did it begin in those early years? I can't be sure. Was her mangy pal Betty her one confidante for a terrible, shameful secret? From time to time I try to recall whether I'd had any sort of suspicions of her father. I think that unappealing dog was my best friend's real bestie.

Her mother died when she was a freshman in college at Wake Forest. She went to college one year after me. I went away across the country. I started a new life. I attached myself to a whole raft of new people. I remember not having time for her. Once or twice we talked from my dorm room and I was at pains to sound older, more sophisticated. I had made myself a round, fluffy Afro in defiance of my mother and my aunt who was a hairdresser.

My friend hadn't yet taken the plunge. I knew she envied me. Though she was more yellow, more light-colored than I was, I was the brown daughter of a woman most people agreed was really good-looking. My friend wore ill-fitting glasses and was gangly. I was plump, pretty, and self-assured. I don't remember feeling this way, but I see it in photographs from that time.

Thinking back to that time, I realize I could have helped my friend. Maybe she needed to talk to me about her mother's illness. Maybe she needed to tell me about her father's intrusions. I graduated from high school on a mission to get out and embrace the world. I came back after the one year at a midwestern, mostly white, though progressive, college to the comfort, care, and creative exhilaration of Howard University. By then she'd gone off to college.

She came home after a year, too, to bury her mother. Her mother had had cancer, one of the fast-moving kinds. I can't recall a single conversation with her about this. What was wrong with me? How could I have abandoned my friend when her mother died? Young people are so thoughtless, uncaring. I was hard at work on building myself, focused on finding someone to fall in love with. Did I attend her mother's funeral? I don't recall, though I'm sure my parents did. I am ashamed to think this, but I have no recollection. Surely, I would remember.

When my friend returned home from Wake Forest to console her father following the death of her mother, she didn't return to college. Her father tied her to himself and consumed her. I've always struggled to write directly about sexual trauma, but here it is. I believe the man made his daughter his drinking buddy and sexual partner. Her parents had always been an alcoholic couple hiding behind a mask of propriety.

One night, in a drunk, my friend came to discuss her father with my father. I was away at school or maybe away in my marriage and child. He never said whether she'd been explicit or only hinted. My father knew something wasn't right but wouldn't discuss it plainly, couldn't find a way to intervene. I can't blame him for not helping my friend though. I ought to have helped her.

The "same block" is how we thought of it. We were friends by association; we grew up on the same block of rowhouses in a neighborhood of working-class strivers, mostly government workers. Her family had a large, completely detached house at the corner. They were on the lighter end of the skin-color spectrum and appeared to be the most successful of all the families on the block. They seemed typical of D.C. and the people who aspired to the middle class.

In her later years — our later years — alcoholism consumed my friend completely. After her father died, she became reclusive and eccentric and was hoodwinked out of the ownership of her parents' home. She hid in a basement apartment, and drank, and died of cancer.

My pleasantest memory of us came before the Beatles. We put on a musical variety show with my younger sister and the four boys who lived in the rowhouses between us. My older sister hung a blanket between the living room and the dining room for our curtain. The adults sat on the sofa. We used our family's upright piano. My friend made a sweeping Hollywood entrance down our staircase while singing along to "Moon River," a sappy song she loved. She made a false start because of nerves and because she had a reedy, timid voice; then she started over.

Sometimes I think back and wonder if I knew something then that I didn't realize I knew.

— Breena Clarke —

79

Quarantine Happy Hour

Surround yourself only with people
who are going to take you higher.
~Oprah Winfrey

here are six of us: Regena, Kemba, Phoebster, Daria, The Silver Fox and me. Some of us have been friends since Sharon Pratt Kelly was mayor, the rest since Jim McGreevey ran for governor of New Jersey. Regena and I have been friends since Jesse Jackson's second presidential bid.

When you're a political operative, you measure most things by candidate races. Our friendship spans many political campaigns and eventually a call higher than public service, a call to ministry. We were licensed for ministry in 2003. Regena, into the Methodist faith, and me as a Bapticostal — Baptist born, Baptist bred, when I die, I'll be Baptist dead — with Pentecostal sprinkles on top. We saw our ministry call as an extension of our public service.

During the campaign, Regena's cousin Pheobe, (Pheobster), came to live with her. She is younger — country as Cracker Barrel and grits, sweet and sassy with a ready smile. During a campaign event, Regena met Kemba, a local pastor who helped her accept the ministry call — they became besties. The Silver Fox was Kemba's friend and eventually became ours. While Kemba is reserved, The Silver Fox is rowdy like us and fit right in. She is older than us, prefers her liquor like her men — brown. We liked The Silver Fox instantly, but the jury was still out on us. Then there was Daria, a professor friend from our days in D.C. politics. A typical intellectual, all brains and beauty but no technical ability whatsoever — we call her Black Amish. Eventually if we love you, you get a nickname.

This gaggle of six women, spanning three generations decided to be friends. In the absence of life partners, we became life partners — keepers of the flames of each other's dreams. We've been through a lot together: breast cancer, depression, aging parents, break-ups with clowns who didn't deserve our tears, and family drama of every magnitude. We fuss but never to harm, always to polish and groom — like those monkeys plucking bugs off each other on the Discovery Channel. It can be uncomfortable, but you sit there, wince a little and end up better, cleaner, stronger. We see things differently and we are not shy in our expression.

We built, as the Fockers would say, a circle of trust — unshaken by anything until COVID-19. When the pandemic hit in March, it shook our lives to the core. New Jersey was a hot spot, Washington, D.C. too — we were in quarantine. About a month in, Regena called and said, "We need to do a weekly check-in. A Friday night happy hour."

Little did we know that this casually planned Zoom would turn into a lifeline as the quarantine dragged on. There was so much we didn't know. What we did know was that we needed each other.

Our first meeting was on Friday, April 3rd, and the ground rules were simple: bring dinner (optional), an adult beverage, and don't be late. We were well past polite conversation and juice boxes after a month indoors alone. We started at 7 p.m. and the laughs and chatter were instant. We talked about all the questions being asked by thinking people. Where is Wuhan City anyway? Why isn't Taiwan scared? What is the path forward? We spent part of our time on the issue that brought us together in the first place, and the rest on us.

Regena decided to move to Kentucky to help care for her mom. She was wading through family re-entry shock. Kemba is a breast cancer survivor and healing from surgery — she shared as she was comfortable. We prayed and then prayed some more. Phoebster is a gifted social worker/educator and deeply involved in her cases. They are complicated and heart-rending—vulnerable kids facing rape, neglect, addiction, failing systems.

It was a lot, but nothing that another glass of something and a tall tale from The Silver Fox couldn't handle. Laughter was good medicine and we needed lots of it. Daria, better known as Black Amish, was exhausted from lecturing or grading papers and faithfully late to the call because she could not figure out how to join the Zoom. I teased her all the time. She is brilliant, tender hearted and kind to a fault. We need more of that in the world. "What happened?" is usually how she joined the Zoom twenty minutes late.

On February 28th, my sweet Weimaraner, Gideon, died. He was friends with all the ladies. Gideon rode shotgun with Regena on a D.C. to New Jersey run. He placed his head under the hand of The Silver Fox even though she wasn't much of a dog person—until Gideon insisted. It was hard for me to be in the house alone.

"So Jill... how you doing?" The Silver Fox began our Zooms by going around the circle for a status update—her sly wisdom on full display. I don't know why she started with me. She calls me Jill aka Jill Scott. I can see the resemblance—caramel skin, big hair, big boobs—I'll go with it.

"I'm good," I began.

"Really?" she said, already knowing differently.

"Yeah." I didn't know how to say that I was lonely—so she said it.

"You miss Gideon today?" she whispered gently.

"Yes, and Daddy too. Every. Single. Day. But I'm trying to push through it."

"Why don't you try sitting with it instead? Be gentle with yourself."

"Yeah, grief has a funny way of sneaking up on you," Phoebster echoed. As we went around the circle, each of us deposited our stressors—then Daria's carryout arrived, so we ate.

"I am sick of all of it," Kemba shouted. We didn't know what "it" was, but we were sick of it too.

As the early days of the pandemic turned into a year's worth of bewildering grief and situational depression, each of us craved connection and looked forward to Friday nights. A safe place where we didn't have to be brave or certain. We could be afraid and mad as hell, until we weren't. I fell asleep on the call and these heffahs texted the pictures — mouth hanging open and all!

Quarantine Happy Hour brought levity to the day's events—whether national news or the most personal details of our lives. I had to attend my birth mom's funeral via Zoom. The Silver Fox lost her sister. Daria's son lost his job. One issue after the other but we faced them together. We watched episodes of *The Chosen*, and the documentary, *Good Trouble* in honor of our fallen elder, the Honorable John Lewis. We traded pound cake recipes (mine is the best) and begged Regena to mail us her famous dinner rolls for Thanksgiving. We figured out how to stay safe. We sent cards and gifts. We laughed until we cried. We cried until we laughed. We sat in silence when words failed us.

Can you join us? Nope. Well, Daria would let you in, but it's The Silver Fox you have to get past.

— Michele Renee Brown —

80

Dancing Around the Question

*The biggest choice for me was surrendering
the need to understand.*
~Iyanla Vanzant, Forgiveness: 21 Days to Forgive
Everyone for Everything

If you were to ask me if God is all-wise, of course I'd say yes. But if He's so smart, why can't He give me a straight answer when I pose questions about life's problems? Where's His wisdom when trying times confront me? It's stressful when I ask God a question and don't get a response. "I know I need a different job, but what should I do?" "Why is this person acting like that?" "How am I going to pay this bill?" Why can't He respond to a simple question? Doesn't He know the answer?

Then there are the weightier matters. The relationship I thought would end in marriage. It did — he married someone else. Bad news from the doctor. What about the Black man sent to prison for a crime he didn't commit? Or the man imprisoned for the crime he did commit — but when you hear his backstory — Mom died young, Dad on drugs, brother killed in a drive-by — you can understand why he broke the law after so many experiences broke his heart. God is good — yes, I believed that, but sometimes I questioned His judgment.

Yet most of the time life is good. When I'm on the dance floor, life is delightfully, deliciously good. One of my favorite things in life is hand dancing. That's the term people in Washington, D.C. use for our variety of swing dancing. My dance partner, TJ, and I were dedicated hand dancers. We'd meet up once a week on Fridays at our favorite spot, The Chateau, and dance away the week's stresses. Most evenings, we dance-dance-danced nonstop but between sets we squeezed in a bit of conversation. One night, I mentioned to him in passing that my sister, Lorraine, had just completed a course in event organizing.

"TJ is planning a party. He wants your phone number," I later told Lorraine. His request had surprised me a little, because as someone who ran his own company, he could easily assign someone on his staff to organize an event.

"Great," said Lorraine. "Have him call me."

About a week or two later I asked her about TJ's party plans. "He never called," she said. But I was pretty sure he had mentioned that they had talked. Whatever.

"Are you close to the people at your job?" TJ asked me one day out of the blue.

"I like them. We get along pretty well," I told him. "Why do you ask?"

But he grabbed my hand and led me onto the dance floor and he never got back to explaining it.

One day while chatting on the phone Lorraine asked, "Can I have Beverly's phone number?" I didn't even realize my sister remembered my neighbor from three addresses ago.

"Sure. Why do you need to call her?"

"A girl at my job knows her and wants to get in touch," Lorraine said.

That seemed peculiar but I passed the number on to her.

All through October, there were little things that she said or did that made me think, "That's odd." And come to think of it, TJ had done and said a couple of things that were off. But I shrugged it off at the time. Who could explain Black folks' behavior? God Himself did things that puzzled me. Why would people be any different?

One Friday in November, TJ said to me, "Are you dancing next week? A friend of mine is having an event here at the Chateau and I'd like to support him. Will you come?"

"Sure," I said, privately wondering what the big deal was. I came every Friday.

When the next Friday arrived, I showed up at the Chateau as I always did. TJ was there already; usually, I was first to arrive. As I settled into my seat, I spotted my former supervisor, a dignified older lady, seated across the way.

What was this devout Christian woman doing in a dance joint?

I got up to go greet her and when I got to that section of the room, "Surprise!" rang out. It was the Friday before my birthday — and this was a surprise party thrown in my honor. And boy, did they pull off the surprise. There were friends from my old jobs, former neighbors, fellow artists, Mom and Dad, and of course, all my favorite hand dancers.

And then the lightbulb switched on over my head. Now, the odd comments made by TJ and Lorraine made sense. In the middle of a dark dance floor in a dark nightclub I had an illuminating thought.

Sometimes God can't reveal to me in the moment everything that's going on. Just like TJ and Lorraine couldn't tell me about their party plans because that would have spoiled the gift.

Things that seemed wrong at the time were actually working to my benefit. People who loved me were working something out that would eventually bless me.

And that's what I now extrapolate to God. That although I can't understand why things are happening to me the way they are — especially things that seem unfair, unpleasant or even evil, I need to remember that God is managing the big picture and that ultimately He is unfolding plans meant for my good. I have to trust that the Master's plan is a wise one, even if I'm not in on it.

After all, I'm pretty sure that God is at least as smart as my sister and my dance partner.

— Joy Jones —

81

Best Trip Ever

*Yes to everything scary. Yes to everything that takes me
out of my comfort zone. Yes to everything that feels like
it might be crazy.*
~Shonda Rhimes

I t was the trip of a lifetime, so we decided to do it up. My sister, my teenager and our three friends decided to make the best of a good situation. Not only would we celebrate the original purpose of the trip, but like people raised by depression-era parents we would not waste one second of our time.

Airport. Subway. Walking the city streets after dark to the hotel, we got lost. We wandered around Washington, D.C. dragging our luggage at breakneck speed. The more we looked at the map on the phone, the faster we walked farther away from the dot.

Finally, one of us said, "We are going the wrong way." We burst out laughing as we stood on the corner of a dark street. Then another person said, "We are the Wrong Way Crew." It became a label that stuck because it would turn out to be something that we did often.

It was December of 2012 which meant Christmas was in full bloom and we wore bright Christmas sweaters under our winter coats as we stood in line for the White House tour. There were Christmas decorations all around so we asked if we could take a picture outside before we went in. It just so happened that on this day, they allowed cameras inside, too, a break from their normal rules! We posed in front of beautiful Christmas trees in every room, each with its own theme.

We photographed the magnificent portraits of former Presidents. We were so snap happy, we even got a photo of the teenager among us who got stuck with carrying all our puffy coats.

More importantly we walked through history in a space that looked huge on television. The moments in history became real. The ballrooms and sitting rooms now were more than words in a book.

That was not enough for us. We decided to take the Megabus to New York City to see the Christmas tree at Rockefeller Plaza. We had never been there before, so it was something that needed to be done. We are from Texas, so a little drive is nothing to us. The bus ride was great. Fresh out of the bus, we hit the New York subway, which is absolutely nothing like the Washington D.C. metro.

Weirdly, everyone in our subway car was a tourist. We looked like tourists with our maps, and we acted like tourists with our giggling. We almost lost our minds when the emergency door opened while the train was running. A man with a black cowboy hat and accordion popped through singing "Feliz Navidad," followed by a man in an orange baseball cap and a guitar, and a third guy with a bass. Not what we were expecting, but we joined in singing with them as everyone else in the car did too.

When the band tried to get off at one stop, a large scary man with a heavy chain beat it against the wall. It sounded like gunfire, and we all understood his message. This was his stop, where he panhandled, and he was not sharing. The band went through the subway car's emergency door to escape. It seemed like an eternity before the main door closed. I don't think anyone in our car breathed until it did and the train pulled out without Mr. Chain Man. Granted, there were six of us and one of him so we probably could have taken him, but we didn't know if living in the subway gave you superpowers.

It was that day my sister, teenager and friends vowed to never go into a New York subway again. We ate at Sylvia's in Harlem and walked around the 9/11 Memorial. As we headed toward Rockefeller Plaza, the crowd became so thick the police closed the streets to traffic. We are from a place where you give people space. You never get in touching range. But this crowd grew thick and once we realized that we could not see each other, we grabbed hands and formed a chain. There would be no photo of us standing in front of that tree because there was no room.

Then it was back to D.C. for the reason we came. My sister was being sworn in to the Supreme Court Bar. She would be eligible to try a case before the highest court in the land. She was nervous just standing inside the walls of this majestic building where African American lives were changed.

Sister Attorney was given two tickets to attend the actual proceedings. I got one automatically because I am her sister. I have spent my life sistering her. I deserve to enter the chamber, to see live justices, to experience this moment in her life. Her legal assistant, one of our friends, got the second ticket. One family. One work associate.

The plan was for the others to wait in the holding room until it was over. Sister Attorney left with the others being sworn in. Legal Assistant and I went inside and sat down. It was so quiet you could hear yourself move. Also, you could not help but notice the officers with the automatic weapons standing in the aisle. We sat still and quiet staring at the nine empty chairs behind the bench in front of us.

As we were waiting for this thing to start, we looked back and saw that all our friends had gotten in after all. They were sitting a few rows behind us. We were all going to see this!

My sister and others to be sworn in were brought into the room.

Our great-grandparents were sharecroppers, maids and porters. Yet a hundred years later, there stood my sister.

The justices came in and took their seats. Chief Justice Roberts, Justices Antonin Scalia, Anthony Kennedy, Clarence Thomas, Ruth Bader Ginsburg, Stephen Breyer, Samuel Alito, Sonia Sotomayor, and Elena Kagan.

This moment cemented something for our group of travelers. We knew our adventures would be life changing. We would laugh and hold onto great moments together. We continue to travel together and we have not been disappointed.

— Karen J. Anderson —

82

We Have Funerals

Faith is the first factor in a life devoted to service.
Without it, nothing is possible. With it,
nothing is impossible.
~Mary McLeod Bethune

I t was a typical Saturday in April. The ladies of the premier social and community service organization, affectionately called "The Society," were pulling up to the community center in which they had their monthly meetings every second Saturday of the month at 4 p.m. Of course, several of them had been there for an hour, greeting and gossiping with each other before the meeting, and to make sure they had prime parking nearest the building. It was the customary setting: greeters at the door, information circulating, ladies hugging and giving side cheek kisses, better known as "sugar."

Even though the women know where they are going to be seated each meeting, it's a social must to canvass the entire room and extend greetings of "Sister!" or "Lady!" with exuberance. The women of "The Society" were some of the most elite and sophisticated women in the city. Membership in this exclusive organization was considered a privilege.

It was an even greater privilege to be the president of this organization, or really, any officer, for that meant you had the respect and trust of these well-established ladies. Madame President, who'd been in charge since January, was no exception. She had been in the organization more than twenty years. She was poised, prepared, and felt confident she would lead a successful meeting. She graciously checked on the rest of the officers as they took their place on the dais at the front of the room and waited for the clock to strike 4 p.m.

Lady Matlock came in at her usual time of about seven till four. Her hair was set in rows of curls from the wash and set she had gotten at the beauty shop the day before. She didn't want the curls combed out; she always preferred that they remained gently loosened and drop on their own throughout the next few days. She had on her customary black long-sleeved suit, embellished with floral applique. She wiped the crown of her brow with her matching black lace handkerchief as she signed in at the greeters' table. Her black dress heels were in her hand, for she had already placed her black ballet slippers on her feet so that she could walk comfortably.

It had already been quite an eventful day for Lady Matlock, for she had been to an eleven o'clock funeral for a distant relative and a one o'clock funeral service for a church member. However, for Lady Matlock, this was a typical Saturday routine. As she took her seat, she greeted several ladies and told them she was going to be leaving the meeting a little early to attend a banquet later that evening.

Madame President called the meeting to order and greeted all the ladies as she did every month. She gave her report and review of the calendar of events. She was usually met with nods of affirmation, expressions of agreement, and even the occasional "Amen" from the audience. Little did she know, this meeting report was going to be met with a different response.

"Ladies, there is a scheduling conflict with next month's meeting. The officers and I would like to recommend to the body that we move next month's meeting time from 4 p.m. to 10 a.m. for just this one month. We promise that the meeting will be brief to allow you to enjoy the rest of your day, and we will be providing refreshments because we know we all need our morning coffee! Ladies, what is your pleasure?"

Madame President was prepared for everyone to agree and vote in favor. However, quite the opposite happened. There was a rumbling throughout the room, accompanied by quick shakes of the head and wrinkled faces. As more women began to whisper and the noise grew louder, Lady Matlock stood up in exasperation and fixed her eyes on

Madam President with a piercing glare.

"To Madam President and everyone assembled, I have been a member of 'the society' for over forty years and we have NEVER changed the meeting time to 10:00 a.m. I believe I speak for EVERYONE when I say we… have… FUNERALS!" Lady Matlock was supported by several well-seasoned members with deep affirming nods and exclamations of "I know that's right!"

Madam President was stunned, yet amused, at the fact that so many members anticipated being at a funeral one month from now for someone who probably wasn't even ill yet.

"Motion died on the floor. That concludes my report."

Madam President learned a very valuable lesson that she carried with her throughout the remainder of her term as president: Southern ladies attend funerals just like any other major event on a weekend. The most coveted hour of a Saturday was the eleven o'clock funeral hour. The meetings remained at 4 p.m.

— Candice Webert and Crystal Webert Mays —

83

Pandemic Pampering

*Caring for myself is not self-indulgence,
it is self-preservation, and that is an
act of political warfare.*
~Audre Lorde

I t started with a simple text. "Heads up that you have something coming in the mail from me. They couldn't include a gift note, and it's unclear if you'd be able to know it was from me, so here's the note in advance (and I hope it gets to you before you leave Sunday — I have procrastinated for the longest.)" She included a photo of the note:

> *Donnette,*
>
> *Just sending some COVID-era love to help you soothe your soul. This is one of my favorite indulgences. Enjoy it.*
>
> *xoxo Melanie*

A gift. For me. For no reason. I immediately texted back. "Ah Mel, really. Thank you so very much. I love it already because you thought of me. I am already giddy."

Melanie and I have been friends for at least two decades. I think we met at a journalism conference, but I'm over fifty now and my memory isn't what it used to be. What's still clear is when we met she was at *The Wall Street Journal* in Dallas and I was in another southern city, although I don't remember which. We commiserated about being New Yorkers who had to move south for work. But for the most part our friendship was cemented based on our careers as print journalists.

Melanie and I were always in different cities, so we communicated mostly through phone calls every couple of months. I always looked forward to those telephone catch-ups: hearing about the cool African art exhibit, fancy NBA parties with the Mavericks or the Nobu restaurant opening.

I was the proudest friend when Mel purchased her first home and happily enjoyed her magical interior design journey. She was meticulous about every purchase — from chests to chairs. Years later, her husband would brag about how spectacular the home was — Melanie's taste is sublime — and how he regretted her having to sell it when Melanie relocated for a new position with *The Wall Street Journal*.

By that time, both our professional and personal dreams had been realized. I too had gotten married and moved back to New York for a position with the *Financial Times* of London.

We still communicated mostly by texts and telephone. Mel's texts were always extensive and crammed with updates. She considered texts the twenty-first century version of letter writing and that gave both of us the freedom to bare our souls using shorthand, as well as newly learned emojis.

Our text chain became deeply personal, maybe because our lives seemed to be on a similar trajectory. She married an older man who was a father and, in true Melanie style, transformed his house into a home. I married a Southern man with adult children and relocated to Louisiana for a year.

Navigating marriage as two independent, ambitious, career-driven women was difficult terrain. As Mel and I leaned into our shared experiences building our blended families, our bond strengthened.

When Mel shared, over a boozy brunch on Manhattan's Upper West Side, that she was getting a divorce, I was heartbroken yet heartened by her resilience. By the time Mel got around to relaying the news, she had the situation handled and was en route to a luxurious cruise to rejuvenate and rebuild.

There was no ex-husband bashing. Instead, we had a heart-to-heart about lessons learned and the thin line between self-care and selfishness.

In fact, over the years, taking time to take better care of ourselves had been a grave concern for both of us. That intensified during the double trauma of the COVID-19 pandemic and the police brutality directed against Blacks. It had been eight months of lockdown, working remotely under quarantine restrictions, and we were both desperate to stay sane.

Our texts became more frequent. And frenetic. Mel confessed to feeling on edge and finding it difficult to unwind as dusk creeped into night and we experienced Groundhog Day again and again and again.

I divulged my husband's threats to quit making meals if I continued to wear pajamas every day. Mel's advice: "These are EXTREME TIMES. I think we all need to show ourselves some grace."

Melanie regaled me with colorful tales about her trip to Maine, cocktails in her courtyard, and pictures of her fancy new monogrammed towels. "They are as soft as the human touch," her text read. "#sheetsontheway."

Melanie's devotion to her self-care was inspiring.

I'm the girl who's always buying the presents and making sure everyone close to me is happy and living their best life. But with Mel's encouragement, I used the time under lockdown to take better care of myself. I splurged on expensive loungewear, Jo Malone scented candles, hydrating masks and scrubs, popcorn and wine.

Mel reminded me we all deserved a reward for making it through perilous times.

A few days after her gift arrived, as I peeled away the pretty packaging of Saint Jane body serum, my spirit shook with gratitude because my friend had not only thought about my mental health but made an effort to do something she knew would bring me joy. It wasn't until I unwrapped her gift that I realized how pivotal Mel had been to my overall self-care and survival during the COVID-19 pandemic. I had come to rely on her check-in texts, extensive updates and general thoughtfulness as a break in the monotony of quarantine life.

Our exchanges, whether arguing the merits of pandemic essentials — bottles of Riesling versus toilet paper — or sharing self-care advice, were the perfect tonic for soothing my COVID-corroded soul.

— Donnette Dunbar —

84

Sisterhood

*Is solace anywhere more comforting
than in the arms of sisters?*
~Alice Walker

What was I thinking? Why was I pursuing membership in a sorority at thirty-seven years old? I kept my desire a secret from everyone close to me, especially my mother. I didn't need the discouragement from her, nor the ridicule from my siblings.

"What do you want to do that for?" Mom would have said in that disapproving tone she used anytime I expressed interest in doing something that she wasn't in agreement with.

"Girl, you ain't in college no more." My older brother would say, followed by a laugh.

"Aww, Charm, you want some fake sisters?" I imagined my younger sister saying.

I had considered joining a sorority when I came across a flyer for interested women at the business college I was attending in the 1990s. I thought about attending for about five seconds but was quickly reminded that I didn't have time. I was a recently divorced mother of a young daughter, working full-time and taking a full load of classes. Besides that, my only exposure to sororities was what I'd seen in the movie *School Daze*, and I definitely didn't have time for that.

In the fall of 2007, the time was right. I was dating Kevin, a proud member of Omega Psi Fraternity, and he dispelled the myth that a person can only attain membership while in college. He encouraged me to pursue membership if it was what I wanted.

With Kevin's support and encouragement along the way, I pursued membership in Delta Sigma Theta Sorority, Inc. through the Detroit Alumnae Chapter. I didn't have any personal connections in the local chapter, so I needed to attend the events that were open to the public so that the members could get to know me. And there were a lot of events: hustle classes, an annual golf outing, a Relay for Life fundraiser, an annual art auction, and political and mental health forums. When certain events allowed for non-member volunteers, like the golf outing, I signed up.

I witnessed the work these women did in the community. I also witnessed the fun they had when they partied with a purpose to raise funds for programs that impacted the community. With every event I attended, I grew more certain that I wanted to be a part of this national organization of educated, accomplished, selfless women who were bonded through their commitment to sisterhood.

Finally, five years later, the opportunity came to apply for membership. The chapter posted the highly anticipated "Informational" notice on their website, inviting all interested ladies to learn about the requirements for membership. Nearly 500 women packed the room. Even with all the networking I had done, I was sure these other women had the advantage of personal relationships with members of the sorority. Some had relatives and some worked with members. Some had attended college with the members. When I overnighted my application, I prayed that what I lacked in personal relationships, I made up for with demonstrated commitment and by surpassing the basic criteria for membership.

A few months later, I was initiated into the largest and most dynamic Black sorority in the world! I couldn't have been more excited and proud to be a part of this sisterhood filled with like-minded, educated Black women. I was ready to work alongside my chapter sisters. I was ready to feel the love that I witnessed them showing to one another over the years that I had been a visitor.

However, when I entered the headquarters of my local chapter for my first official meeting as a Delta, I was immediately overwhelmed and lost. Yes, my sorority sisters greeted me in a sisterly fashion with hugs. I was dressed in our sorority's signature color — red. Yet, I still felt like an outsider. I was immediately reminded of my middle school and high school years where I felt like I was always on the outside looking in. I was amongst them, but not with them.

This was a very hard pill to swallow. I didn't share my disappointment with anyone, not even Kevin, who was now my husband. I continued attending general membership and a few committee meetings, and all the same events I had attended along my journey to membership, hoping that I'd eventually feel the love and sense of belonging that I expected.

I hadn't quite accomplished that when life happened. In March 2015, Kevin was diagnosed with interstitial lung disease. His prognosis was terminal, and I had to slow my sorority life down significantly. Where my husband had once been supportive and excited for my involvement with the sorority, the illness had him angry about that and anything else that took me away from taking care of him.

I would be lying if I said I didn't fear ruining the progress I'd made if I wasn't able to participate in sorority activities. But I had a responsibility to my husband that far outweighed my goals with the sorority.

Caring for my husband proved to be the hardest journey of my life. It was also the loneliest. I was the first in my immediate family and among my friends who needed to care for an ill spouse. Thank God, I found an online support group of caregivers that I could lean on.

A few of my line sisters were there for me during my journey. Some called; some invited Kevin and me out to intimate dinners when he was no longer comfortable going out in public. Some had words of encouragement just for me. But, when Kevin's medical equipment caught on fire in December 2017, we lost him, our pets, and our home. My entire Delta family — near and far — showed up for me in a way I didn't think possible.

The call was put out that a Soror was in need. Sorors from my chapter, as well as our sister chapters from surrounding cities answered that call. My cash app notifications began chiming through the day and night. Most gave $100 or more! A past president of our chapter rounded up a group of Sorors to pull together a collective donation of $2,500! One of my line sisters, who had not always been friendly to me, was the first one to organize a clothing drive for the needs of my family.

I was overwhelmed with expressions of love from my Sorors. That's when I learned the meaning of the sisterhood. A sister may not always be around when you want them to be, but they are always there when you need them.

—LaCharmine (L.A.) Jefferson—

Loving
Black Men

Magically Human

All prejudices, whether of race, sect or sex,
class pride and caste distinctions are the belittling
inheritance and badge of snobs and prigs.
~Anna Julia Cooper

See him over there? He is my brother.
Different dads, but we have the same mother.
And he means the world to me.
Our love is deeper than what you can see.
He's wonderful, indeed he's magic.
And to even think of him harmed is scarily tragic.
In fact, the world might feel differently.
To them, he might not matter.
But my life would absolutely change and shatter.
If they had their way
He might not be here today
Because they see nothingness.
But this is certainly untrue.
He has a heart of gold and he would be there for you.
He'd give you his last.
He'd even make you laugh.
Time with him is a comedy show.
It's a pleasure watching this Black man grow.
But all they see is a body covered 75% in tattoos.
Scared he might not follow racially biased rules?

All they see are gold teeth.
Scared he might rob their home as they sleep.
But that's not true, he doesn't steal.
He works for his desires by his own free will.
They see a thug,
Not someone worthy of love.
But I swear he's the opposite.
Don't judge by appearance — stop it.
See his humanity, let it speak to you.
Look inside yourself if you're human too.
He's an uncle and a brother,
Not a fighter but a lover.
He deserves his life just as you deserve yours.
But in times like today, when it rains it pours
Pouring Black bodies that look just like him
We need them, we love them, let's make a deal.
What will it take just to spare his life?
We'll give the collateral to make these wrongs right.
All we want is justice, we'll pay if needed.
Take the houses, cars, and the accounts, deplete them.
Black lives like his, to us, have value.
Think twice before using deadly force, shall you?
He is loved, he is needed, so think before you accuse him.
Remember, just because he's magic doesn't mean he isn't human.

— SM Nelson —

85

Holding My Prayer Breath

Black women have to know the historical and everyday
struggles of black men, and our men have to know the
struggles of black women in America.
~Ruby Dee

Once again, my beloved was heading out to the garden center to pick up something he needed. I have come to expect these trips on a regular basis to a garden center or one of the large home improvement stores. An avid gardener, working in the yard is his passion as he carefully collects ripe seeds from flowers and propagates from stem cuttings.

Our garage reminds me of a laboratory, with large bags of palmetto vermiculite, peat moss, pine bark nuggets, and topsoil stacked in a corner. There are garden tools and supplies filling the space designated for a second car. On shelves are more bags and containers, everything clearly marked — from bone meal to liquid seaweed to flower food. Too many spray bottles to count, each meticulously labeled with the specific ingredients found within. We have two large tumblers for our composting out back, adding kitchen waste, leaves, and grass. Coffee grinds are collected separately in bowls in our kitchen; he studiously mixes them with soil for certain plants.

I can always tell if he is going into town because he dresses up. Today, he has on crisply pressed khakis and a Polo shirt. Cleanshaven, baseball cap on head, he's ready to go. He won't take the back roads — although faster and with less traffic — but will instead stay on the main highways. It's his routine, one that he learned as a young child. Taught by his father and mother even before he could read, he learned early how to bear this burden: dress neatly, be courteous, be cautious, be on guard, be prepared.

I have listened with an aching heart as my Black male friends and family members have begun to share their stories of the times when they were stopped by the police, painfully reliving each indignity. Some of the incidents occurred over fifty years ago, others within the past few years. Each confrontation has been recounted in great detail, revealing how vulnerable and frightened they felt. I am also hearing a deep anger and a bitterness that even surprises me at times.

"The talk" is given at an early age to every young Black child. As we grow older, we hear a newer and updated version of "the talk" about what to do when: driving a car, walking in a neighborhood, entering a store, starting a new job, moving into a new community. Over time, it is delivered with fewer words but with even greater meaning: "be careful" or "you know what to do" or "I'm praying for you."

I have read that children's exposure to discrimination can harm their mothers' health. I wonder if someone ever will conduct a study on how a husband's exposure to discrimination can harm the wife's health. I also read somewhere that mothering Black boys in America is a special calling. I do not have a son, but I do have a husband. And every time my beloved goes out the door, I find myself unconsciously holding my prayer breath, waiting for the safe return of this Black man whom I love. This is my own kind of special calling, embraced on the day that I said "I do."

And so today, I find myself waiting for my beloved to return safely home from a simple errand to the garden store… holding my prayer breath, yet once again.

— Westina Matthews —

86

The Uppity Black Teacher

Invest in the human soul. Who knows,
it might be a diamond in the rough.
~Mary McLeod Bethune

H e handed me a four-page handwritten letter. I was shocked by what I read on the first page. Me? An uppity black teacher? Dude, you don't even know me. My formative years were in the Forest Houses project in the Bronx. I was raised by a single Black mother who went to college while taking care of her three children. As the oldest, I cared for my brothers.

I was determined not to be a statistic. You know what the world says: Black girls who don't grow up with their fathers are more likely to be young, unwed, mothers. I had a good voice, and I would use it to get out of this ghetto. It wasn't easy, but I realized it was more about the false narrative echoed repeatedly: people of color, who are mostly poor, live in poor neighborhoods and don't know how to take care of themselves, let alone their homes. The truth is it had more to do with government policies and a lack of civic engagement.

I graduated from a highly acclaimed music school and began my life as a working singer. That didn't last long because I wanted to move out of the projects and singing full-time wouldn't pay all the bills. I got an assistant teaching position at a prestigious school where the principal looked at my résumé and said, "If I go by your résumé, I won't hire you. But there's something about you; I am going to give you a try."

That "try" lasted ten years as a kindergarten teacher!

Along the way, I got a Master's degree in Language and Literacy, and I started teaching non-traditional students, just like me, at the college. How could this guy call me uppity? Uppity means arrogant. Oftentimes confidence in Black women can be misinterpreted for arrogance.

When I was invited to teach an English course at a prison in upstate New York I jumped at the chance. I had experience with prison outreach already.

The bus ride to the upstate prison was long — two and a half hours there and two and a half hours back. Twelve professors taught at the prison, and I was the only Black woman instructor that semester. The ride gave me time to reflect on my little brother who was murdered by a "friend" at age twenty-three. Black on Black crime at its finest. Very little was done by authorities: "Black people living in the projects don't even care about themselves." Another false narrative.

I used to sing at prisons for holidays; at one event, the person who murdered my brother was in the same prison for murdering someone else. I openly told him and the rest of the men that forgiveness was for everyone, including him. The correction officers told me not to return until the young man was released.

My class at the upstate prison consisted of twenty-seven Black and Latino men in green shirts. I named them the "Green Shirt Scholars." Every week my class went overtime. No absences unless one of the green shirts had a doctor's appointment. Some green shirts tried to use urban language with me: "What's up, Professor?" "Yo, your boots are fire!" "Come on, you know, you from the hood!" "Professor, you can't give me some slack?"

I introduced them to the concept of double consciousness, to W.E.B. DuBois and his notion of struggling in two worlds by the way we speak and behave. Many of them had never heard of double consciousness, but they understood they were living his theory. As people of color, there is tension in belonging to two conflicting cultures: the Black culture and white American culture.

I had the men read *The Lesson* by Toni Cade Bambara. It's about a Black educator, Miss Moore, who returns to the neighborhood to educate and expose the children to the city outside their impoverished community. After reading the story, many of the Green Shirts saw me in Miss Moore and said they understood why I acted professionally with them. "The other professors are freer with us," some said.

I explained, "As a person of color, in prison or free, we cannot afford to be loose in our language or how we conduct business in the classroom. I am your professor — not your friend." I knew they wanted me to embrace them as a Black woman, a "Sistah," but I needed them to embrace themselves as scholars and respect me as an educator.

That letter that said I was uppity? He said, "You came in here, acting like you knew it all, using words we did not understand." It would be after decoding *The Lesson* that the same letter, on the last page, read, "I see now what you were trying to do. You have taught me the power of books, knowledge, and the pen. By the way, I do not believe you are the uppity teacher, and I thank you."

On the last day of the fifteen-week course, I told my Green Shirts Scholars, "I will see you soon, but not here."

One year later, I received an e-mail: "Professor, I hope you remember me — one of your green shirt scholars; I am released from prison and in college. I saw your name teaching English 201, and I was so excited. I registered for your class. See you soon."

— Rev. Michele Sweeting-DeCaro —

87

Black Momma Power

My mission in life is not merely to survive, but to
thrive; and to do so with some passion,
some compassion, some humor, and some style.
Nothing will work unless you do.
~Maya Angelou

L ast night I sat in my car as I often do to unwind after work before I enter my home. I started watching my young Black male neighbors who were drinking in their yard and being loud and obnoxious.

I people-watch in order to pick up on vibes and energies in order to know what moves I should be making. Plus, I often worry about ignorance and liquor mixing. *Lawd, are they going to start tripping?* I wondered. They were dancing, playing awful music, play fighting in the street, running through my yard, and I felt myself getting heated. I was so tired, and they were so loud, and my thirty-minute unwinding in the vehicle was being disrupted. I wanted to snap on them. But I just sat and watched and judged them. I judged the hell out of them, too!

I thought *Damn, I must be getting old with Alzheimer's, cause that was just us not too long ago.* I stopped and thought about my journey from wild, misguided youth to who I am today. I then started to wonder what greatness was lying dormant and untapped in them as well. Cause I'm pretty dope now. What gifts did they carry that they had yet to discover? Or maybe they had discovered their gifts but not the confidence to present them to the world.

I smiled, then. I started believing in them and seeing those young guys differently. I started giving them all gifts, talents, and goals in my mind. My perspective changed and I closed my eyes and encouraged their youth, said a quick blessing over them, shifted my energy, and started to exit my car.

Then, as I stepped out of the car, I thought, *I hope none of my white neighbors are getting upset with them out here having their version of fun.* Cause then my anger would be redirected even though I'd just been as frustrated with them. So I stayed a few minutes more just to watch over these young people whom I now considered my responsibility.

I thought of ways I could approach them to quiet them before I went into the house, so that I could worry about them less once I lay down. The images of Black male deaths and police brutality flashed through my head. I thought of having to come to their rescue if the police should come. Oh no, I would have to go into full Black Momma defense mode. Don't mess with mine!

Then it hit me on how to quiet them down! Uh, duh… as if they were my own. I had to go into Black Momma mode for them.

I get out of my car and looked at them sternly, "Hey, do y'all need a nap?"

One of them, looking confused, responded, "Huh?"

"Are you tired? Ready to go to bed?" I asked.

Another smirked. "No, ma. I'm sorry, we'll keep it down."

Relieved at the amount of respect I replied, "Okay, I'm 'bout to go in and I don't want to have to send you to your room."

All of them put on the biggest, most bashful, and beautiful smiles. "Yes, ma'am. We'll calm down. I'm sorry, ma."

"Alright now."

One of them adds, "We'll be good, Momma."

"Okay, baby. Good night."

I went in to head to bed and they calmed down. Even when I went back out to my car to grab a forgotten item, they were still playing around and laughing, but much quieter. I'm grateful to be a Black momma equipped with the proper skills, and even though I'm tired and overwhelmed by the state of the world, I have no qualms about helping to raise all our children in any moment that calls for it.

—Vickie Lynn—

88

No One Lives Above the Storm

I get angry about things, then go on and work.
~Toni Morrison

I am a ninety-year-old African American widow, and I am blessed to be healthy and satisfied with my life. I have experienced many things throughout the years, and I believe that the Lord has always been my support and my peace. I have five children, eight grandchildren and three great-grandchildren. They are a joy and a blessing to me.

Before the pandemic, I had attended four classes at a Senior Center program in my community — Acrylic Art, Sculpture, Memoir-writing, and Bible Study. I was fondest of the Memoir-writing course. It was therapeutic for me and it was very helpful during my early period of mourning for my husband, Henry. We had been married for sixty-four years and had enjoyed a solid, loving relationship.

Six years ago, I had an interesting and enlightening conversation with my middle son, Paul. During that time, much was occurring with African American folks in America and we had much to discuss. The day after the conversation with my son, I was preparing for one of my classes, the Memoir-writing class, by writing a happy Christmas story which I had experienced as a child. I had just about completed it, when I heard a commentators' voice speaking from the television, saying gravely that another African American man had been shot and killed by a white police officer.

"Not again," I groaned, trying to deny what I just heard. Then I became angry and muttered, "Will this madness ever end?" The anger developed further into fury. I yelled a question into my empty apartment, "What is the matter with this country?" Even as I asked myself this question, I already knew, and I begin to feel sad and depressed. Racism had reared its ugly head again. I also realized that this was personal. This could have occurred to any of my children.

I discovered that I had lost my desire to share a light, happy tale with the class. I was not in the mood. I decided I would write something more fitting as to what was going on in the world today. I recalled my conversation with Paul the night before, and I decided I would write it, and share it with the class.

Paul had informed me of an experience he had with a white police officer in Houston, Texas. Paul had moved to Texas after obtaining a good position upon graduating from college. I was horrified when Paul told me about this incident, which could have been fatal for him.

What triggered this conversation in 2014 was the news of Michael Brown, an eighteen-year-old African American man who had been recently slain by the police in Ferguson, Missouri. It seemed as if there was an epidemic of similar incidents occurring all over the country. We had also discussed the strained relationships between African American communities and the police.

My son, Paul, gets along well with most people and because of that, he has friends of different races and ethnic backgrounds. Thinking of Paul's seemingly magical ability to live above the storms in such situations, I said, "Of course, I know that you never had a dangerous incident with the police."

"Don't you believe that for an instant," Paul retorted quickly.

"What? I exclaimed in surprise.

Paul said that he often worked late when he first began at his firm, not wanting to leave work undone. Once, at 3:00 a.m., while driving home, he was stopped by a police officer. Paul lived in an apartment in the city of Houston at the time. Paul knew he was traveling at the correct speed limit and he couldn't imagine why he was being stopped.

I believed Paul, because he is the slowest driver I know. If someone comments on his absolute lack of speed, Paul asks, "What's the rush?" You would never believe that he was born in New York City, where everything is done at high speed.

Paul said the man looked angry. He thought he could charm him as he successfully did with most people, but this police officer seemed to be aching for a fight. Paul is extremely intelligent and very wise. He thought about the situation and proceeded to act cautiously.

The officer said, "Do you know that you were driving above the speed limit?"

Paul knew that was not true. Paul also realized that since he had just moved to Houston, he had no one to call if he was imprisoned or worse. He felt strongly that he had to maintain his cool in order to avoid enraging an already-angry man with a gun. His whole career could end tragically before he even had a chance to get a start in life.

Paul was very polite, realizing that his attitude and what he said was of the utmost importance. He felt that his very life was in danger. He also understood that the policeman viewed him as an enemy to be feared, not as a fellow citizen. One hears so often after the killing of an unarmed person, the nonsensical words, "I feared for my life." Paul felt that he had to proceed with great caution. His goal now was to get home safely, and he acted on his instincts.

Keeping his hands on the wheel in plain sight, Paul said, "I'm sorry for any infractions I may have committed. I live in this area and I'm on my way home from work. If you wish, I will show you my license and my work ID." Paul sensed that it was important to the officer that Paul realized who had the power here. Paul later told me, "I didn't care. He could assume the power; I only wanted to get away from him." Actually, Paul was the one fearing for his life.

When the police officer finally left him, Paul felt that he had dodged a bullet. He decided that he would never work that late again. He believed it was a dangerous hour for any Black man to be out and about.

After hearing Paul's account of that terror-filled event, I took a deep breath and realized sadly that no Black man or woman lives above the storm, no matter their level of education or profession, nor how well one gets along with different types of people. African Americans can still be in danger just because of the color of our skin.

A possible exception to this theory may be President Barak Obama, and that is because he still has Secret Service protection.

— Irene R. Granderson —

89

Keeping Score

The power to arrest — to deprive a citizen
of liberty — must be used fairly,
responsibly, and without bias.
~Loretta Lynch

I asked my father if he could recall the cumulative amount of time he had spent in prison since I'd been alive. It only took him a few seconds to rattle off "about eight years and nine months."

I hadn't considered how readily he could identify the lost time. His last release happened the year my daughter was born. I was twenty-four, then. And while I was sure that he was behind bars for a significant portion of my life, I could not put a number to it.

The fact that he could reminded me that no matter how hard it may be for the families of those imprisoned, our bodies are not the ones keeping score. Sure, I spent a third of my life communicating with him through phone calls and letters where he'd correct my grammar. Sure, I wanted more of him than visitation hours would allow. More from him than the beautifully decorated envelopes he'd send my letters in. But my aching pales in comparison to his own. He tells me that doing time requires you to retreat to a certain mental space. I have never asked the amount of time it took for him to get there.

Today, while speaking with one of my older brothers who has been locked up for nearly a year and is still awaiting trial, he told me that the issues he's been having were finally diagnosed as spasms — not kidney stones. Never mind that I didn't know kidney stones were even a concern of his. Never mind that he was prescribed an opioid to address the pain.

He said something about self-medicating in the past and preferring to not use pills. I made a joke about him not coming home with an itch. Or a habit.

Last week, we spent nearly an hour on the phone trying to get me access to his bank account. Hearing him explain to an anonymous call service representative that he was in jail felt a lot like the first time I heard my father address a white man as "sir." He was humble in a way that seemed ill fitting to his stature. He was wearing an orange jumpsuit and looking to take a plea for a crime he did not commit.

At least he said he didn't. And I'm inclined to believe him, regardless of what his record might indicate. I know that the system is broken. I know that we live in a country where Black men are viewed as disposable commodities and given plea deals instead of second chances.

I know that as my family gathered around my father's lawyer once a verdict was reached, my aunt decided to take a stroll down the hallway. I followed. She was staring at a portrait when I caught up to her. As tears rolled down her face, she quietly explained that she didn't want a white person to see her crying. This system will have you believing that white people are an entirely different subset of human.

My other older brother has been in jail since my daughter was born. He's had a hernia for over a year that they are waiting to grow into nearly triple its current size before deeming it operable. Again, there is no rush in rectifying the wrong within a Black body, because Black bodies have been deemed disposable. Especially if said body belongs to a felon.

This is the scariest thing about loving a Black man. Knowing that at any given moment, the world may take him from you. And they don't have to bury them underground in order to make it so.

They can ship them to another state. Make fraudulent charges stick. Send them home in debt and incapable of being hired, then shackle them again when they do whatever it takes to feed their families. The same families these Black men feel responsible to after having already lost so much time.

Despite what America would have us believe about these men, these men are the very ones we know and love. These men have children. And wives. They're our fathers and brothers, grandfathers and uncles. They have passions. And purpose. And value—far beyond what their hands are capable of producing. These men are sensitive. These men tend to project hardness because softness has not proven useful to their survival. These men have thunderous voices and a monstrous notion of what it means to protect their loved ones.

These men are family. They are not what this world says of them. Prison cannot reform men it finds profitable to further damage. Therefore, prison cannot define them, either. These men are enterprising. They are amusing. They are reflective and proud. These men are more than their crimes in the same way that we are all more than our mistakes.

My father has tallied more than his fair share of bad days and bad decisions. Yet, my daughter only sees him as Papa, the man she truly believes is strong enough to lift a house. The decency she sees in him is a direct insult to a system that would rather see him stripped of his joy.

His joy comes with a price tag—at an expense neither of us can ever truly know. When she smiles at him, he smiles back—she reflects a truth that this world has tried to rob him of. The curve of her mouth becomes a disruptor to the ill-informed notions this system seeks to spoon feed us. She reinforces a version of him that this world would have us believe cannot exist.

However, our beliefs are rooted in the knowing that this world is not our home and those prison cells aren't either. We come from a stock of people more than capable of telling their own stories and speaking their own truths. An awful lot of our experience may feel like a gamble, and yet I still bet on Black. Every time.

—Brandi Chantalle—

90

So Unusual and Yet So Very Regular

Love recognizes no barriers. It jumps hurdles,
leaps fences, penetrates walls to arrive
at its destination full of hope.
~Maya Angelou

I was a little over a year old when my parents divorced. As was the standard in the late 1960s, the courts automatically granted custody to my mother. But all that changed the day my dad visited me after work and found me in my crib covered in vomit. From then on, it would just be the two of us.

In those days, a Black single father was extremely rare — but my father didn't flinch from the responsibility.

He has been on my mind lately. Like so many Black people, I'm exhausted by the overwhelming number of negative images I see of Black men. Constant and unyielding videos of Black men being shot, sitting on curbs in handcuffs, or their faces smashed into the asphalt.

We rarely see them as regular men. Cooking dinner. Going to work. Just being fathers and loving their children.

And so, I want to tell the story of my own Black dad, a dad who was both exceptional and also very, very regular. He made his mistakes, but he was always there for me when I needed him. He was a man who knew he was different in many ways but never made his daughter feel like anything was abnormal.

My dad, Lawrence Alfred, was born in 1928 in Morrow, a tiny, segregated town in Louisiana. He was one of ten children, all born at home.

For him to leave that little town and go on to gain a Ph.D. in microbiology and work in some of the most prestigious laboratories in the world all while raising me was nothing short of remarkable.

At the same time, it was all so, well, normal. Saturdays were house cleaning and food shopping. Sundays he watched football while I played with my toys on the floor in front of him. And Sunday nights were dinner, *60 Minutes*, and an early bedtime.

To me, that is what a Black father is.

But at the same time, a Black father is a man who cares deeply for his children but lives with fear just a little deeper than most non-Black parents, because there's more to be afraid of. He's a dad who pushes his kids to be better, because he knows it will be that much more difficult for them.

And so, when George Floyd's daughter heartbreakingly declared "My daddy changed the world!" it was a reminder to me of the many ways our Black fathers affect our lives, whether they intend to or not. That they can love strong and fall hard. That we should sing their praises because often no one else will.

My father traveled the world, first as a Merchant Marine and then as a scientist, and I often traveled with him. One year, when I was in kindergarten, we lived in Paris, and I learned to sing songs in French while he worked at the Pasteur Institute. His travel stories sparked my imagination, and I credit them with my desire to become a writer. He would elaborately describe the town where he grew up. He painted pictures in such detail that years later when he took me to the swamp behind the church where he was baptized, it was as if I'd already smelled the thick, musty air, stepped into the warm, murky waters and seen the moss dripping from the trees. His stories became my stories. And I used them to write, paint and even act for a brief time. He understood that I wouldn't follow in his footsteps, but he never challenged me to do or be anything other than what inspired me and made me happy.

When I became a mother twenty-six years ago to my son, I read him endless books, told him family stories, re-created worlds with his toys and watched movies with him. I was mothering the way my dad fathered — full force, with love and imagination. I believe the way I played with my son as he grew was at least part of the inspiration he drew on to become a visual storyteller using film and photography. Being raised without a mother left me bereft of the comfort that only a mother can give her child, but it also spurred me to embrace my own motherhood, and to heap that lost love onto my son in doses almost too much for him to handle at times.

My father's imprint was indelible on both me and my son, who called his grandfather Boopah, based on his favorite book as a toddler, *Daddy and Me: A Photo Story of Arthur Ashe and his Daughter Camera*, by Ashe's wife, Jeanne Moutoussamy-Ashe. (In that book, Ashe's daughter called her grandfather Boompah.)

In the same way that Boopah taught me, I taught my son how to love traveling and respect differences of opinions and cultures. I taught him, with the help of Boopah, how to be a proud Black man despite the hardships that come with it. It couldn't have been easy to be told that a house you'd like to rent is available, until you show up and they take one look at you and tell you the house has been rented. I watched my dad's face crumble the day we went from house to house in Nashville, when we'd moved to the city so he could teach at Meharry Medical College.

Despite (or maybe because of) the setbacks and discrimination my father faced, he taught me to stand up to injustice and be proud of myself when I did the right thing, and to question myself when I slipped up and went low. I instilled that in my son.

But, like so many "regular fathers," my father was not perfect. He had a daughter with his first wife before I was born, and he was not present in her life. My sister and I became close after we became mothers, and her daughter and my son are like siblings now. If I look for a silver lining in my father's faults, it would be he taught me to love, openly, fiercely. And that's what I'm doing with my sister now.

A few weeks after he died, San Diego State University, where he worked in the College of Sciences as the assistant dean for under-represented students, asked me if they could have a "Celebration of Life" for him. Of course, I agreed.

What my son and I learned that day from the thirty or so students who traveled to the ceremony was that he was as much a mentor to them as he'd been to us. They told stories about celebrating their wins with him and how he pushed them when they doubted the attainable was possible. One student even told a story about how my father had encouraged her to reach out to Congressman John Lewis to endorse her for a teaching position at a historically Black college in Atlanta.

"Why would John Lewis recommend me? He doesn't know who I am," she had said to my dad. My father told her, "Well, he should know who you are because you're worth knowing." John Lewis wrote a letter to endorse her, and today she's a professor at Morehouse.

My son and I sat and listened to story after story from Black, Latino and Indigenous students. It struck us how my father had supported them in their studies and well after they'd launched their careers. And what struck us the most was we didn't know how great his influence was in other people's lives.

We heard a repeated refrain of how impressed they all were that he had raised a daughter alone and was still able to accomplish and give so much to others — despite and because he was a Black man in America. My father did many wonderful things in his life, but the most important thing he taught me was how to raise my Black son with dignity, vision, empathy and grace.

Whenever I look at my son, I see my father's influence and love surrounding us both. Not just a Black father, but a father. And that's what I want this world to recognize now and forever.

— Rebekah Sager —

91

Dear Lawrence Hilton-Jacobs

I embrace mistakes. They make you who you are.
~Beyoncé Knowles

Dear Lawrence Hilton-Jacobs,

You probably don't remember me. Then again, you might. I kind of hope you don't. My name is Nancy, and I owe you an apology.

I, like a kabillion other teenage girls fell in love with you, almost at first sight. I say almost, because the first time I saw your face was when my mom took me and my friends to see the movie *Claudine*. When I saw your picture on the marquee, I thought I was going to lose my mind! You were really fine. But that Charles character you played was mean. And the guy that played Paul was closer to our age, so we spent most of the movie swooning over him; yet I still kept an eye on you.

But then came *Cooley High*, and I was completely smitten. Totally! Man! I mean, you were so doggone sexy. I didn't even mind that you reached in a toilet! Like what kind of mojo were you working with, cause reaching in a toilet is just nasty!

And as if I wasn't already under your spell, two months later the TV gods blessed me with your presence every week on *Welcome Back Kotter*.

Now, I know you're thinking why is this woman telling me all of this and why does she owe me an apology? Well, I kind of did a bad thing. See, my older sister worked in the entertainment industry. She produced some of the greatest jingles ever!

One day when I was babysitting my nephew, I saw her phone book on the table. I began thumbing through it. The pages were filled with all kinds of famous people's names and numbers. I got my phone book and began to copy some. Yeah, you guessed it. Yours was one of the names and numbers I copied. Please understand, I never intended to use any of the numbers I copied. Ever! I just wanted to have the numbers in my book so that I could feel special, because there was so much going on in my life at that point that made me feel like I wasn't.

That summer while I was visiting my mom in California, two of my friends who were more like sisters flew in from New York to visit. It was their first time in California. We went to Disneyland, Universal Studios — but the highlight of the trip was attending a taping of *Welcome Back Kotter*.

This was the first and only time I got to see you live. My intention was to be cool and exercise self-control; after all, I was sixteen and mature. I did well throughout the taping, but at the end when the cast was introduced, and it was mentioned that your birthday was coming up in a couple of days, self-control went out the window and I hollered at the top of my lungs, "What do you want for your birthday, baby?"

Yep. Embarrassing. But as embarrassing as that was, it is not why I owe you this apology.

The next morning, we were in my room talking about the taping and you. As we talked, I got this bright idea. At first, I was like, "Nah." But then, I boldly proclaimed, "I'm going to call him and get his address so I can send him a birthday card."

Brynne looked at me quizzically and asked, "How are you going to call him?"

"I have his number."

"Stop playing."

"I really do!"

I got my bag off the chair, took out my phone book, opened it to the "J" section and handed it to Brynne. Jill moved in closer to see for herself. Their eyes widened, and Jill asked, "Where did you get that from?"

"Out of Debbie's phone book."

"Does she know?" Jill responded with grave concern. I simply shook my head.

"You know she's going to kill you," Brynne said.

"Not if she doesn't find out."

I picked up the phone and dialed, confidently. Brynne and Jill moved in closer so they could hear. The phone rang three times. I almost hung up, but then you answered!

"Hello."

"Uh, hello Lawrence." I was fighting to keep my voice from cracking.

"Who is this?"

"This is Nancy. I was just calling to get your address so I can send you your birthday card."

I grabbed a pen and sat there trembling, twirling the phone cord around my finger in nervous anticipation, when in your mean Claudine Charles voice you said, "Baby, I don't know you!" Then I did what any normal, nervous teen girl who stole a celebrity's phone number out of her sister's phone book would do; I hung up quick.

Jill, being the sweetheart that she is, tried to comfort me with these words: "At least he called you baby!"

I spent the next couple of days anxiously waiting for the LAPD to knock on my mother's door and take me to County. That never happened, and I was able to safely escape back to New York.

I am older and wiser now, with a conscience and a little bit more common sense. I need you to know that I acknowledge my invasion of your privacy and stalker-like behavior was totally unacceptable. I had my reasons, like many young girls who do silly things do. No matter what the reason, I was wrong, and I am sorry.

Oh, and just so you know, I also confessed and apologized to my sister on a dare from Jill and Brynne, who were all speaking on a panel at the Philadelphia Black Film & Media Conference that I hosted. And just so you know, a very famous actress who will remain nameless heard my confession and offered me your new number. I respectfully declined.

— Nancy Marie Gilliam —

92

Raising a Black Son in this World

Racism is a very insidious thing. It's dangerous
to the psyche, to mind and body. It erodes
the self-confidence. And I don't know
how we get through it.
~Ruby Dee

Meet Jordan. Jordan is my son. He is my firstborn child. He is the kindest, sweetest, most genuine person that you will ever meet. Those are not my words. Those are words from his teachers, family, friends, and almost anyone who has ever met him.

We affectionately call Jordan "The Golden Child." His grandmother gave him that nickname. The name was born because she noticed how we rarely had to correct him as a child and even as a teen. Jordan is a rule follower (mostly). He doesn't talk back very much, nor does he grumble when asked to do something. He takes pride in his work, he respects his elders, he works hard, and he's a leader among his peers.

Until last year when he moved away for college, I was pretty confident about keeping Jordan safe in this world. We live in a small town where everybody knows everybody. Other than hanging out with friends, he's usually pretty close to home and is good about removing himself from people or things that might cause him to get into compromising situations.

Jordan now lives on his own. My only hope is that he listens to all the things that we've taught him over the years:

- Say yes ma'am/sir and no ma'am/sir when you're speaking to an adult.
- Make every effort not to get gas at night.
- Don't walk too close to someone in a store, especially a woman who is alone. You don't want to intimidate her. (We were doing this six-feet rule well before COVID-19.)
- If you get pulled over by the police, comply with their demands, keep your hands in view at all times, and make an announcement before you make any moves. Do not, under any circumstances, engage in an argument with an officer.
- Be careful about running or walking too swiftly because that might suggest that you've done something wrong.
- Don't walk around with your hands in your pockets; someone may think you have something that you shouldn't have.

I'm pretty confident that Jordan will stay on the right side of the law, but I also know that he is human. Humans are flawed creatures. Sometimes people and situations get the best of people (even the Jordans of the world) and they find themselves in situations that don't quite fit their character.

I hope that if Jordan ever makes a mistake or travels down the wrong road in life that he is given the opportunity for redemption. I hope that someone doesn't decide that his mistake should cost him his life. I hope that his mistake doesn't cost his father and me the opportunity to talk through his problem and point him back in the right direction. I hope that he is given the same opportunity as people who don't look like him to say he's sorry and to pay for his mishaps accordingly.

I know that I don't have any control over what would happen in a situation like this. I know that no matter what action he takes, he has no control over how someone will view him or how they will respond to him. Even knowing these things, my mind is always busy trying to devise a plan to control the situation anyhow.

Raising a Black son in this world is hard. Real hard.

— Cherith Glover Fluker —

93

In the Long Run

I know why the caged bird sings.
~Maya Angelou

I turned over and rubbed my hand across the curve of the bed's mattress. He wasn't there. There was a knock on the door, alerting me it was 7:32 a.m.

Our fifteen-year-old son, Jeremiah, entered. "Mom, we're ready but I need to take our temperature. Are you or Dad taking us today?"

During the pandemic, two of our four children attended school in-person. We had to take their temperatures each morning, and then my husband Jeff and I took turns driving the kids to school. A 7:35 a.m. departure allowed ample time for breakfast at school and socializing with peers.

"Dad said he would take you today. Let me see if we need to switch." Jeff was rarely late for anything. Even when he seems to cut it too close, my superman swoops in at precisely the right moment.

We relocated from Florida to Georgia a few weeks before schools and businesses began to shut their doors due to the surge of COVID-19 cases. Jeff started running in the morning to shake off quarantine pounds. I rolled back over to my side for a minute and tried to convince myself not to think the worst — to no avail.

We're new to the neighborhood. They don't know us. It's dark out there. When is daylight savings?

My mind took me back to the video of Ahmaud Arbery being

chased during his routine run.

He knows what time the kids need to leave.

The longest two minutes passed. I grabbed my phone and called him in a panic. "Hey babe, I just wanted to know how far away you are. The boys are waiting. Should I go ahead and take them?"

He huffed as he ran. "No! I told them not to bother you. I'll be there soon."

I disconnected, slid back into the bed and burst into tears.

He stepped through the door at 7:38 a.m. and still managed to get each of the boys to school with time to spare—as usual. I was sitting on the bed when he returned.

"What's wrong," he said.

"I called you because I was concerned. I don't understand why that upsets you. With all that's going on, the thought of my Black husband running in an unfamiliar neighborhood is a little stressful."

"Why are you letting that…" he started.

"Because it's real," I interrupted. "I sat here trying not to think the worst but then I realized, I don't know what route you take. How long should I expect you to be gone? If you are gone longer than expected, where do I start looking for you? What do I tell the police? I don't even want to call the police!"

He took a deep breath, paused then said, "I'm sorry. I was frustrated because I specifically told the boys not to wake you."

"It was fine. They needed the thermometer. And I need you to understand how stressed I get when you or Jeremiah go for a run. You aren't simply 'the new neighbor' or 'an innocent teen' out for a jog. To them you are Black men running down the street, obviously up to no good."

"I understand," he said with a hug.

The next morning it was my turn to take the kids to school. The phone buzzed with a text from my husband.

"Good morning dear. I didn't want to wake you. I left earlier than usual because I'm taking a longer run today. I'll be back in about forty-five minutes."

Earlier? That means it was even darker when he left!

He proceeded to tell me his route and then ended with: "I'll look for a gym membership today. Love you."

Instead of inducing a sense of relief and assurance, his message sent me into survival mode.

How are we supposed to be healthy without exercise, and safe while exercising? What if we can't afford the space or the funds for a treadmill or a gym membership? What if my husband is killed or incarcerated for trying to protect us from a physical threat?

These are what-ifs the average middle-class white person does not have to consider.

Once again, we as Black people are forced to adjust our lives to accommodate the discomfort that others experience from our presence and the color of our skin. We constantly adapt to ensure our survival. We focus so much on our physical survival that it sometimes interferes with our efforts to truly thrive.

While my husband and I exchange jokes about growing old together, we fear dying early due to stereotypes, prejudices, and assumptions connected to our skin color. Adding to concern about our personal survival, is the survival of our children as well.

My teenage son could be targeted and killed in his own neighborhood like Trayvon Martin. My third grader could be gunned down by the police for playing with a toy gun like Tamir Rice. My kindergartner could be arrested in his classroom for having a tantrum like Kaia Rolle. If she makes it to adulthood, my daughter and her potential could die like Breonna Taylor.

I think of all the beautiful possibilities, too, to counter my fears of living while Black in America.

My basketball-loving son could make great strides on and off the court like LeBron James. My gifted third grader could be a record-setting entrepreneurial pioneer like Robert Johnson. My charismatic kindergartner could be a two-term president like Barack Obama. In adulthood, my tenacious daughter could reach great heights in her career like Kamala Harris.

We are alive and will continue toward better outcomes. People of color have the daring to see beyond the reality shaped by the hues of our skin. The thickness of our skin ensures our survival and propels us to thrive. We will shine as we continue to defy stereotypes and actualize our bright future, rich with possibilities.

— Elle Dee —

Identity & Roots

W[hole]

You never find yourself until you face the truth.
~Pearl Bailey

It's your father. I need to speak to you and your mother.
December 17, 2017

A text I never could have prepared for.
One that blindsided me completely.
About 18 years too late
Or maybe one too many years too early
Certainly not good timing.

Organic Chemistry Exam
December 18, 2017

A test I was not prepared for
One I fumbled completely.
About a day too early
Or maybe I only felt late
Certainly not good timing.

Growing up I was always asked "Would you want to meet your dad?"
How could I want to meet a stranger?
I was devoid of even a picture to conjure up the encounter in my mind.
Not to mention it was more a matter of "would he want to meet me?"

Like a dog digging up a bone he had buried in the past, put behind him

I defiled phone book after phone book
Made accounts on ancestry sites
Contacted shows to see if my story was compelling enough to be shared
If I was worthy of knowing truth and capable of handling it;
I searched for the missing piece.

Something to fill the hole
Gaping with insecurity, curiosity, and contempt.
Yes.
I wanted to meet him, but not know him.
Stay just long enough so I could tell him about watching my mother sob
Reassuring her time and time again it was not her fault
Deep down feeling as though it was all mine.
So I could show him, all that I have done and become in spite of the
    wounds he left in his wake.

A near perfect student, a reliable employee, a loving sister, a respectful
    daughter, a patient partner.
Well-rounded in every sense of the word yet still rough around the edges.
I'd like to say it made me tough, but it didn't.

It made me soft. Sensitive. Constantly cognizant of the lives people
    lead behind closed doors.
The tears shed when no one's watching.
The weight of empty in a heart that still beats for so many
How one minor detail can sprout complexes of grandeur in a life.

I had just finished a long shift at work.
Anxious about a long night ahead of studying.
When I looked at my phone and saw that message.

My head got hot and my fingers felt numb as I went to respond.
But I couldn't, I had an exam tomorrow.

I had THE exam tomorrow. The bane of many a pre-med existence.
I had gone eighteen years, I could go one more day.
So I left it. Stuffed it all down deeper than I ever needed to before,
    scared it might never come back up.

I stared at the screen.
Past the words and at my reflection.
Did he need money? A kidney?
Had he been lost all these years desperately looking for a way to find me?
The questions came rapid fire, pouring out like a clown car until finally
    I couldn't keep up.

I called. It rang and rang and rang until I was met with hello on the
    other side.
The words rolled in a way so foreign to me.
An accent I only knew from music I used as a bandage to patch up
    my identity.

Suddenly every name, and retort I had dreamt of escaped me.
He did most of the talking.
I learned more names without faces,
Mislabeled "grandma, brother, aunt"
I learned "schizophrenia" runs in the family
And that my ninety-five-average had nothing to do with my work ethic
    but everything to do with his genes.
He came to put his name on a project he never worked on.
A false sense of pride in a thing he didn't partake in
I sat and waited for an explanation that wasn't going to come.
An apology never thought of.
Perhaps for him I wasn't good timing.
Maybe a weight too heavy, an extra piece, a product of his closed doors.
I couldn't hate him though I wanted to.

I barely slept that night, itching to run from that exam.
But I knew better than anyone the implications of running.

Fear would not warrant cowardice in my life.
I would rewrite the story that was given to me.

I failed. For the first time.
But there was good that came out of it all.
Because for the first time ever I realized,
Nothing anyone says, or does, defines me.
Nothing he said or did, didn't say or didn't do, defined or would ever
    define me.

I felt a hole. For years.
And from then on I felt whole.
I am whole, in my own right.
And to think, I always have been.

— Mariah RI —

94

Finding Alfred Clarke

Language can never "pin down" slavery, genocide,
war. Nor should it yearn for the arrogance to be
able to do so. Its force, its felicity is in its
reach toward the ineffable.
~Toni Morrison

I can say for certain now that I know the identity of three of my ancestors who endured enslavement and were freed under the District of Columbia's Compensated Emancipation Act. Now I know for sure. I've recently learned a few precious facts about Alfred Clarke, my ancestor, his mother Lizzie Clarke and his grandmother Mary Ann Clarke.

I'm a fiction writer, a novelist. I write historically based novels about African Americans in the mid-Atlantic region. I've written two novels set in the Georgetown neighborhood of Washington — *River, Cross My Heart*, an Oprah's Book Club selection, and *Stand the Storm*, set in Washington during the Civil War era, a volatile, unprecedented time for African Americans, enslaved and free. Guided by the first-person accounts of enslaved people, filling in the gaps of dissembling and obfuscation, and ferreting out obscure historical facts, I've created my fictional characters.

Sometimes I feel like I have a score to settle with the historical record, an injury to repair. When I discovered facts about Alfred Clarke, I got very excited and came to a pause to consider that there was more to know about one of my direct ancestors. What does a fiction writer do when a historically true family story comes to light? How must she feel? I write historical fiction primarily from an urge to re-tell the past, to rehabilitate the skimpy, fractured, fragmented narratives of the people of the Americas, the so-called New World. Much of the national narrative of the United States is based on limited facts, racially motivated lies, and the visceral belief that all people are NOT created equally.

I've written about the unique path to freedom that the Compensated Emancipation Act of April 1862 opened for people enslaved in Washington, D.C. in *Stand the Storm*. I recently discovered specific information about my Clarke great-grandfather in a webinar produced by a writer and genealogist, Yvette LaGonterie, whose contributions to the historical record and to the Georgetown African American Historic Landmark Project are invaluable. She's done research on Alfred Clarke because of her relationship with a branch of my father's family. Both of my parents grew up in the Georgetown neighborhood of Washington, D.C., an area that had a vibrant African American settlement that included a number of historic Black churches. My father's family was traced to Alfred and his childhood enslavement at the Georgetown Hotel, which also served as a tavern.

Thinking about the 19th century, the period in which the enslavement of African people is legal in this country is a hard moment to inhabit. I am fascinated to learn that my relative was an actual participant in the Compensated Emancipation Act, enacted by Abraham Lincoln to soften the financial loss of emancipation for slave owners who freed slaves in the nation's capital. The plan was that the federal government would pay slave owners who made application.

The act created a free zone sandwiched between Maryland and Virginia, two large slave states. The administrative documents of the transactions created a unique cache of records, stored at the National Archives, that opened a window into the lives of the enslaved. In these records, the ages, occupations, familial relationships, and physical characteristics of the formerly enslaved are set down. This Act was a tiny, tenuous slice of freedom, specific to the District of Columbia, that emancipated my ancestors and roughly three thousand other people.

Alfred was ten years old when he gained freedom in 1862. He worked as a stevedore, as well as at a variety of other jobs. He married Jenny Cole, who was born free, at the segregated Holy Trinity Catholic Church. The couple had ten children, including my grandfather, James Sheridan Clarke, Sr. Decades later, my own father, James Sheridan Clarke, Jr. became the first and foremost altar boy for the Epiphany Catholic Church, built by the African American congregation in Georgetown who did not wish to worship at segregated Holy Trinity.

What do I understand now about Alfred Clarke and my other ancestors? Not too much yet. I know that they remained together in enslavement and freedom, their names appearing on census records. Mary Ann Clarke was enslaved with another woman named Mary; both girls were known to have been sold to Eleanor R. Lang at the age of fourteen in the 1830s. Lang was a widow and the owner of the Georgetown Hotel. Mary Ann was a grandmother when she got her freedom; she had come from a very old settlement in Prince George's County, Maryland called Piscataway and had been sold to Lang by William Marbury. Mary and Mary Ann remained as close as sisters throughout their adulthood.

As sad as the facts are, I was enormously satisfied to learn about Alfred Clarke and pleased that a significant historical event I'd written about in my novel, *Stand the Storm,* had worked to emancipate my ancestor. I've been scratching around in this yard for a while in my fiction. It is gratifying to feel that, through fiction, I told a truth about people in my family though I didn't know it. The discovery of these three Clarkes is a validation of my process. The bits of Alfred's life that have emerged are threads I can take up and spin into a narrative. I've looked at photos and tried to become haunted by the folks staring back. I look long at them and try to absorb their thoughts to embellish my fiction. Now when I look at Alfred, I think I recognize a Clarke soul.

I may never write a straight family history. Without letters or diaries, I'm not likely to learn much more than names, places, and occupations about my biological family. Yet, they inspire me. Knowing about some of the things they did, their answers on census records tell me about their family circle, what work they did and their aspirations, their perseverance, their thrift and their mindfulness of their children's future. But I like the way fiction can put the historical event into the middle of an ordinary person's life and illuminate the two simultaneously.

The D.C. Compensated Emancipation Act of 1862 changed the lives of a few thousand people and its effect rippled much further afield. I enjoy imagining what those effects may have been. Oh, but these people, newly discovered and tantalizingly within reach, are my muses now. Their scant facts are my nourishment.

— Breena Clarke —

95

The Year of Return

*Struggle is a never-ending process. Freedom is never
really won. You earn it and win it in every generation.*
~Coretta Scott King

When I started planning my trip in early 2018, I didn't
know there would be a big push for African Americans
to return to Ghana the following year. 2019 was coined
"Year of Return" by the Ghanaian tourism board. I'd
had a DNA test a couple years prior and decided to explore Ghana
after learning that my lineage was more than 20% Ghanaian.

Upon my arrival in Ghana, I instantly felt at home. I zipped through
the immigration process and was greeted by the immigration official
saying, "Welcome home, sister." I was thrilled to get the Ghanaian
stamp in my passport. And then my joy continued to overflow as I
heard the live jazz band playing a roaring, upbeat melody of piano
strings and bustling horn tunes in the airport hall. I thought to myself,
"Well, this is a first!" In the almost fifty countries I'd visited, I'd never
seen a live band greeting travelers at baggage claim. My next thought
was, "Now this is the kind of greeting a girl can get used to." This all
strengthened my belief that this was where I was meant to be.

Even though my initial "homecoming" reactions were filled with
glee and excitement, these were not the emotions that were felt through-
out my trip. One of the main reasons I wanted to visit Ghana was to
see the massive slave castles along the coast. I needed to stand in the
pain. I needed to feel the horror that my ancestors faced hundreds of

years prior.

When I entered Cape Coast Castle, I felt a slow ache that became more and more menacing as I approached the dungeon. My guide explained the lineage of the slave trade as we stood outside the male dungeon, which he told me could hold 800 kidnapped Africans.

As we entered the dungeon, the first thing I noticed was the overarching stench. It was as if death was still upon those underground dungeon walls. I couldn't even fathom how hundreds of years later, the smell could still be so strong. My guide pointed out the one miniscule opening in the dungeon wall, where a ray of light shined through in that moment. Now the dungeon was bright with light fixtures, but back then it had been almost completely black inside.

I was the only person on the tour, so my guide shut off the lights so I could get a feel for what it was like for the prisoners. They had stood in the dark, tightly packed in the cold, damp underground cells. I could feel my and many others' ancestors in that moment, and I instantly broke down. My guide gave me a gentle hug, saying, "It's okay sister. It's okay."

As I exited the chambers into the sunshine, I decided it only right to hold my head high. I did what my ancestors could not. It was a full circle moment, and in that moment, I felt truly free, determined to live out my ancestors' thwarted dreams.

— Nicole T. Brewer —

96

Secrets, DNA, and Traces of the Diaspora

Our feelings are our most genuine path to knowledge.
~Audre Lorde

My grandmother was my favorite girl, as I called her, but there was one thing that left me confused. She'd kept the identity of my dad's father a secret. My father had asked my grandmother over and over, but there was no name, no picture — nothing.

I flew to Trinidad, my family's home country, to spend some time with her after she suffered two strokes. We gossiped about old neighbors, laughed and exchanged stories, but I couldn't muster the courage to ask her, at age ninety-one, who my grandfather was.

Shortly after my visit, my grandmother was transferred to hospice after suffering a third stroke. I traveled back to Trinidad to say my final goodbye and to hug and hold her one last time. She passed a few weeks after, still holding onto her secret.

Some time passed, and I was home on maternity leave with time and curiosity on my side. My father had accepted he would never know his father, but I was not so easily discouraged. Even without the slightest clue, I always remained hopeful — and kept faith the size of a mustard seed, a biblical reference older folks often talked about. After watching yet another commercial about DNA testing, I figured I'd give it a try even though it wasn't likely that my grandmother's generation were eager to spend ninety-nine dollars on a DNA test.

Four weeks later, I got my results, and shockingly, found my DNA was a match to a large group of people with the same surname. These people were listed as aunts, uncles, and first cousins! I took a deep breath, sent an e-mail, shut my laptop, and went to bed.

To my surprise, a response came. This person, who was listed as an "uncle," was also looking for his paternal grandfather, who had gone missing after immigrating from Trinidad to New York City. Excitedly, he thought I was the great-granddaughter of his missing kin. After a few exchanges, his grandfather's dates and timeline were not aligning with my information.

But my father's dates and timelines were matching with this gentleman's. One year after my father's birth, this man's father had moved to the United States. His father was married with twelve children, the last daughter being born five months before my father. He was educated and a highly respected person in the community, and I guess he hadn't acknowledged the birth of my father, a child he had out of wedlock. More conversations ensued, and facts and dates were fitting. The man listed as my uncle promised to send a photo of his father. My heart was racing. It came through my phone, and my jaw dropped. The resemblance to my father was striking.

There was only one thing left to do. Convince my father to take the DNA test.

My father is a staunch Rastafarian with antipathy to Western medicine and doctors. So the thought of sending his saliva in a tube, through the mail, was laughable. But, I had to convey that he needed to test without having to spill all the details. What if these newfound relatives were matches to my mother and not my father? I thought about how traumatic it would be to instill a false sense of hope in this sensitive situation. It felt like I had done the impossible, but I eventually convinced my dad to test, then I waited five long weeks. The results came back.

The family was a match to my dad. They were his half-siblings. Eureka!

I had a sit-down with my father, who I anticipated would be

excited, relieved, and flushed with emotion. I showed him the picture of his dad, and he just smiled. After a lifetime of yearning and hoping, he just... smiled. *He's internally processing this,* I thought — *that's fair.* I went on to share that his father had passed thirty years ago, but he had twelve half brothers and sisters who were looking forward to connecting with him! My dad was numb — and had been so for decades. He wasn't ready. I was naïve to think otherwise.

I corresponded with my newfound uncle, and he rejoiced at having new family members. My uncle shared beautiful photos — displaying what appeared to be a large and loving family. There were photos of my newfound grandfather perched on a lawnchair with his twelve children — happy, smiling, and looking at peace. I warmly welcomed stories that gave me some insight into my long-lost family and this man — my grandfather — who to some extent, will always be a mystical figure. Six months later, I boarded a plane to Canada to meet my uncles and their families. My dad wasn't coming; I only hope that someday he will be ready to take that step.

My uncles and their wives greeted me (and my sister, who also came along) with open arms and a feast. We quickly bonded over the culture of our "home country" — outsinging each other over the blasting but sweet melodies of soca and calypso, the deliciously flavored and prepared curried food, and sweet Caribbean delicacies. We talked about our love for Trinidad Carnival and the good vibes of Caribana, Canada's version of carnival.

For whatever reason, it wasn't meant for my grandmother and my grandfather to face the realities of their past, and fate granted their wish. While my family could never make up for the lost time, I feel blessed beyond measure to have the opportunity to know them going forward — all made possible by a DNA test.

— Inika Pierre Williams —

A Waste of
Good Skin and Hair

*I'm convinced that we Black women possess a special
indestructible strength that allows us to not only get
down, but to get up, to get through, and to get over.*
~Janet Jackson

I prayed that you wouldn't look like me. When you were born, I
was relieved when your butternut skin was just light enough. I
checked your ears to predict how dark you'd get and watched
closely over the next few weeks.

I brushed your hair religiously, trying to undo the coils that God
might give you, as if it was possible for her to make a mistake. "Please
stay soft, please stay straight, please stay good," I prayed.

As you grew older, I was thankful that you didn't develop my
large breasts and round nose. I had been teased, touched and shamed
for my womanly body.

My mama used to squeeze my nose when I was little. She always
said it was so it wouldn't spread all over my face. She had a "keen"
nose and said it had gotten that way because her mama would squeeze
her nose every day. She said you have to do it while you're still little
because your nose is soft enough to be molded. She was a dark-skinned
woman. She never went in the sun or attended outdoor activities,
saying she didn't like the heat. No one ever talked about it, but we all
knew the reason she avoided the sun was so she wouldn't get blacker.

Later in life, I learned that a keen nose meant one that was slim and narrow. That was in contrast to a nose that was "all over your face," which meant wide, fat, ugly and Black. In the hierarchy of Blackness that I saw, having dark skin with a wide nose and big lips was at the bottom of the totem pole.

My husband's family was what we New Orleanians call 7th Ward. That means you have light skin with "good" hair, but we can still tell by your features that you're Black. Some people call themselves Creole, some *passe blanc*, which means passing for white. They often used words in casual conversation that had some resemblance to French Creole. They typically had French last names like LeBlanc or Boutté.

They were the descendants of the Black Bourgeois who were descendants of house slaves and free people of color. They were members of exclusive clubs and attended lots of parties, typically owning their own businesses and homes. No one ever talked about how their skin color became so light, what that meant had happened to their female ancestors.

People in the Creole community are expected to do well, be prominent members of society, go to college, and achieve success. When they don't, they bring shame to their families. I've heard people say about their family members who've achieved less than expected were just "a waste of good skin and hair."

Sitting across from them, with my kinky coils and dark skin, made me wonder. What was I?

From the time Black babies are born, people begin to assess every feature on their bodies. Their skin tone, their features, their hair. Is it possible for Black babies to enjoy some fraction of their lives being innocent and pure? Absolved from the harshness and judgment of the world?

I've had lots of conversations with parents about the right time to talk to your kids about racism. My response: As soon as possible. If you don't, the world will do it for you.

— Ashley Hill Hamilton —

98

$3,000 vs. $300

I am deliberate and afraid of nothing.
~Audre Lorde

Besides being a New York City police officer, I also perform a one-woman show called "Harriet Tubman Herself" at colleges and schools across the country. With some bookings scheduled in the Las Vegas area, I flew there on March 17th, 2020. Upon landing, I learned that only hours before, due to COVID-19, the governor had shut down the state.

Well, if Las Vegas is shut down New York City will follow suit, I thought to myself, and sure enough, two days later it happened. Unable to fly home, I decided to rent a car and explore the West Coast. While in San Diego, I noted on my GPS I was only twenty-four minutes from the Mexican border. Not realizing how much this might change my life, I decided to go to Mexico for the day.

I arrived in this beautiful country and drove around for a few hours, then ended up in Tijuana. After walking around, being serenaded by mariachi bands, and buying postcards, I decided to head back to San Diego before nightfall. The GPS said to proceed on 5 North and, after driving a while, I noticed about fifty men in the middle of the street, cars everywhere, and people walking about looking confused.

As I slowed down, thinking it was a car accident, five men approached my car. One gestured to me to stop, so I stopped the car and rolled down the window. Another man, with a gold sheriff's badge in his hand, came to my window and, as I was examining his shield to confirm the validity of it, a small man about 4'11" reached behind the guy, stuck his hand in my car, and popped open my door.

Then, the man with the shield quickly grabbed my shoulder and shoved me across the armrest to the passenger side. Although bewildered, I wasn't alarmed, since I thought he was the law. I just said, "Hey, be gentle, I'm a lady!" The little guy hopped in my back seat and sat leaning between the driver and me. Then the man with the shield started driving my car in reverse at high speed, away from what I took to be an accident on the highway.

As I was recording my journey on Facebook Live, the driver realized this was being filmed and told me "No camera!" so I stopped my video. Thus, for the next forty minutes I was under their control and no one would know what was happening. Then the driver said, "If you don't give us 3,000 US dollars you will never leave Mexico!"

This sounded ludicrous to me so I said, adding the little Spanish I knew, "That's okay because Mexico is a *bonito pais* so I will *trabajo aqui* and teach English, voice, and history lessons to the children."

The man with the shield yelled, "No! If you stay in Mexico, you will never teach anything or help the children in anyway."

Still not comprehending the danger I was in, I said, "Fine, I won't teach, but I will visit Cancun and Cabo. I hear they are both beautiful!"

The driver yelled again and said, "No, you will not travel, you will not teach, and you will not like what is done to you!" That was the moment I realized I was being threatened and my life might be in danger.

Mind you, this entire conversation is taking place while he's still doing approximately 38 miles per hour in reverse. At this point, I said firmly, "May I please see your badge and shield?"

He looked in the rearview mirror at the little man behind us, then said, "Well, I'm not actually with the police, we are the cartel!" I said, "Oh, wow, the cartel! I heard of you on the hit Netflix show, *Narcos*."

Then I reached into my clutch, grabbed my New York City police badge and ID card, and threw it open on the dashboard. I said calmly, "*Soy un oficial de policía de Nueva York!*"

The driver looked at my badge, then at the man behind him, gave a nervous smile, and then said. "Okay, Mommy, then you don't gotta give us $3,000, just give us $300."

I said, "Bless your heart, you're charging me ten percent of my own ransom? Well, I'm still giving you *nada!*"

At this point, the driver reversed the car to the right and drove onto another roadway and, for the first time, we were going straight. After about four more minutes I saw a police barricade with a gate closing off this quiet road. We pulled up to the barricade and a man in uniform walked to my side of the car. I saw from his badge that he was an officer of the law and I rolled down my window. "*Por favor, ayúdame.* Please help me. I am in danger here!" I said in Spanish and English.

He did not even look at me but beckoned to the driver who was texting something on his cellphone. As he passed what was clearly a message to the officer behind me, I tried to see what it said but couldn't. The officer read it, handed the cellphone back to the driver and said curtly, "Let her go!" He walked back to his pillbox, touched a lever, the gate went up, and we drove through.

Within a few minutes we were back on the main highway where traffic was moving swiftly. After about half a mile, the driver pulled over and the two men hopped out. After telling me to stay in my seat, they ransacked my car, searching the glove compartment and the trunk. They got away with a twenty-dollar bill and four dollars in quarters and, as they pocketed the quarters, I was livid thinking, "Hey, they're for my laundry in San Diego!"

Barely eleven minutes later, I reached the United States border where the U.S. officer asked me why I traveled to Mexico today. I said "Because I wanted postcards…" hardly remembering what I had just gone through. I crossed the border and was driving along quite calmly when it hit me. I had been kidnapped by the cartel, held for more than forty minutes, and I hadn't even mentioned it to the officer. I pulled over on the highway and started shaking uncontrollably. I put my right hand over my heart to control my breathing and felt a lump. Reaching my hand into my bra I realized I had put eighteen $100 bills in there, in case of an emergency.

Lessons learned: I will never drive to Tijuana, Mexico again; I will not be so trusting the next time I see a police shield, and I will identify myself sooner when in unfamiliar territory. However, it is interesting to know that as a Black lady in Mexico I'm worth $3,000, although as a U.S. police officer I'm worth only $300!

— Christine Dixon —

99

A Natural Reflection

It's so clear that you have to cherish everyone.
I think that's what I get from these older black women,
that every soul is to be cherished,
that every flower is to bloom.
~Alice Walker

I t was the late 1980s and early 1990s. It was a time of reclaiming the true narratives of the words and deeds, journeys and accomplishments of peoples of Africa, the Caribbean nations, the Indigenous people — all who needed their stories told. It was a time to feature the voices, art, music, inventions and writings that speak truth to the false histories of a people determined to marginalize and mitigate us. It was a time when schools in Black communities were engaged in seeking out the scholars, writers of books for adults and children, creators of toys and games that were positive in their messaging and imagery.

Books poured forth for children with stories and illustrations of beautiful Black and brown faces, clothes that were colorful and fancy, artfully drawn to showcase the fabrics and creative designs of other cultures. They showed homes that housed families in a diverse array of settings that, no matter how rich or poor, uplifted the reader.

Dolls of all types were readily available for girls and boys of all ages. Baby dolls, rag dolls, dolls with beautiful clothes and accessories, she-roes and heroes complete with tales of their places in our stories.

I created a space where children and adults could come and find in one place as many of the independent and commercial products as I could find. Local artists brought a wealth of dolls, greeting cards, and educational materials that were amazing.

In this sacred space came Black writers, including Eloise Greenfield, Walter Dean Myers, Lucille Clifton, and a host of others. Buses of school children came, parents came with children, and during the afternoons of quiet time, The Elders.

I watched from my desk after greeting them, as they drifted around the store and touched, held and perused the books and other offerings. Eventually they would turn and look in my direction, although it seemed to me they were looking far off into another time and place. A gentleman who may have been in his seventies or eighties spoke in that place of reverie. "You know," he said, "I never had any toys or books when I was a child. I never thought there could be anything that looked like me. I never could have imagined any of this." He looked up at me as if suddenly aware of my presence. "Thank you" he said. "I will bring my grandchildren here."

My most enduring memory was of a tall, thin, dark-skinned elderly woman with short wispy white hair. She came in so quietly, almost timidly, and asked if she could look around. "Of course, you can; welcome to Natural Reflections," I replied.

She walked around the store in awe of what she was seeing, hesitantly touching the spines and covers of the books. I watched her as if I too were seeing everything for the first time. With a spiritual energy, she walked to the rocking chair as if called by it. In her arms she had a doll. A hand-sewn Black doll with a pretty white eyelet dress and long braids of black yarn. It had a face that was hand painted with bright eyes and a secret smile — made by Julie Brown of Brown Spices.

As she rocked and held the doll in her arms, she began to tell me of her life. "We never had beautiful dolls when I was a child. Only the white children had those pretty dolls with dresses like theirs. We had homemade dolls of rags or cornhusks. I never saw myself as pretty," she said. "I thought they never made dolls like us because we were not beautiful."

Her gaze moved over the books as she said with tears in her eyes, "Now I know that is not true."

— Rabiah Nur —

The Day I Learned
I Was Black

It's not enough to just survive something, right?
That's not the point of life. You've got to thrive,
you've got to feel happy.
~Meghan Markle

I t was the last day of summer break and Amber Walsh was hav-
ing a sleepover for some of the girls in the class. I could not
believe that she had invited me.

Amber was the prettiest, most beautiful being in the whole
school. She had big blue eyes and fine blond hair that flowed down
her back. She wore the cutest pink outfits and her mom even let her
wear light pink lipstick. Amber was bossy, though, and we did what
she said. When we finished playing with Barbies and moved on to
Spice Girls, I wanted to be Baby Spice, but she forced me to be Scary
Spice. I didn't make a fuss or think anything of it; I mean, I was lucky
to even be her friend.

I didn't learn that I was Black until the second grade. It was the
first day of school and Ms. Stuart said she wanted to get to know us.
She began passing out colored paper, crayons, markers, colored pencils,
stencils, glue, colored sticky tape, and scissors. I was excited and had
been working on arts and crafts all summer with my grandma. My
mom and aunt had convinced me that I was the next Picasso. This was
my chance to impress all the girls. Amber may have been the prettiest

girl in second grade, but I just knew I would be the envy of them all once they saw my impeccable art abilities.

I anxiously waited for Ms. Stuart's directions. "Draw yourself as what you want to be when you grow up," she said. I grew even more excited; I knew exactly what I wanted to be. I grabbed all the pink and purple glittery paper, some gold sticky tape, rhinestones, and a box of markers; then I went to work. When I was done, I was impressed with my masterpiece, a pretty princess just like my idol Princess Diana.

I silently inched my drawing over on the desk toward Amber, who was one of my three desk mates patiently waiting for her to rant and rave over my museum worthy piece. Amber took a glance at my picture and began laughing uncontrollably.

"Don't you like my shiny crown and my glittery pink dress," I asked looking for approval.

"It's nice, but don't you know, there's no such thing as a Black princess," said Amber.

"She's right, you know," added Tina.

My other desk mate Jennifer stood with her hands over her face. I knew she felt bad for me due to this revelation.

I didn't say anything, I just sat there fighting back my tears. At seven years old, all my career aspirations had been shut down and I now had to come up with a whole new life plan.

I spent the rest of the day quiet, thinking and contemplating. I wonder if the Princess of Africa was Black. That was it! I'd just have to move to Africa.

At the end of the day Mrs. Stuart came over and said, "Raneesha, beautiful picture, I can't wait for you to be the princess."

I corrected her. "It's 'Raneeseeya,' and I'll never be a princess."

Mrs. Stuart look puzzled, so I went on. "Amber said there's no such thing as a Black princess and she's right."

Mrs. Stuart paused then smiled, "Well I guess you'll be the first."

I smiled back and she walked away.

Mrs. Stuart gave me just what I needed at that moment: hope. A reason to go on and look forward to what would one day come.

I ended up becoming a teacher just like the new idol I gained on the day I learned I was Black.

Though I didn't become the next Princess Diana, I'm proud to say Meghan Markle did; and as for Amber, let's just say her dreams of being the Pink Power Ranger didn't happen either.

—Ranecia Dee—

Bella in Black

I was in the most beautiful country I had ever seen but I had cramps out of this world. I felt awful for not being able to go with my class to the Vatican museum. I love museums, and for once we were taking a bus and wouldn't have to walk there.

At first, I was upset, but then I realized how much I enjoyed the quiet time. I took a warm shower and looked at the view from our hotel. The colorful buildings, the street view, and the people passing by never got old.

When I made my plans to go to Italy, I searched the Internet to learn about the experiences of other Black Americans in Italy. I found a girl from Ohio named Tia who moved to Florence for her career. She has a gorgeous rich brown complexion with dark, long, straight hair. She's a YouTuber, and in her videos she said that she didn't feel any racism or oppression in Italy. I soon became a superfan of hers.

I also researched how Italians treat Africans, which seemed to be the same as the way many Americans treat Mexicans and other Latino immigrants. I found another YouTuber who was a Black Italian, an African born in Italy, who said she experienced a lot of racism in grade school. I started to think that I had done too much research and I would just take it as it came.

That day I stayed behind in the hotel we were about halfway through our trip. I reflected on how things had gone for me in Italy so far. As a Black woman, for the first time in my life I felt exotic. Though some of the Italians were tan, none of them were as brown as I am. People had been very, very kind to me. I felt safe, unlike at home, where I worried about dying from police brutality.

Our first day in Rome had been an eye opener for me. I was standing at the corner with my classmates waiting for the walk light when I heard a high-pitched sound. I looked around and saw one car at the light. The sound stopped. I focused my attention back on the light. Then I heard the sound again. I looked around but the sound stopped. Again I noticed that the car at the light had five young men squeezed inside it. I looked away and finally caught a guy in the back seat yelling and looking our way. We crossed the street and a few seconds later they drove away still yelling *bella*. As we walked, I turned to my translator app to find the meaning and learned that *bella* means beautiful.

No one had ever catcalled at me before and I didn't know how to feel about it, but my friends brushed it off, so I did too for the moment.

It was also on my first day that the waiter at Chicco di Grano, the restaurant where we had lunch, had caught my eye. He had amazingly thick eyebrows, he was a dark tan color, and he spoke very clear English. The way I dressed and did my hair made me feel confident while I was there. I wore bright red, loosely curled, long hair, I penciled my eyebrows red, I wore a gray beret, a white sweater, a leather jacket, and jeans with combat boots. I'd looked up some European styles before I packed so that I could blend in a little, but the girls in my group wore leggings and denim jackets that gave us away.

My roommate and I were the only two minorities on the trip, and we stuck together pretty tight most of the time. I was the only Black in a group of twenty-two students from the University of Delaware, and she was the only Korean.

The second night we were in Rome, she and I found a Black hair shop, which surprised me. I thought about buying some of their products to do my natural hair but decided against it. Then we went back to Chicco di Grano and I officially met Steve, the waiter. We chatted, exchanged numbers, and my roommate and I got free shots of limoncello. Things with Steve didn't last long and later I met an African guy in Florence who was also nice to me and we chatted for a little while once I returned to America.

Overall, my experience was amazing, and I still think about how natural it felt to be in Italy versus how I feel at home. There I didn't feel like a color. I felt safe and comfortable and beautiful.

— Rahsel Holland —

Meet Our Contributors

Taifha Alexander was born and raised in South Jamaica, Queens and is a graduate of Georgetown Law. Her passion for building coalitions and appreciation for diversity among students stems from the racial and ethnic diversity within her own family. She hopes to inspire others to challenge their stereotypes and biases.

Karen J. Anderson received her Master of Arts from the School of the Art Institute of Chicago in 2020. A writer, filmmaker, artist, and photographer, she loves to tell stories. She and her sister host a podcast about television, movies, and culture. She has an adult daughter.

Mia Y. Anderson is a proud Jamaican, born in the Republic of Brooklyn. She is a multi-hyphenated working artist who is currently living in Manhattan. She loves house music, hip-hop, dance hall and old school music. She proudly holds the title of #1 fan of President Obama in the whole wide world.

Wanda G. Anderson is a wife, mother, co-pastor of a church and an attorney. She has been writing for most of her life and discovered her love for words as a child. Known at times throughout her career as a poet laureate, she is an advocate for justice and for gender equality. Wanda lives in Colorado Springs, CO.

Quantrilla Ard, aka The PhD Mamma, is a personal/spiritual development writer, speaker, and author who resides in the metro Atlanta area with her husband and three children. She is a storyteller who advocates for the voices of the unheard. She lives by the saying "Protect Your Peace" and encourages others to do the same.

Tonya May Avent loves to write encouragement for overcoming the struggles we face in life. She lives in New Jersey with her husband

and two daughters, and enjoys sports, traveling, and reading. Her first book, a devotional for young athletes, will be published in 2021. She blogs inspirational content at destined4thedub.com.

Judy Belk has a passion for exploring stories focused on families (especially the dysfunctional types), community, race and social change… which means she never has a shortage of material. Her work has appeared in the *Los Angeles Times*, *The New York Times*, *Washington Post* and numerous other publications.

Nicolette Branch holds a B.A. in Economics from UCLA and MBA from the University of Michigan. She is married with a teenage son in The Woodlands, TX. Nicolette has led several strategic and marketing initiatives as a consultant and entrepreneur. She enjoys staying active, creative endeavors, and inspirational projects.

Nicole T. Brewer is an English language teacher, travel blogger, author, and freelance writer. She has traveled to over forty countries and lived abroad in South Africa, Germany, South Korea and presently in Oman. She is the author of *A Guide to Landing an English Teaching Job Abroad* and co-founder of I Luv 2 Globe Trot.

Dr. Edna Faye Moorehead Briggs is a retired Los Angeles County and joint commission healthcare administrator who holds a doctorate from USC. She serves as a self-appointed historian. Born on a farm in Gethsemane, AR, she is a widow who has two adult children, and currently resides in Los Angeles, CA. E-mail her at ednafbriggs@att.net.

Debra L. Brown received her bachelor's degree from Howard University. She took an early retirement from the New York City Health and Hospitals Corp. to travel and pursue her writing. Over the years she won several prizes and participated in many writers' workshops and retreats. She is in the process of completing a novel.

Erica Brown is a "Bona-fied" Blues Woman and has performed worldwide. She is also an accomplished actress and speaker. She loves her family, community, country and world, and is still working on delving deeper into having a Servant's Heart.

Michele Renee Brown is a master storyteller and purveyor of words. She is the author of *Adventures in Gideon: Kingdom Principles & Life Lessons My Dog Taught Me*. She has two master's degrees from

NYU in cinema studies and cultural studies. She is the only daughter of Woody and Marina Brown and a passionate dog lover.

Exodus Oktavia Brownlow is a Blackhawk, MI native, an HBCU graduate of Mississippi Valley State University with a B.A. in English, and a Mississippi University for Women graduate with an MFA in creative writing. Her work has been published with *Electric Literature*, *Booth*, *Hobart Pulp* and more. She plans to write exceptional novels.

Brandi Chantalle is an educator, author and public speaker. She facilitates workshops that prioritize the healing/experience of BIPOC, particularly women. Motherhood inspired her upcoming book *Love Notes for Our Daughters*. Brandi enjoys the outdoors, live music, and pretending she isn't too sleepy to indulge in a good book.

Shawntae Chase is a social worker who graduated from the University of Central Missouri with a Bachelor of Social Work and also has a Master of Social Work from East Carolina University. She is married and has three sons. She has a blog where she shares about her life as a military spouse, autism mother and follower of Christ.

Rozelle Clark, mother of three, received her bachelor's in health and wellness in 2006, graduating with honors, while maintaining a full-time position as a respiratory therapist. She lost over 100 pounds, changed her lifestyle and daily habits. She completed two half marathons in 2010 and her Yoga Teacher Training 200-hour training in 2017.

Cheryl Clarke is a Black lesbian feminist poet, essayist, and educator. With her life partner, Barbara Balliet, she is co-owner of Bleinheim Hill Books, a new, used, and rare bookstore in the Catskills village of Hobart, NY. She is the author of five books of poetry and a sister of Breena Clarke, co-editor of this book.

Yolande Clark-Jackson is a writer, educator, and author of the award-winning children's book, *Rocko's Big Launch*. She holds an MFA in creative nonfiction from Converse College and an English degree from Morgan State University. She lives and writes in South Florida and has a memoir in progress.

Coretta Collins is a family nurse practitioner who serves patients with cancer and blood diseases. She is married with three children and lives in Alabama. Coretta enjoys reading, writing, movies and traveling.

She currently writes her blog, Confessions of a Nurse Practitioner, at www.ccthenp.com.

Courtney Conover is a writer and certified yoga instructor who, since the pandemic, lives for dark-chocolate covered almonds and Zoom happy hours with friends. She and her former NFL lineman husband are proud, grateful, and tired parents of an elementary school-aged son and daughter. She blogs at courtneyconover.com.

Good trouble is a passion in **Cora Cooper's** life that inspires her quest for a justice that isn't focused on just us. She studied law at U.C. Berkeley. Cora exists in alternate realities: fighting for social justice and antiracism by day and writing fantasy and romance by night. She is a member of the RWA.

Morgan Cruise believes in creating art with intention. Whenever she picks up a paintbrush or pen, her goal is to use her gifts as a form of healing for herself and her audience. She is a two-time graduate of Howard University, children's book author, and currently teaches high school in Washington, D.C.

Rachel Decoste is a software engineer, educator and immigration policy expert from Ottawa, Canada. She received her master's in public administration from The George Washington University in 2017. Ms. Decoste runs an online store specializing in Afro-centric apparel. She plans to write a memoir. Learn more at www.racheldecoste.com.

Elle Dee, Ph.D. is a Florida native and a Georgia resident. She met and married her college sweetheart at Florida State. They are entrepreneurs who host "Meet the Mitchells," a podcast about their life as a family of six. Elle Dee enjoys traveling and helping others. She plans to write short stories and nonfiction books.

Ranecia Dee is a spoken word artist, curriculum writer and English professor, originally from Milwaukee, WI. She is an HBCU graduate and holds a master's degree in education and professional development. Ranecia enjoys vintage fashion, anything nineties, fine dining, literacy advocacy, and poetry.

Jeanine DeHoney is a freelance writer whose work has been published in magazines, online, and in several anthologies. She's had stories appear in three *Chicken Soup for the Soul* anthologies and is currently a blogger at "WOW! Women On Writing." She writes hoping her words will land into the hearts of others and inspire them.

Sonya Carol Vann DeLoach, whose family is her muse, has written for *The New York Times, Chicago Tribune* and *Detroit Free Press*, where she was a copy editor. She has a B.A. in journalism from Wayne State University in Detroit. Sonya lives with her husband, Shawn, in Ann Arbor, MI, where she's writing a memoir about life after Tokyo.

Christine Dixon is a member of the NYPD, Sag-Aftra, NY. She is a woman in film and TV, and for years has starred in the one woman show *Harriet Tubman Herself*. She also portrays Harriet in the short film *Era*, that has won awards in film festivals worldwide. Christine enjoys scuba diving. E-mail her at harriettubmanherself@gmail.com.

Kitsy Marie Dixon holds several degrees, including a Bachelor of Arts, Master of Arts, Master of Divinity, and a doctorate degree. She currently serves as a licensed pastor to three United Methodist congregations in Alabama. She also works in the fields of mental health and pastoral counseling.

Ronada Dominique is a young woman who loves reading, writing, traveling and education. A career student, she's currently in the twentieth grade with hopes of obtaining her Ph.D. by the twenty-third grade. Her excitement for completing this stage of education is coupled with parenting her toddler daughter, whom she calls her "Greatest Gift."

Donnette Dunbar helped launch the U.S. online platform of the *Financial Times*. Her role as an editor took her to six continents. Donnette holds an undergraduate degree in literature and an MS in journalism from Columbia University.

Regina S. Dyton credits writing and the music of Nina Simone with saving her life, a best option to self-harm, substance abuse or other treacherous responses to trauma. Her public readings began in the 1970s as a tool for social justice advocacy and have continued as such.

Liseli A. Fitzpatrick, Ph.D. is a Trinidadian poet and professor of African cosmologies and sacred ontologies in the Africana Studies department at Wellesley College, MA. In 2018, Liseli made history as the first Ph.D. in African American and African Studies at The Ohio State University. She currently lives in Massachusetts.

Cherith Glover Fluker received her Bachelor of Arts from Auburn University in 2001, her Master of Science from Jacksonville State University in 2013, and her Doctor of Education from Samford University in 2018. She is married and has two children and works as an instructional specialist for a school district.

Ashonti Ford received her Bachelor of Arts from San Francisco State University. She is a well-traveled journalist with stories published around the globe. When she's not chasing a lead, Ford likes to plan spontaneous trips, eat good food and collect new music from people she meets along the way.

Zorina Exie Frey is an author, essayist, screenwriter, and spoken word artist. She works as a copywriter, graphic designer, and publisher. Zorina is an MFA candidate at Converse College. She's also the recipient of the 2021 Palm Beach Poetry Festival's Langston Hughes Fellowship. She likes traveling, designing journals, and cats.

K E Garland is a creative nonfiction writer based in Jacksonville, FL. She uses personal essays and memoir to de-marginalize women's experiences with an intent to highlight and humanize specific issues. She has a husband and two daughters and is a community college professor.

Stephanie J. Gates is an educator and published writer. Her work has appeared in a number of anthologies, including *Chicken Soup for the Soul: Inspiration for Teachers: 101 Stories About How You Make a Difference*. Stephanie enjoys spending time with family and friends and traveling.

Nancy Marie Gilliam is an award-winning performer, educator, producer and teen girl advocate. She made her Chicken Soup for the Soul debut in *Chicken Soup for the African American Soul*. Her greatest accomplishment and joy is being mother to seven and grandmother of eight beautiful humans.

Autrilla Gillis is a life-long Long Beach resident currently pursuing a doctorate degree in educational leadership. As an educator she's been a history teacher, curriculum specialist, vice principal, principal and district director. In her spare time, she enjoys reading, walking, and traveling with her daughter Aubree.

Alexa Goins works as a writer in Indianapolis. She received a Bachelor of Arts in Journalism & Digital Storytelling in 2016. When she's not writing, you can find her reading nonfiction works, doing embodiment yoga, or planning her next trip to Paris.

Irene R. Granderson is a retired social worker who has been writing since she first started attending a memoir class in 2006. Irene's work has been published in two literary journals. She also enjoys painting and sculpture. Widowed six years ago, Irene feels blessed to have the caring support of her large family.

S. Mayumi "Umi" Grigsby is a graduate of Georgetown University and Northeastern University School of Law. She published her first book, *EmpowHERed Health: Reforming a Dismissive Health Care System*, in December of 2020 and describes herself as a joyful warrior, author, advocate, and attorney.

Cherise Haggerty is an accountant by day who enjoys telling stories through photo books and videos. She is currently helping her father write his memoir and is in the process of researching her family ancestry. Next on the list is her own memoir.

Ashley Hill Hamilton is a native of Uptown New Orleans and mother of two with a sixteen-year age gap. She is a reproductive justice activist, lactation counselor and doula. Ashley's writing is a tool for dismantling oppression and unlocking freedom through an unfiltered portrayal of the nuances of the Black experience.

Robin D. Hamilton is the author of *Shedding Negativity, Gaining Grace*. She enjoys writing books, stage and screen plays, and dabbling in tab art. When not writing, Robin enjoys spending time with family and friends. She currently lives in North Carolina. E-mail her at Sheddingnegativity@gmail.com.

Samantha Hawkins is a Christian. A black woman. A daughter. A sister. She works in 911 dispatch in northwest Georgia. Samantha regularly contributes to MadameNoire (a lifestyle website for millennial women of color), and the blog "Black Superwoman Chronicles." Her writing has also appeared in *The Atlanta Journal-Constitution*.

Rahsel Holland is an alumnus of the University of Delaware where she majored in English and public policy. She enjoys traveling, roller skating, and volunteering. She plans to publish a poetry book. She has been published in *Caesura* and *Main Street Journal*.

Lavinia Nanetta Holmes is a licensed cosmetologist, with twenty-four years of experience, and the owner of It Is Written Hair and Nails Salon. She is married with two children. Lavinia enjoys singing, traveling, writing, reading, cooking and trying out new cuisines. She is looking forward to completing her first inspirational book.

Sharonda Hunter is a proud 2003 graduate of the HBCU Morris Brown College, where she earned her Bachelor of Arts with honors. However, her greatest honor is being Mom to her son, Chase, and daughter, Hunter. Sharonda has worked in educational administration for fifteen years and loves traveling, yoga, fashion and writing.

Halona Jackson, a Chicago native, studied English language and literature at Howard University and is a student at McCormick Theological Seminary in the Black Church Studies Certificate Program. She enjoys reading, engaging with people, and music. Halona plans to continue writing her story to inspire the world.

LaCharmine (L.A) Jefferson is the author of two contemporary women's fiction novels. She is a widowed mother of two and grand-mother of one. Ms. Jefferson is currently writing her third novel and first memoir. She is a proud and active member of Delta Sigma Theta sorority, Inc. Learn more at http://www.lajefferson.com.

Naomi E. Johnson received her Bachelor of Applied Arts in Integrative Public Relations from Central Michigan University in 2016. Outside of her career in marketing and event planning, Naomi enjoys singing, yoga, and time spent with family and friends. She plans to continue spreading love and hope through storytelling.

Sydney Ann Johnson has always had a passion for advocacy and writing from a young age. Sydney received her bachelor's degree in history from St. John's University in 2015. Her parents stressed the importance of knowing your history as a person of African descent. That same year Sydney self-published her first book entitled *Wounds Heal to Wisdom*.

Margaret Johnson-Hodge is the author of nineteen published works, many receiving national acclaim and making multiple bestseller lists. She has garnered rave reviews from the likes of *Publishers Weekly*, *USA Today*, and *Booklist*, to name a few. Learn more at www.mjhodge.net.

Dr. Angelle M. Jones holds a bachelor's in African American studies., master's in theology and a Doctorate of ministry in the philosophy of Dr. MLK's Beloved Community. She is an adjunct professor who uses the written and spoken word to reconcile racial division. E-mail her at globallifeconsultants@gmail.com.

Joy Jones is a playwright, author and popular speaker in Washington, D.C. Her most recent book, *Jayla Jumps In*, is a novel for young people. This is her second contribution to the *Chicken Soup for the Soul* series. Learn more at www.joyjonesOnline.com.

Sharisse Kimbro is a writer, mother, and lawyer who lives in Evanston, IL. She is the author of *Beyond the Broken* and her work is featured in *We Got This: Solo Mom Stories of Grit, Heart, and Humor*. Sharisse earned a B.A. in English, an M.A. in sociology from Stanford University and a law degree from University of Michigan.

Ruth King, MA, is an educator, meditation teacher, and the founder of Mindful of Race Institute. She is the author of several publications, including *Mindful of Race: Transforming Racism from the Inside Out*. Ruth is an elder and heart activist, and wife to Dr. Barbara Riley residing in Charlotte, NC.

Billie Joy Langston earned a Bachelor of Arts in anthropology/journalism, and Master of Education, with honors, from Howard University. Billie is a contributor to the Guideposts book *Miracles Do Happen* (2019). Her publishing credits include Wesleyan Publishing House, CrossRiver Media, and ChristianDevotions.us.

Aya de Leon teaches creative writing at UC Berkeley. Kensington Books publishes her award-winning feminist heist series, and her stand-alone novels, *A Spy in the Struggle* and *The Queen of Urban Prophecy*. She has written for *Harper's Bazaar*, *Essence*, and *Guernica*. She's currently at work on a Black/Latina teen girl spy series.

Dara Joyce Lurie is co-director of Black Stories Matter programming with the TMI Project in Kingston, NY. Her first book, *Great Space of Desire: Writing for Personal Evolution*, is a memoir on race, identity and healing.

Vickie Lynn is a mother/grandmother from Rockford, IL, currently living in Beloit, WI. She is a standup comedian, spoken word artist, entrepreneur (Noni Lynns Naturals) and is the founder of Black Women in Business Expo Beloit. She credits her mother for her love of all things word.

Crystal Marie is a chaser of good, engaging, can't take your eyes or ears away stories. She writes about race, motherhood, politics, and faith. Crystal Marie holds a master's degree from the University of Southern California and a B.S. from Howard University and can be found on Twitter @CrystalMarieCom.

DaNice D. Marshall attended Carleton College. In 2016, she lost 50% of her hearing due to illness, stopped writing and began painting as therapy. Her paintings have been on exhibit in Boston's Piano Craft Gallery, with sales abroad and domestic. DaNice has two adult daughters and is married to Ben, the love of her life.

Melissa A. Matthews is an entrepreneur, writer, and artist born and bred in Brooklyn, NY. She received her Bachelor of Fine Arts in painting from Howard University in 2008. She owns several small businesses with her twin sister. She now lives, works and is raising her family in her cultural home of Trinidad and Tobago.

Westina Matthews, Ph.D. is an author, public speaker, retreat leader, and theologian. Through her thoughtful, poignant, humorous, and authentic writings, she has found a way to connect with audiences around the world. E-mail her at matthews@gts.edu.

Crystal Webert Mays is an educator, wife, and mother of two. Her sister, **Dr. Candice Webert**, is also an educator. Both are from Shreveport, LA, having completed studies at Louisiana Tech University and Louisiana State University at Shreveport. They enjoy music, traveling, and are avid lovers of history and culture.

DW McKinney pens a column at *CNMN* magazine and serves as a senior nonfiction editor for *Raising Mothers*. Her writing has been featured in *Narratively*, *JMWW Journal*, *Los Angeles Review of Books*, and elsewhere. Born in California, she now lives in Nevada, where she writes and gardens. E-mail her at dwmckinney.com.

CaSandra McLaughlin is a native of Marshall, TX. CaSandra is the morning drive host at a gospel radio station in Dallas. She's also a national bestselling, award-winning Christian fiction author. CaSandra is married to Richard McLaughlin and they have two children, Nick and Chloe, and one beautiful granddaughter, Nova.

A life-long New Yorker and vegan eating Knicks fanatic, **Katheryne McMullen** once upon a time wrote relationship themed pieces on assignment for magazines. Then she traded facts for fiction with two screenplays that have yet to be greenlighted. Now nothing inspires her more than real life.

Sharon Moore, retired educator, pursues her second act as an artist. Moore sings, writes, designs cards and sketches. Her new memoir collection is titled, *Kaleidoscope: Journey of the Sharecroppers' Granddaughter*. Awed by aviatrix Bessie Coleman, Moore wrote a script and performs a first-person reenactment. She resides in Delaware with husband Julius Jackson. E-mail her at classysounds@comcast.net.

Aja Moore-Ramos is a writer, educator, and proud mother of three based in Oakland, CA. She graduated with a BFA in Writing from Emerson College and an M.S. in Education from Hunter College. Aja enjoys journaling, family time, and social justice work.

Dr. Kimberly Mucker-Johnson was born and raised in Louisville, KY. Dr. Mucker-Johnson has been an educator for over nineteen years. She holds a Bachelor of Arts in Humanities, Master of Arts in Business, Teaching, Educational Technology, and Counseling, and a Doctorate of Education in Educational Technology.

SM Nelson is a mother, wife, and educator who feels honored to have those roles. She is an educator, professional development consultant, researcher, and author. She enjoys authoring various genres of writing, with poetry being her favorite. In her spare time, she reads, travels, and writes poetry for publication.

Dr. Crystal E. Newby received her Ed.D. from Johns Hopkins University in 2020. She is also a two-time graduate of the University of Scranton with a B.A. in communication and an M.S. in human resources. She is a diversity, equity, and inclusion advocate who loves candy, college football, and most important, her niece Cora.

Rabiah Nur is a seventy-one-year-old mother and grandmother.

She is an Indigenous healer, activist, storyteller, speaker, and writer. Her work heals and empowers women through a connection to nature, to Spirit, and to their innate wisdom to facilitate a rebirth of new and healthy societies where the whole of women is valued.

Rebecca Olayinka resides in the UK. Rebecca has been a qualified social work practitioner for nine years. Rebecca is also a freelance writer and is currently writing her own personal powerful memoir to inspire Black foster children to live a life of their own creation. E-mail her at rebeccaolayinka@outlook.com.

Temeka S. Parker is a licensed clinical social worker with several years of experience serving children and families impacted by trauma. She received a bachelor's degree in social work from Bowie State University and a master's in social work from University of Maryland. Temeka enjoys reading, swimming, biking and running.

Rachel R. Perkins is the author of "The Well-Adjusted Adult," a blog that celebrates the chaos of life while encouraging everyone to find the balance between who we have to be for others and who we are for ourselves. Rachel is a wife and working mother of four daughters. She enjoys writing, traveling, and connecting with others.

Aerial Perkins-Good is an award-winning published author from Virginia. She loves writing, music, dancing and photography.

Ellen Pinnock is a Newport, RI native who works in education and racial equity. She is the mother of a sixteen-year-old daughter and devotes her time to community work and advocacy. Ellen enjoys reading, writing, cooking and baking. Her dream is to become a published author and poet.

Sheila L. Quarles has degrees in psychology and drama. A traumatic brain injury led her to study indigenous and natural techniques of healing. She became a Reiki Master and partnered with Kathy Morris to establish Inner Journeys, LLC, a natural healing center. Learn more at www.innerjourneys-heals.com.

Terri Redwine, a native of Detroit, is the mother of three. She graduated from Eastern Michigan University and worked most of her life teaching on various fronts. Currently she volunteers, helping four-year-olds, kindergarteners and first graders learn to read fluently, and is humbly engaged in entrepreneurship.

Lexcee Reel was raised in Bailey, NC. She is a veteran educator who is a wife and mom to some wonderfully made souls. Reel enjoys reading, writing, and traveling. She authors blogs, stage-plays, fiction novellas, poetry, inspirational books and devotionals. She's desperately in love with words and their power to inspire.

Kamala Reese received her B.A. in communication and earned an M.S.Ed in her quest to teach writing. Now, she works in the field of Edtech while homeschooling her seven-year-old son and four-year-old daughter. Kamala is married to her husband of almost ten years, loves writing and listening to music, and plans to publish more of her work soon.

Mariah RI received her Bachelor of Science, with honours, from the University of Toronto in 2021. She enjoys traveling, writing, baking, cooking, being outside and spending time with friends and family. Her dreams are to become a physician and author, work with underserved communities, contribute to health policy, and teach.

Cynthia A. Roby is a writer and adjunct professor with work published in *Bacopa Literary Review*, *The Penmen Review*, *Black Denim Lit*, and *The Lindenwood Review*. She earned her MFA from Lindenwood University. A lover of great books, black-and-white movies, and yoga, Roby lives in Connecticut.

Rebekah Sager is an award-winning journalist with over a decade of experience covering politics, lifestyle, entertainment, and human-interest stories. Sager has contributed to *The Washington Post*, *The Hollywood Reporter*, *Playboy*, *VICE*, *HuffPost*, *Sisters from AARP*, *Zora*, *Cosmo for Latinas*, *Bustle*, *Dame*, the *Los Angeles Times*, and more.

Mae Frances Sarratt RN retired after forty-three years. She received her degree in counseling and human services from Gardner Webb University, Boiling Springs, NC. She is married with two children and four grandchildren. She feels blessed God called her to write. She enjoys decorating and reading.

Lisa Marie Simmons is an American singer/songwriter, essayist, and published poet currently based in Italy. She was a speaker and performer at the 70th Conference on World Affairs at the University of

Colorado and has signed with the American Grammy award-winning label Ropeadope Records that released her album *NoteSpeak* in March 2020.

Pat Simmons is a multi-published Christian romance author of more than thirty titles. She is a self-proclaimed genealogy sleuth passionate about researching her ancestors, then casting them in starring roles in her novels. She is a three-time recipient of the RSJ Emma Rodgers Award for Best Inspirational Romance.

Roslyn D. Smith is a program manager for V-Day, a non-profit organization that has vowed to end violence against women, girls and the planet. She is using her personal experience from long-term incarceration as a vehicle for her work as a criminal justice reform advocate. She received her bachelor's degree from Mercy College.

Rev. Michele Sweeting-DeCaro is a college educator, gospel charting vocalist, and New York City pastor. She uses her gifts and talents to inspire, encourage and motivate people worldwide. Michele is happily married for over twenty years to Dr. Lou, and they have an amazing son, fifteen-year-old LouMike.

TAH is a mother, Army veteran and researcher who resides in Illinois. She is both community driven and mission focused and has a Ph.D. in community psychology, where she is able to work in her passion of helping others heal. TAH enjoys traveling, reading, playing darts, dancing and writing.

Cassandra L. Tavaras is an aspiring writer from Lynn, MA. She is passionate about all things natural hair, empowerment, positive affirmations, education, music, dancing and living her best life. She is currently a youth development program evaluator and Zumba instructor.

Andrea Taylor received her B.S. in journalism at the University of Maryland in 1990. She later decided to pursue a master's in school counseling at Bowie State University. She has been a counselor for twenty-four years. She is married with two daughters. She is currently working on an inspiration book for young girls.

Sarai Ashari Thompson received her Bachelor of Arts in English with a minor in journalism from Georgia State University and a Master of Arts in magazine, newspaper, and online journalism from Syracuse

University. She currently works at CNN as an editorial coordinator for CNN Underscored.

Courtney Tierra is an educator, servant leader, writer, and ice cream connoisseur. During the COVID-19 lockdown in 2020, she wrote and published her first children's book, *Worthy! A Book for Kids of All Ages*. She is an award-winning storyteller, has a ridiculous giggle, and did she mention her adoration of ice cream?

Casandra Townsel is a social worker and has been assisting those in need for over twenty-two years. She received her Bachelor of Arts in psychology and her master's in social work. Casandra is a wife and mother of three who works with many philanthropic organizations. She loves to read and travel, hoping someday to live abroad.

Born on the beautiful island of St. Croix, U.S. Virgin Islands, **Cassandra Ulrich** received a Bachelor of Arts in mathematics, with honors, from the University of the Virgin Islands and a master's in computer science from Penn State. She is married and has two sons. She enjoys singing, learning new languages, and writing.

Dr. Kamaria Washington is a proud product of Detroit, MI and is a doctor of physical therapy who is passionate about pelvic health rehab and the peri-partum journey. She began sharing her writing during graduate school and plans to use poetry for facilitating empathy in healthcare and for community healing. Read her blog at TheFreeDPT or visit her on Instagram @dr.kwashington.

LaTonya R. Watson received her Bachelor of Art from the University of Toledo, and master's of human resources and healthcare management from Herzing University. She served four years in the United States Marine Corps. She has a son and two dogs. She loves swimming, warm weather, and the beach.

Dana Tenille Weekes navigates the world of law, policy, and politics in Washington, D.C. Over the years, she has been answering her inner calling to use her voice to amplify others, including Black women, through storytelling and writing. She is a graduate of Wellesley College and the University of Virginia School of Law

Alicia F. Williams is a wife, daughter, sister, friend and mother of two beautiful daughters. She practices law in New Jersey and has enjoyed writing as a form of expression since childhood. She received her B.A. from Rutgers University and her law degree from New York Law School. E-mail her at aliciaw909@gmail.com.

Chenelle Williams is a Clinical Director from New Jersey. She has a master's degree and completed undergraduate studies at Delaware State University. She enjoys obstacle course racing and community service and is an active member of Delta Sigma Theta Sorority, Inc. She is also the founder of Black Spartans, an OCR community.

Inika Pierre Williams is a Trinidadian-American who was raised in a culture of calypso, carnival, and remnants of the diaspora. She is a university program director working to increase enrollment for first-generation students. Inika enjoys traveling, reading, and spending time with her husband and two sons, JR and Ivan.

Hailing from Akron, OH, **Jasmine J. Wyatt's** public service career spans from the Midwest, to the halls of Congress, to the U.S. Mission to the United Nations. A passionate advocate for empowering marginalized communities in U.S. foreign policy, Jasmine received her B.A. in Government and South Asian Studies from Harvard University.

Kuukua Dzigbordi Yomekpe is a multidisciplinary artist and scholar. She holds several degrees in English and theology and has worked in various areas of higher education. She loves to do art and crafty things, write in her journal, and blog at www.ewurabasempe.wordpress.com.

Meet Our Authors

Breena Clarke is the author of three novels, most recently published, *Angels Make Their Hope Here*, set in an imagined mixed-race community in 19th century New Jersey. Her debut novel, *River, Cross My Heart*, was an October 1999 Oprah's Book Club selection and was named by Publishers Weekly as one of the seven essential books about Washington, D.C. Her critically reviewed second novel, *Stand The Storm*, was named one of 100 Best for 2008 by *The Washington Post*. A graduate of Howard University, Breena's recollections of her hometown are included in *Growing Up In Washington, D.C., An Oral History*. Her short fiction has appeared in *Washington Post Magazine, Kweli Journal, Stonecoast Review, Nervous Breakdown, Mom/Egg Review, The Drabble, Catapult*, and *Now*, the Hobart Festival of Women Writers online magazine that she co-edits. She is co-founder of the Hobart Festival of Women Writers, an annual celebration of the work of women writers. She has been a member of the fiction faculty of Stonecoast MFA in Creative Writing at The University of Southern Maine since 2013.

Amy Newmark is the bestselling author, editor-in-chief, and publisher of the *Chicken Soup for the Soul* book series. Since 2008, she has published 174 new books, most of them national bestsellers in the

U.S. and Canada, more than doubling the number of Chicken Soup for the Soul titles in print today. She is also the author of *Simply Happy*, a crash course in Chicken Soup for the Soul advice and wisdom that is filled with easy-to-implement, practical tips for enjoying a better life.

Amy is credited with revitalizing the Chicken Soup for the Soul brand, which has been a publishing industry phenomenon since the first book came out in 1993. By compiling inspirational and aspirational true stories curated from ordinary people who have had extraordinary experiences, Amy has kept the twenty-eight-year-old Chicken Soup for the Soul brand fresh and relevant.

Amy graduated *magna cum laude* from Harvard University where she majored in Portuguese and minored in French. She then embarked on a three-decade career as a Wall Street analyst, a hedge fund manager, and a corporate executive in the technology field. She is a Chartered Financial Analyst.

Her return to literary pursuits was inevitable, as her honors thesis in college involved traveling throughout Brazil's impoverished northeast region, collecting stories from regular people. She is delighted to have come full circle in her writing career — from collecting stories "from the people" in Brazil as a twenty-year-old to, three decades later, collecting stories "from the people" for Chicken Soup for the Soul.

When Amy and her husband Bill, the CEO of Chicken Soup for the Soul, are not working, they are visiting their four grown children and their three grandchildren.

Follow Amy on Twitter @amynewmark. Listen to her free podcast — Chicken Soup for the Soul with Amy Newmark — on Apple Podcasts, Google Play, the Podcasts app on iPhone, or by using your favorite podcast app on other devices.

Thank You

We owe huge thanks to everyone who submitted stories and poems for this book and cheered us on as we pored through them. There were way too many great stories, so we've sent some of them off to inspire the readers of other Chicken Soup for the Soul collections that will be published in 2021 and 2022. And we "violated" our normal rule about only including 101 pieces by taking 12 great poems and using them as appetizers at the beginning of the book and at the beginning of each chapter!

We spent a lot of time this winter reading stories, making chapters, and shaping this new collection of heartfelt, honest, and ultimately inspiring and encouraging pieces that reflect the experience of Black women today in the United States, Canada, the Caribbean, and beyond. We know that our readership will go beyond the BIPOC community and include everyone who seeks to better understand what is happening in our world.

We want to thank Breena's literary agent Cynthia Cannell for her support of this undertaking even as it took some time away from Breena's next novel. Brian Allain at Publishing in Color was a great help in spreading the word about this writing opportunity. And we want to thank the sales team at Simon & Schuster for their enthusiasm for this important book that we've worked so hard on.

Chicken Soup for the Soul's associate publisher D'ette Corona was the third member of the team that went all out to get this over the finish line. She worked with every contributor to make sure they loved the quotes we put at the top of each poem or story, and also to approve whatever edits we suggested.

The rest of the Chicken Soup for the Soul crew jumped in to help, and that includes senior editor Barbara LoMonaco, editor Kristiana Pastir, editor Elaine Kimbler, senior director of marketing Maureen Peltier, vice president of production Victor Cataldo, executive assistant Mary Fisher, and graphic designer Daniel Zaccari, who designed the beautiful cover and interior.

— Breena Clarke and Amy Newmark —